SEEING
TO THE HEART

*English and Imagination in the
Junior School*

BY

MARIE PEEL

*Senior Lecturer in English,
Avery Hill College of Education*

1969
CHATTO & WINDUS
LONDON

Published by
Chatto and Windus Ltd
40 William IV Street
London W.C.2

*

Clarke Irwin & Co. Ltd
Toronto

First published 1967
Second impression 1968
Third Impression 1969

SBN 7011 1014 7 boards

SBN 7011 1015 5 paperback

Printed in Great Britain by
Cox and Wyman Ltd
London, Fakenham and Reading

CONTENTS

PLATES

1 Children improvising. 2 (*a*) Boys watching trains; (*b*) Children fishing. 3 (*a*) *La Premiere Sortie* by Renoir; (*b*) Detail from *The Pond* by Lowry. 4 (*a*) Detail from *The Graham Children* by Hogarth; (*b*) *Storm in the Jungle* by Rousseau. 5 *Totes Meer* by Paul Nash. 6 Extract from *Tales from a Forced Landing* 7 (*a*) Miner and pit pony; (*b*) Victorian pit boy. 8 (*a*) Replica of the Mask of Agamemnon; (*b*) the Gokstad Ship, Norway.

The plates appear between pages 144 and 145.

AUTHOR'S NOTE

I wish to express my very warm thanks to Mr. G. E. Offord, J.P., Headmaster of Kidbrooke Park Primary School, for allowing me to come and go so freely in his school and for the encouragement of his own liberal attitude and understanding of children; and to Mrs. S. V. Banfield, now his Deputy Headmistress, for her unfailing helpfulness and co-operation, and for the exciting stimulus of all her work. I am also grateful to the children in her class, whom I much enjoyed teaching and who taught me much.

I also want particularly to thank my ex-colleague, Mrs. Claire Ash, now Lecturer in English at Sidney Webb College, to whose creative ideas and practice in improvisation and drama work with children I owe a great deal.

ACKNOWLEDGEMENTS

I SHOULD like to express my grateful thanks to the following people for permission to reprint copyright material in this book: Mr. W. H. Auden and Her Majesty's Postmaster General for lines from *Night Mail*; Mr. George Barker for *Miners Above Ground*; the Owner of the Copyright and Methuen and Co. Ltd for an extract from *Clayhanger* by Arnold Bennett; Mr. Edward Blishen and Thames and Hudson Ltd for an extract from *Roaring Boys*; Mr. Edwin Brock, the Scorpion Press and Penguin Books Ltd for lines from *A Moment of Respect* from 'With Love from Judas,' subsequently reprinted in Penguin Modern Poets 8, and Mr. Brock the editor of *Ambit* and Penguin Books Ltd for lines from *Symbols of the Sixties*, originally printed in *Ambit* and also reprinted in Penguin Modern Poets 8; William Heinemann Ltd for an extract from *The Secret Garden* by Frances Hodgson Burnett; the County Council of the West Riding of Yorkshire and Chatto and Windus Ltd for an extract from *The Excitement of Writing*, edited by A. B. Clegg; Mrs. H. M. Davies and Jonathan Cape Ltd for lines from *The Cat* from 'The Complete Poems of W. H. Davies'; the Literary Trustees of Walter De La Mare and the Society of Authors as their representative for lines from *Done For, Five Eyes, Myself, The Ride-by-Nights* and *Silver;* Faber and Faber Ltd for an extract from *The Use of Poetry and the Use of Criticism*, and for lines from *Virginia* from 'Collected Poems 1909–1962' and from *The Song of the Jellicles* from 'Old Possum's Book of Practical Cats', by T. S. Eliot; Miss Eleanor Farjeon and Michael Joseph Ltd for lines from *Cat* and *It was long ago*, from 'Silver, Sand and Snow', and Miss Farjeon and Oxford University Press for extracts from *Tales from Chaucer*; Jonathan Cape Ltd for lines from *The Line-Gang* from 'The Complete Poems of Robert Frost' and Holt, Rinehart and Winston, Inc., New York (Copyright 1916 by Holt, Rinehart and Winston, Inc. Copyright 1944 by Robert Frost); the Society of Authors as the literary representative of the Estate of the late Rose Fyleman for lines from *Alms in Autumn*; Mr. Roger Lancelyn Green and Penguin Books Ltd for extracts from *King Arthur and His Knights of the Round Table*; Mr. Frederick Grice and Oxford University Press for extracts from *The Bonnie Pit Laddie*; the Trustees of the Hardy Estate and Macmillan and Co. Ltd for lines from *The Fallow Deer at the Lonely House* and from *The Strange House*, from 'Collected Poems' by Thomas Hardy; Miss Cynthia Harnett and Methuen and Co. Ltd for an extract from *The Woolpack*; Mrs. Hodgson and Macmillan and Co. Ltd for lines from *Time You Old Gypsy Man* from 'Collected Poems' by Ralph Hodgson; Mr. David Holbrook and Cambridge University Press for an extract from *The Wakefield Second Shepherds' Play of the Nativity* from 'Thieves and Angels'; Miss Lilian Hollamby and Longmans, Green and Co. Ltd for an extract from *Young Children Living and Learning*; Miss

SEEING TO THE HEART

Marjorie Hourd and Heinemann Educational Books Ltd for extracts from *The Education of the Poetic Spirit*; Mr. Brian Jackson and Chatto and Windus Ltd for extracts from *Good English Prose, Book II*; Hodder and Stoughton Ltd for an extract from *The Story of My Life* by Helen Keller; Mrs. George Bambridge and Macmillan and Co. Ltd for extracts from *The Jungle Book* and *Puck of Pook's Hill* by Rudyard Kipling; Mr. James Kirkup and Oxford University Press, for lines from *The Lonely Scarecrow* from 'Refusal to Conform'; Mr. Philip Larkin and Faber and Faber Ltd for *Days* from 'The Whitsun Weddings'; Laurence Pollinger Ltd and the Estate of the Late Mrs. Frieda Lawrence for an extract from *Hymns in a Man's Life* from 'Selected Literary Criticism' by D. H. Lawrence, published by William Heinemann Ltd; Mr. Christopher Leach and the *Times Literary Supplement* for *Blackbird*; the Executors of C. S. Lewis and Geoffrey Bless Ltd for an extract from *The Silver Chair* by C. S. Lewis; Mr. Rutgers van der Loeff and University of London Press Ltd for an extract from *They're Drowning Our Village*; Mr. George MacBeth and Macmillan and Co. Ltd for lines from *Noah's Voyage*; Mrs. Sybil Marshall and Cambridge University Press for an extract from *An Experiment in Education*; Mr. Christopher Middleton and Longmans, Green and Co. Ltd for lines from *For a Junior School Poetry Book* from 'Nonsequences'; Mr. Henry Miller and Peter Owen Ltd for an extract from *Books in My Life*; Mr. Ogden Nash and J. M. Dent and Sons Ltd for lines from *The Child Is Father To The Man But With More Authority* from 'The Private Dining-Room', and Curtis Brown Ltd for the same lines (Copyright 1949, the Curtis Publishing Company); Mr. Norman Nicholson and Faber and Faber Ltd for *Five Minutes* from 'The Pot Geranium'; John Murray Ltd for lines from *A Song of Sherwood* from 'Collected Poems' by Alfred Noyes; Miss Sonia Brownell and Secker and Warburg Ltd for an extract from *Road to Wigan Pier* by George Orwell; Miss Philippa Pearce and Constable Young Books Ltd for an extract from *A Dog So Small*; Miss Barbara Leonie Picard and Oxford University Press for an extract from *The Iliad of Homer*; Mr. R. W. Purton and Ward Lock Educational Company Ltd for an extract from *Surrounded by Books*; Mr. John Crowe Ransom, Eyre and Spottiswoode Ltd and Alfred A. Knopf Inc. for lines from *Janet Waking* from 'Selected Poems of John Crowe Ransom' (Copyright 1927 by Alfred A. Knopf Inc. Renewed 1955 by John Crowe Ransom.) Mr. Michell Raper for lines from *Morning Glory*; Mr. James Reeves and William Heinemann Ltd for *Snail* and lines from *Mr. Tom Narrow*, from 'The Wandering Moon', and Mr. Reeves and Oxford University Press for lines from *Cows* and *Uriconium*, from 'The Blackbird in the Lilac'; Mr. M. R. Ridley and Edmund Ward (Publishers) Ltd for extracts from *Sir Gawain and the Green Knight*; Mr. E. V. Rieu and Penguin Books Ltd for lines from The Penguin Classics New Translation of *The Iliad*; Mrs. Theodore Roethke and Secker and Warburg Ltd for *Child on Top of a Greenhouse* from 'Words For The Wind', and Doubleday and Company, Inc. for the same poem (*Child on Top of a Greenhouse*, copyright 1946 by Editorial Publications, Inc., from 'Words for the Wind' by Theodore Roethke. Reprinted by permission of Doubleday and Company, Inc.); Miss Doris Rowley and Messrs. Novello and Co. Ltd for lines from *The Other Me* from

ACKNOWLEDGEMENT

'In Poem-Town'; Mr. William Saroyan, Faber and Faber Ltd and Harcourt, Brace and World, Inc. for extracts from *Snake* from 'The Daring Young Man on the Flying Trapeze'; Mr. Vernon Scannell for lines from the original version of *Hide and Seek*, and Mr. Scannell and Putnam and Company for lines from *Autobiographical Note* from 'A Sense of Danger'; Mr. Jack Schaefer and Harold Matson Company, Inc. for an extract from *Shane* (Copyright 1949 by Jack Schaefer. Reprinted by permission of the Harold Matson Company, Inc.); Mr. Ian Serraillier and Oxford University Press for *Anne and the Fieldmouse* from 'Happily Ever After' and *The Headless Gardener* from 'Thomas and the Sparrow', and for lines from *The Fox Rhyme* from 'The Tale of the Monster Horse'; Mrs. Iris Wise and Macmillan and Co. Ltd for *Seumas Beg* and lines from *The Snare* from 'Collected Poems' by James Stephens; Mr. Hal Summers for lines from *Out of School*; Miss Rosemary Sutcliff and The Bodley Head Ltd for extracts from *Beowulf*, and Miss Sutcliff and Oxford University Press for an extract from *The Eagle of the Ninth*; the Literary Executors of the Dylan Thomas Estate and J. M. Dent and Sons Ltd for an extract from *A Visit to Grandpa's* from 'Portrait of the Artist as a Young Dog' by Dylan Thomas; Mrs. Helen Thomas for *A Cat* from 'Collected Poems' by Edward Thomas, published by Faber and Faber Ltd; Professor J. R. R. Tolkien and George Allen and Unwin Ltd for an extract from *The Hobbit*; The Society of Authors and Miss Pamela Hinkson for lines from *August Weather* by Katherine Tynan; Chatto and Windus Ltd for extracts from *Use of English*, Vol. III, No. 3, and Vol. X, No. 3; George G. Harrap and Company Ltd for an extract from *Tales From The Eddas* by E. M. Wilmot-Buxton; Mr. M. B. Yeats and Macmillan and Co. Ltd for lines from *The Coming of Wisdom with Time* from 'The Collected Poems of W. B. Yeats'.

I should also like to thank the following for their permission to use work by child writers: Mr. Michael Baldwin for *The Tramp* by Christine Elliot, and *Big Sisters*; Mrs. J. B. Ellison; the Headmistress of Bromley High School for Girls, G.P.D.S.T.; the Headmaster of Kidbrooke Park Primary School and the Inner London Education Authority; the Headmaster of Slade Green Junior School, Erith; the Headmaster of Temple Hill C.P. Junior School, Dartford, Kent.

Acknowledgement is also due to the following for permission to reproduce illustrations:

The Trustees of the National Gallery and S.P.A.D.E.M. for *La Première Sortie* by Renoir; the Trustees of the Tate Gallery for details from *The Pond* by Lowry and *The Graham Children* by Hogarth; the Paul Nash Trust for *Totes Meer* by Paul Nash; Mr. and Mrs. Henry Clifford Radnor P.A. and the Art Institute of Chicago for *Storm in the Jungle* by Rousseau; The Ashmolean Museum, Oxford for a photograph of a replica of a Mycenean mask in the National Museum, Athens; Universitetets Oldsaksamling, Oslo for the photograph of the Gokstad ship; Mr. Peter Epps of Avery Hill College and Mr. Tom Stabler of the Ward Jackson Junior School, West Hartlepool for photographs of children doing improvisation; The National Coal Board, Mr. Richard Dykes and Mr. Roger Mayne for other photographs.

The very essence of the imagination is already defined to be the seeing to the heart; and it is not therefore wonderful that it should never err; but it is wonderful, on the other hand, how the composing legalism does *nothing else* than err.

RUSKIN: *Modern Painters*

For all knowledge and wonder (which is the seed of knowledge) is an impression of pleasure in itself.

BACON: *Advancement of Learning*

Now the great and fatal fruit of our civilisation, which is based on knowledge and hostile to experience, is boredom. All our wonderful education and learning is producing a grand sum-total of boredom. Modern people are inwardly thoroughly bored. Do as they may, they are bored.

They are bored because they experience nothing, and they experience nothing because the wonder has gone out of them. And when the wonder has gone out of a man he is dead. He is henceforth only an insect.

D. H. LAWRENCE: *Hymns in a Man's Life*

I · INTRODUCTION

IMAGINATION AS VISION AND DISCIPLINE

TODAY children of junior school age are regarded very much as individual people. One feels this on entering most schools and the children certainly take it for granted themselves. Usually also they are regarded as *whole* people, not potential specialists or assumed failures. School gates do not shut out the world; rather, good teachers seek opportunities to relate what they teach to life outside. Education is not partitioned into exclusive subjects but seen as offering children varied and related experience of which, all the time, fresh knowledge forms an exciting part. A good teacher seeks to arouse a child's interest and curiosity; to lead him to discover for himself; above all to call forth his strong sense of wonder, which Bacon described as 'the seed of knowledge', so that what he learns may take root and grow.

The situation twenty or thirty years ago was very different and the revolution is almost entirely an imaginative one. For it was brought about by the imagination of teachers and others concerned with primary education; by their awareness of the need for change; by their power to see connections, integrate different aspects of knowledge and present them imaginatively in the classroom. In so far as they have contributed, teachers believe at least unconsciously in the creative individuality in each child. They believe that each possesses what still lives in themselves, an active imagination. In some measure at least they have retained their own power to wonder.

The whole meaning and power of primary education is still rooted in this central conception, however practical its application. The imagination is both a seeing and shaping power; 'The seeing to the heart' was how Ruskin defined it. Coleridge spoke of the 'shaping spirit'. In so far as it operates among intangibles, human relationships, ideas – for instance, the issues in primary education just discussed – it is an adult power. We have the word *insight* to express it. It always brings with it awareness of emotional as well as intellectual implications. In children, imagination is much more a vivid kind of *outsight*, a marked capacity for the intent absorbed seeing of the actual, accompanied by strong responsiveness of feeling. A child picks up a hamster, a guinea-pig, a kitten, holds it in his hands, feels its throbbing body. The direct sensory experience is strong. Feeling will be present throughout, the intelligence watchful rather than active. The whole being is momentarily concentrated and absorbed in a way that the expression shows. This full 'seeing' means something to the child. Much the same happens when he is gripped by a play, film or television. Involvement is usually intense. Also, though children have little insight in the adult sense, they usually have an instinctive clearsightedness where adults are concerned. They invariably detect humbug. They form their judgements though they do not always express them.

It is this directness of apprehension in children that a good primary school harnesses, but also allows free rein. It is through this that a creative discipline of the imagination works. For in whatever sphere it operates this power, possessed in some measure by all of us, is a creative shaping one. The fusion of mind and feeling at its heart always produces pressure towards expression of some kind. In school the teaching provides experiences that demand creative outlet. The children are moved to paint or model or write in a very personal way. This is valuable for children in itself. It also creates an atmosphere of feeling attentiveness in which the intellect develops no matter what its measured range. Whenever the imagination is stirred concentration is heightened. Children want to find out more and are led profitably to do so.

Unfortunately this does not happen in every school. Imagination is always opposed by what Ruskin called 'composing legalism', by which he meant some artificial pattern accepted from without, with no individual life or spirit; and although much exciting work is going on in junior schools now, in many imagination has clearly faltered. The strong educational and social pressures exerted by selection at eleven, the accompanying streaming in many schools, often descending to children as young as eight years old, attitudes to discipline which deny individuality as soon as it becomes necessary to respect and understand it, all these have led to compromise and sometimes denial of vision. Often the flame burns in isolated classrooms but lacks any central accepted source of fuel. Yet despite this there remain important distinctions between most primary and

almost all secondary schools which would make one rather see
the primary influence extend upwards than the other way about.
Particularly it would be valuable if primary methods could
influence new comprehensive schools. For there is usually more
continuous concern in primary schools for the whole child, a
more continuous awareness of his individuality. Also, because of
the need to envisage knowledge in terms of meaningful experience for the child, there is usually a much more vivid sense of
its relatedness.

Paradoxically the main failure of imagination in the junior
school has been with English, which should be one of the most
imaginative subjects. It now presents the most urgent challenge,
for if the new sense of purpose towards it abroad in many
schools can be focused through a strong unified vision of its
central significance and power, primary school work as a whole
will rise up with certainty, and be ready to play a full creative
part in coming changes. This will be particularly important
should these involve, as many hope they will, some change in
the age of transfer. As things now are, one would be delighted
to have children staying on until twelve or thirteen in many
schools but certainly not in others.

No one ever denies the importance of English, but many
junior school teachers seem uncertain where it stands in their
work; what knowledge it offers comparable with what children
learn in geography, history or science, what activity to stand
beside games, dance, or craft. They accept as they must that
it is, with number, the foundation of all their work, but only in
the limited sense of being a necessary tool for expression in
other subjects. They often allow a narrow concern for technical
correctness to blind them almost completely to its proper
function.

It is easy simply to blame the eleven plus for all this yet,
although its pressures have encouraged concentration on arid
trivialities, it has also provided a strong external sanction for
them. It has kept many teachers from facing their deeper inner
uncertainty about English, about what as a subject it could and
should be doing. *As a subject*: the first confusion comes at once.
Is English a subject at all in the primary school? The original
revolution said no, and swept away — or thought it did — the
old, wrong, establishment conception of it as written and
literary, a storehouse of treasures from which children supposedly
derived acceptable ideas, aesthetic pleasure and above all the
foundations of a 'good style'. Of course gifted teachers always

conceived it differently, chose what would concern and involve their pupils and brought the subject vividly to life. But most teachers, paying only lip-service to the traditional conception and equipped by nothing in their experience at grammar school or training college to make them see and feel it differently, tended to find English artificial and boring, and made it so for their classes.

The revolution brought relief and release. Now English was openly proclaimed not a subject but, as George Sampson called it in his fine book, *English for the English*, 'a condition of school life'. 'It is probably true to say,' wrote Mr. Cutforth in *English in the Primary School*, a useful handbook published in 1954, which marked the first stage in the post-war primary achievement, 'that a good primary school makes its best contribution to English almost indirectly, by treating it not as a subject but as an expression of the very lives that children lead.' (It is worth noting that this book was designed for those who found teaching English 'difficult and troublesome'. There were obviously many who did.) No more so-called 'imaginative' compositions to be forced on unresponsive children. No more days in the lives of pennies, puppy dogs or postage stamps. Now teachers had the incentive of the actual, the 'real' rather than the 'imagined'. Children would now describe what they had seen or done for themselves, the model they had built, the flowers they had picked on a nature walk and had before them on the desk. They would compile books based on information that they themselves had sought in reference books and supplemented by writing to living authorities outside school. This gave a sense of purpose to junior school work that was badly needed, aroused the interest of children and led to improved standards in their written work. For they were stimulated to record accurately and sensitively what they had directly observed. Honest recording of this kind is of great value and importance in a child's education.

But thoughtful teachers soon realised that this approach is only rewarding when there is considerable interest and involvement on the part of the child, and that this will very largely depend on the teacher's imagination, on his insight and creative power, both in the original conception occasioning the search for information, and in its presentation and development. Whatever his subject matter, he must be able to make it real *for the child*. Facts do not necessarily absorb and interest young children, especially not girls, nor are children inevitably excited by their own environment. One needs the catalyst of an active imagination in the teacher, to relate the facts to the child's experience, to bring the environment to life *in the child's mind*. It must be presented to him in personal terms so that he can enter into it and as the project proceeds live in it *in his own imagination*. Then he will come with sharpened apprehension to whatever further first-hand experience his teacher offers him. In their excitement at the new approach, some teachers pursued the actual, the everyday, with relentless zeal but not much imagination. In any case many educated people then, as now, actively distrusted and misunderstood the imagination, equating it with the imaginary, the unreal, the false, with everything in fact that they were so relieved to have swept away.

During the next ten years the effects of this banishing of English as a subject made themselves disturbingly felt. Many schools found less and less time for poetry or story beyond the graded readers thought essential for practising this necessary 'skill'. (Some schools even instituted 'tool reading lessons'.) Writing tended to be more and more objective. Dramatic work rarely took place in the average classroom. The only province left to English in its own right became the dreary abstract one of 'comprehension' and work on 'English' exercises, enticingly packaged by enterprising publishers throughout the fifties in a succession of bright all-purpose course books. New teachers coming into primary schools still often thought of English in terms of 'O' level clause analysis, précis, set books, for although a new spirit was active in many training colleges, many remained more narrowly academic in their approach than good grammar schools, while the effect on students of general attitudes to written English among lecturers rarely made for confidence and idiomatic ease. So unless a teacher was very courageous and imaginative himself or fortunate in his school, he tended to accept the routine and grow depressed. 'I don't really like teaching English,' a young teacher told me quite recently, 'it's so abstract.' No one had ever made her see and feel it differently. Far more experienced teachers distrusted the imagination, failing to realise or accept that it can have its own kind of reality and integrity. 'All this creative English, however you approach it, it's so artificial,' was one headmaster's comment. 'I never sit down to write a story. They won't when they grow up. Yet we're supposed to keep making them.' He was genuinely worried by the mediocre quality of his children's writing and was trying to work out with his staff what their aims and teachers have used their imaginations and seen the connection between a full and rich experience in English *as a subject* and the ability to use it freely and expressively *as an instrument*. Long before 1964 individual writers of vision concerned with English at this level, Marjorie Hourd, for instance, Sybil Marshall, Margaret Langdon, Dora Pym, in different ways urged the need for a unified conception of English not as a mere tool but a creative source. For readers who are interested I give details of their books and others I have found valuable in the appendix on page 274. Since *The Excitement of Writing* came out many more teachers have ventured to test the truth of this vision in their own work. Others who venture will discover that a powerful means of making the often impersonal material of many projects more alive and real for children may lie in English; not the literature earlier associated with junior school work, the poetry of the average anthology, *Alice in Wonderland*, *The Wind in the Willows*, the little book of form room plays, but in stories, poems and other writing directly concerned with some aspect of their theme, which draw children into it in a personal way. If a class has been living for some weeks in the world of the Greeks or Vikings or Pilgrim Fathers, creating their own play based on some incidents in this world makes it real for them in their own terms, gives it added depth and texture, like country one has walked over rather than driven through. Even more important, teachers will discover that stories, poems, playmaking, in their own right, feed and strengthen and delight just that part of a child's being on whose responsiveness and power all their other work depends: his power of feeling, his imagination, his capacity for wonder. Rooted in these, a child's intellect is more ready to respond than if sole attention is given to training it. Other expressive subjects, art, craft, music, movement, are tremendously important in this sphere, particularly art, and it is no accident that in schools where English has a central place they will be very much alive, although not always the other way about. But only English is consciously and articulately concerned with 'the very lives that children lead', working personally and intimately through language, the child's own language. The experience it offers in story and poetry, when this is well-chosen, can sharpen a child's awareness of the world about him and much more explicitly than other arts extends his knowledge and experience of life. It also has the power to enter and affect his private and personal worlds, to move him imperceptibly to new awareness, to make

him begin seeing to the heart there also. Writing enables him
to express this awareness in many different ways, and gives
him opportunities to express himself, to find outlet and pleasure
in the creative process of making. It also often helps children
explore and establish some kind of mastery over what as purely
private experience might be disturbing and intractable. Most
teachers, as they read the following, will recall parallel instances
in their own work:

One day after my real mother had died Daddy came into my
bedroom. 'Hallo Michael' he said in a sorrofoll voice I came in
because I wanted to ask you if you would like a new mother. He
drove strait to the point. '*No*' I said flatly I would not. Well he
said youre going to have one. 'I dont want one i said flatly 'I am
engaged to Miss James my secuarty at the office' Why must I have
another mother? I wont have one. 'Look Michael' he said I am going
to marry Miss James in two weeks time!' The quarrel was settled.

All this plays a vital part in developing children's sympathies
and understanding as people. At the same time it is always
vitally concerned with language — not grammar, for that is a
purely intellectual analytical activity which offers children no
experience and as I argue later should never be taught to
junior children, but the language that we all speak every day
and have done from our earliest years. This is never isolated
from us as people, unless we have to act a part, but in speech
or writing reveals immediately something of the kind of people
that we are. Unless our subject matter is completely dead for
us, it can never be an entirely neutral instrument. It should
certainly never be this in a junior school, where nothing that is
to be real for the child can be impersonal. Yet many teachers
still treat the English language as if it were and as if a child
must learn to use it solely to avoid grammatical errors, to
punctuate and spell correctly, and ultimately to fill in forms
and apply for jobs. 'Of course children from this area can't
cope with anything imaginative,' teachers sometimes say apol-
ogetically when mentioning how much time has to be spent on
'remedial' work, but one knows whose imaginations are defi-
cient. For one's own language is not a utility like gas or water,
but a condition and agent of growth. It should be central and
exciting for teacher and child. Both need some command of it
to be fully alive. If English is to be alive for the child it must
be alive for the teacher, which means the teacher's being alive

to the nature of English, to the spirit of the language. This means having nothing to do with text-books that are quite insensitive to this. It also means always being aware of English not as a negative body of rules, but as a living spoken tongue, continuously developing and changing, having a rich but not necessarily hallowed past. English is spoken much more than written. Everyone talks far more than they write and usually much more easily. Teaching young children, primary teachers know intimately what a vital part is played at every stage of a child's growth by his growth in language, in his individual power to express himself in words. They know also, though not all may want to admit it to themselves, that the success and value of their teaching depends entirely on a good relationship with their class, and that this must be based on some genuine personal relationship with each child. Not all teachers seem aware that the nature and quality of these relationships are largely shaped through English, through everyday talk between themselves and the children. Explanatory and exploratory, continuous in its ebb and flow, talk is at the heart of good primary teaching, to say nothing of its importance in all teaching, especially of English. Through natural serious talk about whatever is the heart of the matter in poem, story, starting point for writing, episode to be dramatised, children are helped towards understanding. If only negatively, teachers are also helped by talk, in choosing what to offer children. For they must not cheat. They must never choose what they cannot take seriously at the level for which it is intended. It must always be what they are prepared in some measure to enter into themselves. It must be what they can talk about with sincerity to children. I remember supervising a student who would take no poetry with his class of second-year juniors because all the poems in their book were, to use his phrase, 'pretty crumby poems'. Better to take no poems than 'crumby' poems, no story than 'crumby' stories, but only a lazy teacher will be content with such negative honesty. Children brought up in the kind of atmosphere I have described grow accustomed to take the experience of English seriously, which does not mean solemnly, and also naturally to associate talking and writing. This helps them develop confidence in their own written work and to express themselves easily and idiomatically. Their 'use of English' will have its roots in living language which a good teacher helps purge of vague approximation by kindling wherever possible individual concern to be exact.

All teachers want children to be responsive to experience, to develop in sympathy and understanding, to express themselves fluently in speech and writing. They must now work their own imaginations and recognise that the quality of the experience they give children in English in these four important years itself plays a decisive part in shaping the responsiveness, the development, the power of expression. The quality of this experience affects to some extent the kind of person each child becomes. On the narrower but most immediately important educational issue of a child's ability to write competently, they must see that most children, unless they take some positive pleasure in English, remain clumsy and indifferent craftsmen.

For the child pleasure comes immediately enough provided his teacher knows what to offer him; for English is full of shaped experience of the most varied and interesting kind and children are rarely bored by experience. It has not always the intensity of pleasurable experience in life nor its physical immediacy, but neither has it the rawness, the distress, the sheer injustice of so much that happens to them. Pleasure comes to children from words and rhythms and a peculiar heightening of consciousness in poetry; from the fascination of entering other people's lives in story; from projecting themselves in drama into some action more satisfying than life offers them; from using words to explore and express their own experience of all kinds in talk and writing. It does not come from filling in gaps in a text-book, from 'opposites', 'comprehension', grammar (the word still occurs on a number of timetables and students are quite often told to 'take nouns and adjectives' with eight and nine year olds, usually because they have 'such poor vocabularies'). Pleasure, 'this grand elementary principle', as Wordsworth called it, 'by which. . . (man) knows and feels and lives and moves', is nowhere more vividly attainable than in English, yet in many schools is nowhere so conspicuously absent. 'A dead subject consisting of spelling, grammar and now and again an essay. . . . No story, no poetry. . .' This is still typical of some comments made by students after a teaching practice. Yet following a practice at the same time as the student just quoted, another wrote: 'English had an important part in the class I taught. The children enjoyed reading and were encouraged in this. They were read to frequently—both prose and poetry. Their English writing was very good. The children had good imaginations, their writing was full of feeling. They especially enjoyed writing poetry that did not rhyme.' The average verdict suggests considerably more life than the first of these comments, but remains far in spirit from the second. The general aim still seems limited, remedial, utilitarian. Yet all teachers would probably like to achieve the atmosphere and response of the second class. All know, too, that the second set of children have much more chance of developing all their abilities and of doing themselves justice when examinations come. The obvious connection cannot be stressed too often. The second teacher clearly enjoyed English herself and at least unconsciously realised its essential unity and interrelatedness *as a subject*. Her class enjoyed its many forms of expression. She saw that each strengthened the other. Once there is this insight and pleasure on the teacher's part, English comes alive for the children, though for them it will not be a subject but to use the definition of the recent (1965) Schools Council Working Paper 'an activity permeating their lives'.

Teachers cannot enjoy English unless they genuinely experience it in some form themselves, both at the level at which they are choosing for children and at their own level. The second experience profoundly affects their capacity for the first. Unless some form of literature means something to them now, they cannot genuinely believe in the kind of experience they are offering children. The same mistrust, unease and lack of personal commitment that may have deadened English for them at school or college will begin to affect their class. On the other hand, if they had good teachers, they know that literature did not stop for these men and women when they left the classroom but was part of their lives. It is natural after some years teaching that one falls into a routine, but one should particularly guard against this happening with literature. One must be ready to reassess, which means to experience afresh books and poems that one takes for granted. They may not be right for children now, they cannot be the same for oneself as they were ten years ago. There is no danger of routine but some temptation to live on past pleasure for the many married women coming late to junior teaching. Only by all teachers giving themselves sometimes to the power of a good play or novel, or to reading some poetry, can they know the heightening of consciousness, the increased awareness which this can bring. This is a fusion of illumination and exhilaration, an access of energy, an increase in one's own capacity for living. For literature is not a storehouse of eternal values, nor a moral gymnasium, nor a sanctuary from debasing modern pressures, though many teachers seem to see it as one or more of these. Most great writers are highly subversive of convention in thought and feeling, if not in action. We are the better for reading them only in that our imaginations have been profoundly stirred, our sympathies drawn forth, and we have been made to see to the heart. After this experience we are less likely to be bored or apathetic towards actual living, though whether the increase of energy in us is translated into good or bad action depends entirely on other factors.

Much adult fiction, many television plays, films and West End successes fail to intensify awareness in this way. They have little precision or truth in observation, feeling or language. Stock characters, situations and reactions abound. Dialogue often becomes a trick or habit, outwardly 'true to life', but not coming from genuinely imagined characters reacting upon each other in a developing situation. All this fulfils tired expectations, never shocks into new seeing. However incidentally amusing, inventive or spine-chilling, such works lack imagination. They often appear full of energy, but this is external and spurious. There is no inner imaginative life. Because of this, it seems to me vital that teachers, as they read novels or watch plays, should find themselves naturally and spontaneously making their own living response. Then they will find that they have little time for the shoddy or secondhand, and will not be content to draw on it in their work with children.

Many teachers will need no suggestions for their reading. Others may welcome some, and for these I include the brief discussion and annotated lists in Appendix I. I offer suggestions for drama and poetry as well as the novel and short story, for these two older forms are a vital part of literature and for many people far more important and exciting than the novel. The latter has always tended to be stressed most in schools, partly because it lends itself most easily to extended classroom use, and probably even more because it is the form we traditionally associate with private reading. But this may not remain so. Certainly in England since the war there seems to have been a significant shift of interest from, and a certain tiredness in attitude towards the novel as a form. It badly needs a major talent. There is less vigour in English writers than in American or Commonwealth or South African ones. There is more power in modern drama. No fictional character in the novel has been as significant as Osborne's Jimmy Porter. No novel that I know has created the peculiarly modern paradox of isolation and dependence as memorably as Harold Pinter's *The Caretaker*. This may well mean that the novel is less suited than drama or poetry to reflect and explore the mood of modern English society, so pragmatic and materialist on the surface, yet probably more individually reflective and questioning than any preceding one. The novel has always tended lovingly to re-create the past, and vividly to celebrate and explore the present, often during the nineteenth century with the kind of documentary purpose that has now partly been taken over by certain kinds of television programme, or more scientifically if less movingly by sociology. It has been concerned with individual men and women in society more than with man and his relation to the universe. Novelists far more than dramatists have drawn heavily on their own childhood in their writing. More novels and stories are concerned with childhood and growing up than plays. This naturally makes the form of particular importance and value in school, but it also suggests that teachers need first-hand experience themselves of literature in all its forms if they are to see this in its proper perspective, and not greatly to limit their own pleasure and the pleasure they can bring to children.

Most of the writers I suggest are of this century. This is deliberate. Literature and drama always start by being of their age. Their tensions and energy must spring from writers being aware of their own time in a profound way, even though the whole emphasis of their work may be to show their lack of sympathy with it. At its greatest, literature and drama speak beyond their time because of the power of their energy, the power of their imaginative life. Greatness is rare and unless one experiences it one can never genuinely measure the impact of lesser achievement. But the writers of one's own time speak more immediately and intimately to most people than those of earlier periods, no matter how great. Even more important, they sometimes seem to speak *for* us. Their concerns are often peculiarly our concerns. Also, our experience of our own time makes us able to judge the genuineness of an author's awareness in a way that we cannot do with earlier writers without very extensive knowledge of the period, and not only of its literature. Even then, our awareness lacks something vital and irrecoverable, actual experience of living then. My final reason for choosing mainly modern writers is that we cannot fully experience our own time without some experience of its literature. Some awareness of it first-hand is part of full living in our time.

Where the novel and drama are concerned, I have deliberately not recommended particular authors as touchstones (for this is depressing if one fails to enjoy them) but chosen some themes that seem to me important and suggested some books and plays that explore these, though without this necessarily having been their authors' main conscious purpose. Teachers can then more easily decide for themselves the relative imaginative power of the books they read, or the plays they may be able to see, and will have no difficulty in exploring further any writers whom they find particularly interesting. The works are not by any means all masterpieces, but I think that all have some genuine imaginative life.

There is no easy formula for recognition here, we can only be ready to respond to the work. It must make its impact on us as individuals or not at all. Critics can help in various ways towards our seeing with the author, they cannot feel for us. They positively hinder if, by some pattern of 'composing legalism', they tell us what we ought to feel, what we should or should not be enjoying.

However, one recognises genuineness first, I think, from sensing an underlying seriousness, which will be there with a comic writer like Shaw as much as with more tragic or earnest ones. What he is trying to do must matter to him before it can begin to matter to us. With a novelist or dramatist, his characters and their situation must concern him, be real for him as he imagines them. We must sense some excitement, delight or creative tension at work as he imposes shape on their inter-action and development. We can also expect, particularly with dramatists, a powerful intellectual excitement: some idea or vision, significant for him and, in his view, for us as well. Whether the writer's excitement is matched by a correspondingly genuine quality of insight, thought and shaping power is an-other matter; and recognition here must partly depend on our own understanding and experience. Only we ourselves can know how much we are moved and in what way by a book or play. Only we can know how much our picture of the world as it is has been illuminated, how much our sense of what it could be like has been heightened. Certainly, most good novels and plays have a continuous moral concern, for they are about people, their beliefs and ideas, their thoughts and feelings at every level of being; and about their individual and social relationships and values. Much of our pleasure is in response to this, and in the interaction between the author's values and our own. But the final effect of reading a good novel, or of seeing a fine play well acted and produced, is on our whole being and is much more one of vision. We respond to the writer's total imaginative energy, to what – with his individual creativeness – he has *made*. If teachers for whom literature has hitherto meant little can find time to read with feeling attentiveness only a few of the books suggested, and manage to see only one or two of the plays, I think that they will begin to sense this for themselves. If they do, I am sure they will find themselves wanting more than they may have done in the past to give the beginnings of such experience to children.

Teaching is a practical art. I have written this book not only to stir teachers' imaginations but to help with specific suggestions towards their implementing their own vision. I also want to provoke some reassessment of ordinary everyday assumptions about English as a subject to be taught.

For instance, what do teachers think of the poetry in the anthologies in use in their school? Is it genuine? Does it in some way heighten our senses? Or is much of it the kind of decorative and wordy nothing that makes many English people ignore or feel embarrassed by it? If it is good poetry, is it also good poetry for children? Again, how much imaginative life do teachers find in the stories in their class libraries, or in the graded readers that they may be using, or in the stories that they have recently chosen to read to their class? If they have read no stories of late, are they confident that they can justify the omission? Above all, what do teachers consider *good* English generally, and for the level at which they teach? How important do they think correctness? What do they want to encourage in their children's writing? How much in practice are they working through negatives, concerned more with what children should avoid than what they should strive for? What do they think of the quality of language in any course book they are using?

This is the kind of question I want teachers to ask themselves as they read, not because I expect them to accept my views, for one cannot be dogmatic in these matters. But if they disagree after genuine consideration, their teaching will be based on individual conviction, which is worth far more in English and makes more impact on children than dutiful imitation. Above all, it should help some teachers to be clearer in their own minds about the nature and purpose of the subject, and to be freer and happier about teaching it. Once they genuinely enjoy it, the children certainly will. They need not fear, as I know some teachers do, the effects on discipline of freedom and enjoyment.

A consistently imaginative approach is never disruptive of discipline. An occasional excursion into drama or a half-hearted trial of 'free' writing with a class usually kept tightly under control, or generally drifting, will be; but here it is the personal commitment and the need for effort that is feared, and not the freedom. If the teacher's whole attitude is informed by conviction and concern and genuine respect for the individuality of his children, there will be order as well as freedom. For imaginative work in English, as in any subject, produces its own order, the 'more than usual order' which Coleridge discerned, together with 'more than usual excitement', at the heart of all creative activity.

POETRY

MANY junior school teachers are unhappy taking poetry and
some make no attempt to do so, especially not in the fourth
year, while students who enjoy poetry are sometimes asked to
take lessons with classes in addition to their own. Some teachers
may have tried and been disheartened through unwise choice
or presentation. Many are more likely to be people who do not
expect children to have time for poetry because they have no
time for it themselves. They probably have dreary memories of
poetry lessons at school, particularly at secondary level. They
are almost certain to be saddled with an anthology that confirms
their worst suspicions about its pointless artificial nature. All
these teachers tend to isolate poetry from their other activities,
their mistrust infects their class and when conscience occasionally pricks them into doubtful action, the children – not surprisingly – are unresponsive or hostile. And so their own
attitudes are perpetuated. Unless something happens. Unless
their class has another teacher for whom poetry is an exciting
urgent form of expression; who knows good from bad, and
especially what is good for children; who reads poetry well,
and is well read in it; above all who knows that it intensifies
ordinary experience, and so relates naturally to most other
activities.

When poetry *is* discovered at school, it is almost always due
to an individual teacher and years later the revelation remains
vivid. A student put it like this: 'I have very little recollection
of any poetry being read to me until the third year of the junior
school. I can vaguely remember a rhyme or short poem being
read, but the occasions were rare, and they left no impression.
The teacher who took the class in the third year enjoyed poetry
and his attitude greatly influenced me and the rest of the class.
I clearly remember the occasion on which he read *Silver* to us.
The poem was read once, and then we all put our heads on the
desks and closed our eyes. I remember picturing almost every
word as he reread the poem. We wrote on a loose-leaf sheet
any poems that were read to us, and then mounted the sheets

in a folder that we ourselves had made in craft lessons. I was
particularly proud of this anthology and would often read it in
my spare moments.'

Junior school teachers have a marvellous opportunity, which
many take with both hands. They recognise that all young
children naturally delight in poetry and deserve the best that
one can give them. Others who do not care for poetry may at
least be helped in their work in the classroom by some consideration of what gives children pleasure. If as imaginative
adults they begin to give poetry a chance they may find that
they begin to get pleasure from it too.

What do children like? This, for instance:

> When cats run home and light is come
> And dew is cold upon the ground
> And the far-off stream is dumb,
> And the whirring sail goes round,
> And the whirring sail goes round;
> Alone and warming his five wits
> The white owl in the belfry sits.

Or this:

> In Hans' old Mill his three black cats
> Watch the bins for the thieving rats,
> Whisker and claw they crouch in the night
> Their five eyes smouldering green and bright.

Or this:

> Four o'clock strikes
> There's a rising hum,
> Then the doors fly open,
> The children come.
>
> With a wild cat-call
> And a hop-scotch hop
> And a bouncing ball
> And a whirling top . . .

For children delight in the directness of poetry, its sharp exact
appeal to the senses, which makes the poet's world, if he is a
good poet, strangely kin to their own: all presentation and *outsight*, no analysis. There is often an explosive magical quality.
The poet is so excited by what he is writing about that he

makes the words dance and sing, the lines move in formation
of some kind. Enjoyment is as immediate and real for them as
watching and hearing telegraph wires from a train. There is no
conscious appreciation of the separate elements that cause the
excitement: rhythm, rhyme, repetition, pattern, sheer sound of
words; but intense response varying in emphasis with individual
children. As children grow older, their pleasure becomes slightly
less immediate and explosive. There will still be sharp exact
outsight, but there will also be a first stirring of insight. They
will begin to share the poet's imaginative excitement, experience
a little of what made him want to write, although not consciously. In James Reeves's *Snail*, for instance, there is immediate
participation and at the same time slight withdrawal and wonder
as children watch:

> At sunset when the night-dews fall
> Out of the ivy on the wall
> With horns outstretched and pointed tail
> Comes the grey and noiseless snail.
> On ivy stem she clambers down
> Carrying her house of brown.
> Safe in the dark, no greedy eye
> Can her tender body spy,
> While she herself, a hungry thief,
> Searches out the freshest leaf.
> She travels on as best she can
> Like a toppling caravan.

The same is there in reaction to Emily Dickinson's *The Bird and
the Crumb*:

> A bird came down the walk:
> He did not know I saw;
> He bit an angle-worm in halves
> And ate the fellow, raw.
>
> And then he drank a dew
> From a convenient grass
> And then hopped sideways to the wall
> To let a beetle pass.
>
> He glanced with rapid eyes
> That hurried all abroad, —
> They looked like frightened beads, I thought.
> He stirred his velvet head . . .

POETRY 31

And with the element of wonder much more strongly marked,
it is there in Walter De La Mare's *Silver*, so vividly remembered
by the student I quoted:

> Slowly, silently, now the moon
> Walks the night in her silver shoon;
> This way, and that, she peers and sees
> Silver fruit upon silver trees . . .

Many poems in more old-fashioned junior anthologies
(of which plenty are still in use especially in the first two
years) have none of this poetic life, so that it is worth considering some of its elements in more detail. For instance, if one
contrasts the Emily Dickinson just quoted with a verse from
a poem I have seen in more than one anthology, *The Procession
of Flowers*:

> First came the primrose,
> On the bank high,
> Like a maiden looking forth
> From the window of a tower
> When the battle rolls below
> And saw the storms go by.

The average adult would probably say that this is more 'poetic'
than *The Bird and the Crumb*, yet there are no words in it that
make one see the flowers as precisely and delicately as the lines,
'He bit an angle-worm in halves', and 'rapid eyes that hurried
all abroad', make one see the bird. None that appeal to the
sense of touch as *velvet* does, and *raw*. The second poet has
visualised nothing sharply, his elaborate simile adds no particularity to the primrose it is meant to be describing, as Emily
Dickinson's 'like frightened beads' does to the bird's eyes. Instead it takes one away to a literary never-never land. Eleanor
Graham includes Rose Fyleman's *Alms in Autumn* in *A Puffin
Book of Verse*, of which this is one stanza:

> Ashtree, ashtree, throw me, if you please,
> Throw me down a slender bunch of russet-gold keys,
> I fear the gates of fairyland may all be shut so fast
> That nothing but your magic keys will ever take me past.
> I'll tie them to my girdle and as I go along,
> My heart will find a comfort in the tinkle of their song.

If one sets beside this Katherine Tynan's *August Weather*:

> Dead heat and windless air,
>   And silence over all;
> Never a leaf astir,
>   But the ripe apples fall;
> Plums are purple-red,
>   Pears amber brown;
>   Thud! in the garden bed
>   Ripe apples fall down

one immediately knows which would more heighten a child's sense of what autumn is really like. *Alms in Autumn* creates no genuine experience but merely elaborates a fanciful idea in the poet's mind. There is nothing to talk about except the personification, which is still thought of by many teachers as inherently poetic and to be admired and imitated. Poetic devices should never be considered at this stage in this way. If one is forced into talking about them, they are not working properly. For they should always be directed towards making real the experience which the poet has felt urgently compelled to create and explore. If there is no urgency in the poem, one should not waste time on it and, worse still, make children associate poetry with the decorative and artificial. Personification of course often does serve imaginative pressure but then it is like a fly-over, not a hold-up while the Lord Mayor's Show goes by.

> All round the house is the jet black night;
> It stares through the window-pane;
> It crawls in the corners, hiding from light,
> And it moves with the moving flame.

Stevenson undoubtedly gains in immediacy here through personifying *night*. On the other hand, though Brighty Rands calls the following, *The Race of Flowers*, the personification is too elaborate to give any sense of speed (as well as being suspiciously full of echoes from Tennyson's *Maud*):

> The trees and the flowers seem running a race
>   But none treads down the other;
> And neither thinks it his disgrace
>   To be later than his brother.
> Yet the pear-tree shouts to the lilac tree,

'Make haste for the Spring is late!'
And the lilac cried to the chest-nut tree,
  Because he is so great
'Pray you, dear Sir, be quick, be quick!
For down below we are blossoming thick!'

Urgency or lack of it is nowhere more strongly revealed than in
the quality of a poem's rhythm. Yet rhythm is easier to respond
to than define. It is there in my first three quotations, Tennyson's
Owl, De La Mare's *Five Eyes*, Hal Summers's *Out of School*, but
less markedly in the next two. It is there strongly in Blake's

     Tyger! Tyger! burning bright
     In the forests of the night
     What immortal hand or eye
     Could frame they fearful symmetry?

in W. H. Auden's

     This is the night mail crossing the border
     Bringing the cheque and the postal order.

and the anonymous *Sir Patrick Spens*:

     They hadna' sailed a league, a league,
       A league but barely three,
     When the lift grew dark, and the wind blew loud
       And a gurly grew the sea.

It is not there in *To The Cuckoo*:

     Though babbling only to the vale
       Of sunshine and of flowers,
     Thou bringest unto me a tale
       Of visionary hours.

Yet Wordsworth uses exactly the same ballad form as the
writer of *Sir Patrick Spens*. It is not simply that certain stanza
forms are powerful rhythmically and others not, though this
comes into it. Rhythm always has a recurrent recognisable
pattern of sound that arouses our expectations. When it reflects
genuine feeling, it also profoundly satisfies them. English poetry
works by speech stress not metrical feet. For a rhythm to have

C

life stress must fall on words that matter, so that genuine urgency of meaning decides how you say the poem, not the tired 'tum-ti-tum' expectations of external pattern. The stresses in the ballad show this. *League* matters, so does *lift* and *dark* and *gurly*. In the Wordsworth unimportant link words are stressed as they never are in speech, *to*, for instance, and *and* and *unto*. Singsong easily results and teachers won't need telling how quickly children fall into this in choral speaking when they have no concern about the meaning. Wordsworth's greatness as a poet does not lie in his rhythms, nor is it accessible to children, yet the *Puffin Book* has more poems by him than any writer except Anon.

What about:

> Then the little Hiawatha
> Learned of every bird its language
> Learned their names and all their secrets?

Children always respond to a marked rhythm and may well enjoy it but they should not come to associate something so easily imitable, so much a kind of trick or habit, with good poetry. Longfellow's rhythm bears no relation to the way we stress words in speech. Genuine rhythm almost always has an organic natural quality. It never becomes a straitjacket. Some rhythms seem tremendously vigorous yet this may not be produced by the inner life of the poem but whipped up consciously by the writer. *A Wet Sheet and a Flowing Sea* strikes me as an instance, as does the pseudo-straining at the leash of:

> I'm a lean dog, a keen dog, a wild dog and lone,
> I'm a rough dog, a tough dog, hunting on my own!

Teachers will naturally give children all kinds of rhythms. It is only important that they themselves should realise these distinctions, and that there is always a connection between genuineness of feeling and the rhythm that embodies it. False rhythm invariably means false feeling. Alfred Noyes, for instance, in *Sherwood*:

> Hark! the dazzled laverock climbs the golden steep!
> Marian is waiting: is Robin Hood asleep?
> Round the fairy grass-rings, frolic elf and fay,
> In Sherwood, in Sherwood, about the break of day

is pretending to himself about the past as much as to his reader. The traditional Robin Hood ballads quickly reveal this as does a very little knowledge of the traditional May-Game. (The Oxford Companion to English Literature describes Maid Marian with delightful circumspection as 'a female personage'.)

Falseness of feeling and thought in a writer reveals itself in falseness of language as well as rhythm. During Noyes's period, which still exercises strong sway over traditional anthologies, false language often shows in pseudo-contractions like *'twixt, 'twill, 'tween,* and tired or contrived alliteration like 'frolic, elf and fay'. There is addiction to archaic verbal forms kept alive by nineteenth-century hymn writers especially. For instance:

> Where the sunny Lindis *floweth,*
>   *Goeth, floweth*
> From the meads where melick *groweth,*

from Jean Ingelow's much anthologised *High Tide on the Coast of Lincolnshire.* Repetition is usually there to fill out a stanza as with 'In Sherwood, in Sherwood', and rarely has the deep cumulative force of 'Tyger, Tyger' or 'They hadna' sailed a league, a league', which corresponds to how strong feeling works upon our speech in life. Generations of children, since become adults and some of them teachers, have come to associate the poetic with this kind of insincerity and unnaturalness, which is the very opposite of the truth. Junior teachers who care about poetry can do much to reverse this conventional view.

The satisfaction of pattern, rhyme and sound is almost always closely linked with rhythm and for children is quite unconscious. They usually prefer simple patterns to elaborate ones, except where there is a singing lilting quality as in *The Owl and the Pussy Cat* or *The Jumblies.* They love any element of magic and incantation as in:

> Jellicle Cats are white and black,
> Jellicle Cats are of moderate size;
> Jellicles jump like a jumping-jack,
> Jellicle Cats have moonlit eyes.

Other patterns that genuinely reflect and reveal meaning work with children as much as adults. James Reeves's *Cows*, for instance:

Half the time they munched the grass, and all the time they lay
Down in the water-meadows, the lazy month of May,
  A-chewing,
  A-mooing,
To pass the hours away.

'Nice weather,' said the brown cow.
  'Ah,' said the white.
'Grass is very tasty.
  Grass is all right.'

And Walter De La Mare's *Done For*:

> Old Ben Bailey
> He's been and done
> For a small brown bunny
> With his long gun.
>
> Glazed are the eyes
> That stared so clear,
> And no sound stirs
> In that hairy ear.

Children expect poetry to rhyme although they write much better poetry themselves without it. Only towards the top of the school, when a class is ready for some detachment from and feeling about the experience, as well as strong participation in it, do they enjoy free verse. They like humorous rhyme but less than some adults think. Browning's effects in the *Pied Piper*, and other nineteenth-century ingenuities abounding in the *Laughter* sections of anthologies, are beyond most of them. They respond much more to a deeper unconscious appeal, akin to that of satisfying chords in music, or to the power of rhyme as a kind of spell which James Reeves catches in his

> There was a man of Uriconium
> Who played a primitive harmonium;

They respond intensely, for instance, to Eleanor Farjeon's *Cat*, in which rhyme works very closely with pattern and rhythm to give the directest of presentations:

Cat!
Scat!
Atter her, atter her,
Sleeky flatterer,
Spitfire chatterer,
Scatter her, scatter her
  Off her mat!
Wuff!
  Treat her rough!

They also love poems that are full of sounds, such as James
Reeves's *Grim and Gloomy*, with words like this and 'slim and
slimy' or 'salt and oozy', 'Huge and snuffling', to be mouthed
and enjoyed.

These elements, rhythm, rhyme, pattern, sound, all release
children at once into a world of heightened consciousness but,
save in the pure not-to-be-explained delight of nonsense poetry,
there must be genuine experience for their consciousness to
play upon. It must first be genuine *for the poet*, otherwise there
will be no poetry but it must also be experience of potential
reality, interest and concern *for the child*. A swift glance at the
contents of *A Puffin Book of Verse*, *The Open Window*, Book II of
James Britton's *Oxford Books of Verse for Juniors* (this series varies
very much from book to book. Book IV, for instance, could not
be cited in this way) reveals little such experience. Old wives
and wagoners still trudge the highway, together with wandering
fiddlers and wise old gypsy men. Shepherds and milkmaids toil
cheerfully, sometimes breaking off to enjoy well-earned leisure.
Poems about poverty and content provide suitable moral background while sluggards and other naughty boys are either solemnly
warned or humorously put in their place, usually the corner of
some upper middle-class Victorian schoolroom. Most modern
children, born for better or worse into the second half of the
twentieth century and into towns and suburbs, not rural communities, couldn't care less and one is not in the least surprised.
In their hearts most teachers don't care either about these
themes, which is why so many keep away from poetry altogether. There are obviously many poems in these books of
much intrinsic merit, many that penetrate beneath the surface
picture I have given and some that individual children enjoy
and remember. But very few have genuine urgency for children.

Many poems are unsuitable less because of their subject than
the poet's attitude towards it. Adults often find this kind of

unsuitability difficult to recognise. Nostalgia may keep them
from clear-sightedness or strong personal response to what they
fail to see are entirely adult themes. Poems about time and
dreams tend to be corrupted by nostalgia and of little concern
to children. Walter De La Mare's *Nod*, for instance, and Ralph
Hodgson's

> Time, you old gypsy man,
> Will you not stay,
> Put up your caravan
> Just for one day?

I have seen this taken in conjunction with a film strip, supposed
always to make things 'real' for children. By the end of the lesson
the class knew a little more about the gypsy way of life. They had
no inkling of the point of the comparison for the poet. For
children live in the moment. They never think of time as
devouring our years or vaguely, distressingly, leaking away. On
the other hand they have their recollections, some very early
ones stand out vividly and at nine and ten there is a feeling of
grown-upness towards five and six. Eleanor Farjeon's poem, *It
was Long Ago*, in *A Puffin Quartet of Poets*, explores time with
vivid awareness of what it is beginning to mean to a child.
Nine year olds are interested. They are held by the conversational manner of the reminiscence, as the poet searches the
recesses of her mind for the details:

> A dusty road in summer I remember,
> A mountain, and an old house, and a tree
> That stood, you know,
>
> Behind the house. An old woman I remember
> In a red shawl with a grey cat on her knee
> Humming under a tree.
>
> She seemed the oldest thing I can remember,
> But then perhaps I was not more than three.
> It was long ago.
>
> I dragged on the dusty road, and I remember
> How the old woman looked over the fence at me
> And seemed to know
>
> How it felt to be three, and called out I remember
> 'Do you like bilberries and cream for tea?'
> I went under the tree

And while she hummed, and the cat purred, I remember
How she filled a saucer with berries and cream for me
So long ago.

Ordinarily no teacher would think of reading children a poem
about death. Philip Larkin's deceptively simple one, *Days*,
which I quote in Appendix I would hold and puzzle them but
they would not understand. But many children come upon dead
animals or have pets who die. By the time they are nine or ten,
death has more concern for them in many ways than time,
especially if they look back to the death of a beloved pet a few
years earlier. John Crowe Ransom's poem, *Janet Waking*, about
a small girl who discovers that her beloved hen has died, is
sufficiently moving for its difficult precision of vocabulary not
to be a handicap:

> 'Old Chucky, Old Chucky!' she cried,
> Running on little pink feet upon the grass
> To Chucky's house, and listening. But alas,
> Her Chucky had died.
>
> It was a transmogrifying bee
> Came droning down on Chucky's old bald head
> And sat and put the poison. It scarcely bled,
> But how exceedingly
>
> And purply did the knot
> Swell with the venom and communicate
> Its rigour! Now the poor comb stood up straight
> But Chucky did not.

Christopher Leach's *Blackbird*, included in the excellent recent
anthology, *Happenings*, compiled by David Grugeon and Maurice
Wollman, is equally moving and objective and also simpler.
The setting has immediate meaning for most children while
the ending brings in questions of relative value that thoughtful
ten year olds are ready to think and talk about.

> My wife saw it first—
> I was reading the evening paper.
> Come and look, she said.
>
> It was trying to drink
> Where water had formed on a drain-cover,
> It was shabby with dying.

It did not move until I was very close —
Then hopped off, heavily,
Disturbing dead leaves.

We left water, crumbs.
It did not touch them
But waited among the leaves,
Silently.

This morning was beautiful:
Sunlight, other birds
Singing.

It was outside the door.
I picked it up
And it was like holding feathered air.
I wrapped what was left
Incongruously
In green sycamore leaves
And buried it near the trees,
Inches down.

This evening
I find it difficult to concentrate
On the paper, the news
Of another cosmonaut.

Many children have been cruel to an animal at some time
themselves. Experience may not have made all realise the extent
to which they can arouse fear in creatures infinitely powerless
before them. A poem that explores this aspect of a child's
relationship with animals is Ian Serraillier's *Anne and the Field
Mouse*, with which *Happenings* opens.

We found a field mouse in the chalk quarry today
In a circle of stones and empty oil drums
By the fag ends of a fire. There had been
A picnic there; he must have been after crumbs.

Jane saw him first, a flicker of brown fur
In and out of the charred wood and chalk-white.
I saw him last, but not till we turned up
Every stone and surprised him into flight,

Though not far — little zigzag spurts from stone
To stone. Once, as he lurked in his hiding-place,
I saw his beady eyes uplifted to mine.
I'd never seen such terror in so small a face.

I watched, amazed and guilty. Beside us suddenly
A heavy pheasant whirred up from the ground,
Scaring us all; and, before we knew it, the mouse
Had broken cover, skimming away without a sound,

Melting into the nettles. We didn't go
Till I'd chalked in capitals on a rusty can:
THERE'S A MOUSE IN THOSE NETTLES. LEAVE
HIM ALONE. NOVEMBER 15th. ANNE.

One notices how the last four poems quoted explore meaning
very much as a story does, rather than excitingly reveal it.
The tone in each is conversational, rhythm and rhyme are
muted, for they would distract, but there is still loving exactness
in the choice of word. There is much in them that children
want to talk about. That they are a kind of free verse in contrast
to much of what they may have read can be validly touched on
in this context.

The important criterion for teachers always is that there
should be objective presentation. Poems about nature should be
concerned with nature at work in a particular setting, as John
Clare, for instance, always is, not about the pageant of the
seasons. Poems about animals should direct the senses to the
creature, as W. H. Davies does in *The Cat*:

> Within that porch, across the way,
> I see two naked eyes this night;
> Two eyes that neither shut nor blink,
> Searching my face with a green light.

Christina Rossetti in *What can lambkins do?*, which is in *A Puffin
Book of Verse*, invites readers to share the animals' feeling in a
way that becomes a little sentimental and wrong for children.
This writer's childlike intensity makes her immediately accessible to them but her quite frequent morbid indulgence of feeling also shuts them out. *The Sound of the Wind* is objective and
delightful, *My Heart is like a Singing Bird*, subjective and embar-
rassing. In the same way, if one contrasts De La Mare's laconic
Done For (quoted on page 36) with the better known poem
by James Stephens *The Snare*:

> I hear a sudden cry of pain!
>   There is a rabbit in a snare:
> Now I hear the cry again,
>   But I cannot tell from where,

the second would obviously appeal to many, especially girls, but one knows that there is more truth and strength in the former, and that most ten year olds would get more satisfaction from it. What about Edward Thomas's *A Cat*?

> She had a name among the children;
> But no one loved though someone owned
> Her, locked her out of doors at bedtime
> And had her kittens duly drowned.
>
> In Spring, nevertheless, this cat
> Ate blackbirds, thrushes, nightingales,
> And birds of bright voice and plume and flight,
> As well as scraps from neighbours' pails.
>
> I loathed and hated her for this:
> One speckle on a thrush's breast
> Was worth a million such, and yet
> She lived long, till God gave her rest.

Children tend to resist this. It has none of the immediacy of W. H. Davies or Eleanor Farjeon. It is quiet and conversational and reflective. But it is not self-pitying or nostalgic. Thomas asks one to register certain facts, then forces what is probably a new awareness about the nature of animal life and offers an outlet in strong feeling – 'I loathed and hated her for this.' There is complexity for children in sharing this feeling for they may well be deeply attached to a particular cat, whom they must now see in a new light. Children of ten and eleven, however become increasingly aware of complexities of feeling and the occasional poem that allows these to be talked about is valuable although it will not be widely enjoyed.

Poems about people must be equally objective in presentation and are best read when the class is actively concerned with observing and writing about people, people in their own families, people they notice on trains and buses, people they for some reason remember vividly. The occasional poem, however good, about a person who has no part in their world or with any project may well fall flat. Most of the people in poems in older anthologies are very remote from them. Yet children are vividly aware of adults, if not very interested in what goes on in their minds. James Stephens's *Seumas Beg* comes alive as this otherness registers upon the boy in the poem:

A man was sitting underneath a tree
Outside the village; and he asked me what
Name was upon this place; and said that he
Was never here before—He told a lot

Of stories to me, too. His nose was flat!
I asked him how it happened, and he said
—The first mate of the *Mary Ann* did that
With a marling spike one day—but he was dead,

And jolly good job too; and he'd have gone
A long way to have killed him—Oh, he had
A gold ring in one ear; the other one
—'Was bit off by a crocodile, bedad!'

That's what he said. He taught me how to chew.
He was a real nice man. He liked me too.

As an unusual character, if children are concerned with these,
he holds their interest. Otherwise teachers would do well to
explore more modern poets whose insight can sharpen a child's
awareness of people around him. To start with the open road,
B. S. Johnson's *Song Of The Wagondriver* means something to a
modern child, especially if he lives near a main trunk road, or
sometimes goes long journeys by car. The feeling it establishes
between the driver and his wagon, the monotony but also the
hold of his job upon him, and the way that this conditions his
family life, are realistically established in rhythm and idiom.
After reading it, a ten year old would look with new eyes at
passing wagon-drivers, and with some understanding. Closer
to most children's own lives, Edwin Brock's *A Moment of Respect*
is moving in a completely objective way:

> Two things I remember about my grandfather:
> his threadbare trousers and the way he adjusted
> his half-hunter watch two minutes every day.

Michell Raper, in a poem called *Morning Glory*, stirs feeling even
more important:

> My father would begin each day
> By standing in the backyard door
> And giving one tremendous sneeze
> Mid-way between a gasp and roar.

These three poems are all in the 'Portraits' section of Hutchinson's anthology of modern poems, *Here Today*, introduced by Ted Hughes, which I warmly recommend. It is intended for secondary children so only some of the poems are suitable for juniors but in its own right I think it would give many teachers pleasure.

A person can be presented from inside, voicing his own otherness, and still be an objective creation separate from the artist creating him. A scarecrow is a kind of man, always fascinating to a child. James Kirkup brings this out in his poem *The Lonely Scarecrow*:

> My poor old bones – I've only two –
> A broomshank and a broken stave,
> My ragged gloves are a disgrace,
> My one peg-foot is in the grave.

Mr. Scarecrow, on the other hand, by a writer called Sheila Braine, has none of this inner integrity nor does it respect the individuality of child readers:

> There's a ragged old man in the garden to-day
> And Gardener, laughing, says there he can stay;
> His coat is in tatters, he wears an old hat,
> And the birds do not like him, I'm quite sure of that.

The writer foists on the child the conventionally arch attitude of appealing childishness, the falseness of which is given away by the trite *Teddy-Bears Picnic* rhythm. There is often an equally false pathos, yet pity is very rare in children. I am reminded of a grim story of a friend of my sister's, whose mother died one Christmas Eve while with the family. When she told her children on Christmas morning, their first question was 'Did she leave our presents?' This is close to the world of James Reeves's *Mr. Tom Narrow*:

> A scandalous man
> Was Mr. Tom Narrow,
> He pushed his grandmother
> Round in a barrow.
> And he called out loud
> As he rang his bell,
>   'Grannies to sell!
>   Old Grannies to sell!'

Children live immediately and often carelessly. They can take oblique hints of adult complexities, they have to all the time, but these can be tossed aside when new experience comes – unless they are personally affected, when their reaction may be out of proportion to the event's significance. Where fantasy or magic comes in, as it often does with seven and eight year olds, the poets must be as childishly involved and as serious as children, they must genuinely believe in the world they are creating. The fantasy must be as real as a dream is real while we are dreaming. Walter De La Mare believes in his witches in *The Ride-By-Nights*:

> Up on their brooms the Witches stream,
> Crooked and black in the crescent's gleam;
> One foot high, and one foot low,
> Bearded, cloaked, and cowled, they go.

But one does not need much of a poem called *The Sand Castle*:

> I'm building a castle,
> A lovely sandcastle,
> Down by the edge of the sea;
> And I *think* that a mermaid,
> A shy little mermaid,
> Is timidly peeping at me . . .

to know that its writer does not for a moment really believe in her mermaid but thinks that it would be nice to play a game of *Let's Pretend* with child readers. A moment watching a group at play makes one feel how real *pretending* is for them. Adults who want to play must lose themselves in a new reality. One must never cheat children, least of all with poetry and at a time when their attitudes towards it are beginning to form. Yet many anthologies for first and second years do cheat almost all the time. 'There is no cruelty in these books,' says one of them. 'Nothing but kindness from cover to cover.' But life is not a joyous *Golden Road* despite the book's title and unconsciously children already know this. 'I am Stephen Dedalus. I am walking beside my father whose name is Simon Dedalus. We are in Cork, in Ireland. Cork is a city. Our room is in the Victoria Hotel . . . ' So James Joyce makes his hero repeat to himself, just as he writes his address in his geography book, as most of us have written, ending with Europe, The World, The Universe.

This concern with identity, this feeling of the separateness of oneself, perceived detachedly by a strange second self, possesses most children at some point. It is a secret and rather frightening feeling. Walter de la Mare captures it in *Myself*:

> Along the lovely paths
> A little child like me
> With face, with hands like mine
> Plays ever silently.

But one would not want to read the poem aloud. There is no such delicate integrity, only conscious archness in Doris Rowley's *The Other Me*:

> When I go visiting and sit
> With mother in a train:
> It's fun to see another me
> Inside the window pane . . .

There is no hint here of the occasional real terror of childhood, that one has no identity. In general, though, children have no interest in poems about childhood, for the state of being a child has little meaning for them until they are on the verge of leaving it. On the other hand they respond at once to the sense of excitement and guilt in Theodore Roethke's *Child on Top of a Greenhouse*:

> The wind billowing out the seat of my breeches,
> My feet crackling splinters of glass and dried putty,
> The half-grown chrysanthemums staring up like accusers,
> Up through the streaked glass, flashing with sunlight,
> A few white clouds all rushing eastward,
> A line of elms plunging and tossing like horses,
> And everyone, everyone pointing up and shouting!

Equally, to the speed and sharp focusing of Hal Summer's *Out of School*, the opening of which I quoted earlier. Older ones appreciate the insight of Ogden Nash in *The Child is Father to the Man but with More Authority*. The ordinary inconsiderate children in this are suddenly left free to look after themselves on an island holiday. Everything goes wrong so that they are forced into being less selfish. Yet

... when their parents returned to their native heath,
Why, the first thing these children did was to leave the
   window open so it rained on the piano, and
   go to bed without brushing their teeth.

This looks outwards, pictures vividly yet children individually
know themselves implicated and take pleasure in this objective
moralising. For many children, though, Vernon Scannell
would speak more directly to their experience in his *Autobiographical Note*:

> Beeston, the place, near Nottingham;
> We lived there for three years or so.
> Each Saturday at two o'clock
> We queued up for the matinée.
> All the kids for streets around
> With snotty noses, giant caps,
> Cut down coats and heavy boots,
> The natural enemies of cops
> And schoolteachers. . . .

Children love stories, but poetry is only sometimes a good
medium for them. Teachers should be particularly critical of
the indifferent narrative verse in the story sections of many
anthologies. Its diction is usually remote from everyday speech,
its humour elaborate, the rhyme pattern and rhythm complicated and the event or incident being commemorated of little
concern today. Before choosing a story poem one must feel
certain that the words and rhythm matter, that the story could
not be as well told in prose. Something ominous or mysterious
or nonsensical is heightened in effect by strict form. The quite
elaborate form of some narrative poems, like *The Jackdaw of
Rheims* or Tennyson's *Revenge*, lessen the impact of what happens,
though good teaching can overcome this. But one questions the
choice. Ballad rhythm is simple and strongly stirring when
genuinely related to content. It can be monotonous and trite
when not. Our most powerful narrative poetry is traditional
ballad poetry, whose strong impersonal presentation makes it
exactly right in tone for children. But it is invariably adult in
feeling and the Scots dialect is difficult. Some ballads, though,
are fine material for dramatisation and I discuss some of these
in a later chapter. Ballad has become important again in
modern poetry and music, and teachers will want to present it

sometimes in their programmes. Ballads like Charles Causley's
Nursery Rhyme of Innocence and Experience or Henry Treece's

> Oh come, my joy, my soldier boy,
> With your golden buttons, your scarlet coat

affect children strongly without needing talk or explanation,
and linked with suitable music or not will stay in their minds.

Most children enjoy Cautionary Tales and nonsense verse,
especially the latter, which is often close to the power of
incantation. Lear and Lewis Carroll have a kind of rapt
seriousness in a world free of ordinary circumstance. Their form
and sentences always have a delightful dancing precision, highly
logical, yet at variance with meaning. It is quite severed from
a child's ordinary expectations of feeling. Some more modern
writers of nonsense verse seem to me oddly irresponsible here.
What does one make, for instance, of *The Headless Gardener*, by
Ian Serraillier, one of the *Puffin Quartet of Poets*?

> A gardener, Tobias Baird,
> Sent his head to be repaired;
> He thought, as nothing much was wrong,
> He wouldn't be without it long.
>
> Ten years he's weeded path and plot,
> A headless gardener, Got wot,
> Always hoping (hope is vain)
> To see his noddle back again.
>
> Don't pity him for his distress —
> He never sent up his address.

Or the same author's *Fox Rhyme*?

> Aunt was on the garden seat
> Enjoying a wee nap and
> Along came a fox! teeth
> Closed with a snap and
> He's running to the woods with her
> A-dangle and a-flap and —
> Run, uncle, run
> And see what has happened!

Be with it, presumably, and conclude that both are good for a
laugh, which they certainly get, but the kind of laugh one

provokes in children matters. I feel rather the same at times about Ted Hughes, a very much finer poet than Serraillier, when he writes for children. For he clearly finds a strange liberation in seeing things with a child's surrealist vision yet indulges some cruel as well as comic fantasies in *The Earth-Owl and Other Moon-People*. On the other hand he peoples the moon with wonderfully alive, grotesque, luxuriant foliage: moon-cabbages, moon-hops, moon-freaks, jungles of moon-nasturtiums, all of which children love.

One comes back, as one always does in actual choice, to the quality of language and rhythm, to the ordering of the whole that makes it poetry, not prose, to the strange dancing power or quieter illumination that makes what it says take on a new dimension in the mind, which cannot always be defined. Once teachers feel this for themselves and grow more confident and adventurous in exploration and choice, they will find no difficulty in making poetry live for children in the classroom. And it must live, not set apart from other activities but connected with and enhancing them. Then it will be accepted naturally. Poems about animals, for instance, are positively *needed*, if children are talking and writing about them, collecting coloured photographs of them, compiling and illustrating their own books. This activity could then lead to some climax, if one chose, for instance, to mime and act a poem like George MacBeth's *Noah's Journey*, written both for children and for acting. MacBeth, like Ted Hughes, occasionally finds genuine liberation from the cruelty and pain of adult life in recapturing a child's vision and this work, which I discuss further in the chapter on mime and drama, has much to offer. Similarly poems about people can illuminate many projects or themselves be the centre of a project. In this situation of concern and related interest, poems can be read and enjoyed about most projects that engage juniors, poems about the sea and ships, the moon or the seabed, other countries, innumerable different aspects of nature. In fact where there is no poetry, the project may well be too one-sided and impersonal to be really suitable for children. Sometimes the contrast will be marked between the poetic and other content – I am thinking of the moon, space, the seabed, where poetry has not, for the most part, kept pace with the amazing and exciting developments of science. But then the strange creatures of Ted Hughes's imagination free the children's imaginations to make their own response to this new world.

Although poetry gains enormously through this natural

D

relatedness, it should never become simply a useful adjunct and it easily can, if it has no place of its own. One may be always meaning to explore and read relevant poems but may let other more immediate necessities crowd it out. In any case poetry is not utilitarian. Its own life justifies it. Therefore I think that one also needs regular short periods for poetry on the timetable. Two or three of fifteen or twenty minutes are better than fewer longer ones and it is good to have them associated with a particular time of day, probably the end of the morning or afternoon, when work is almost done and one can relax and simply enjoy. This is the time to bring together and reread poems recently enjoyed, and to introduce new ones less closely connected with their other work; a time for children to compile and illustrate their own poetry anthologies, and at intervals to present in groups their own short poetry programmes. They enjoy devising these, with or without a connecting theme. If one can ensure that the school and class library have a variety of *good* poetry books in them, this helps enormously. I give some suggestions in Appendix III at the end of this book. It is important that the feeling behind their reading should come from within, that they should read for meaning, not with some misconception of an outwardly applied 'expression'. These programmes can be made more of an occasion and more pleasurable, if one arranges some music to go with them, either on records or where possible from the children themselves. It is also well worth using a tape-recorder if one can, for children respond excitedly to the chance of making an occasional recorded programme and this has, too, a good effect on speech. Children sometimes want to chant a poem, a sort of spontaneous group response very different from planned and practised choral speaking. The latter they enjoy as well, with the right kind of creative control, and gifted teachers produce striking results. A poem like W. H. Auden's *Night Mail* is one that is particularly suitable for this.

These lessons are also times to improvise plays from story poems or ballads and to mime others and I discuss this later when talking of mime and drama. With such a wealth of activity naturally connected with poetry, there is no need for neglect or misgivings such as inevitably come to teachers who rely only on telling children to open their desks and get out their poetry books. In fact there is much to be said for having no class poetry books at all and using the money saved to build up more varied and attractive selections in class libraries, and

also to buy good records of poetry reading. The more one
grows interested and explores poetry oneself, the less one will
want for ideas. The BBC's sound programmes are very helpful
here, not only those designed for juniors but sometimes those
meant for slightly older children. Television on the other hand,
unless used particularly creatively, seems to me to work against
a child's using his own imagination actively while living in
the poem.

To consider very briefly what one might offer children oneself in a short poetry programme, I would suggest two, at the
most three related poems or one longer one with a brief coda
where appropriate. Usually, though, a story poem wants to be
alone. Often these programmes will bear some relation to other
work but sometimes will have their own theme. This, I think,
should always be connected with an area of experience important to the child: with his home and closest family relations, his
holidays, his pets, some of his hopes and fears; with special
times of year, like Christmas, and Easter, special freaks of
climate like fog and frost and snow, and with the seasons. In
such programmes one poem can balance or heighten another
or be thrown into relief by it. *Snare* and *Done For*, for instance,
or Edward Thomas's *The Cat* following the sharp visualising of
Christopher Leach's *The Blackbird*, to restrict oneself for the
moment to poems already talked about. One may enjoy putting
different kinds of incantation together:

> You spotted snakes with double tongue,
> Thorny hedgehogs, be not seen

with *Jellicle Cats* or Tennyson's *Owl*; or the Shakespeare with
a poem like Ben Jonson's *Witches' Charm*:

> The owl is abroad, the bat and the toad,
> And so is the cat-a-mountain;
> The ant and the mole both sit in a hole,
> And the frog peeps out of the fountain.

Contrast often sharpens apprehension, especially of the senses.
Katherine Tynan's *August Weather* with Shakespeare's

> When icicles hang by the wall,
> And Dick the shepherd blows his nail,
> And Tom bears logs into the hall,
> And milk comes frozen home in pail

would do this; or a contrast in a specific way of looking at something: in a train, looking out at a flying landscape, in Stevenson's *From a Railway Carriage*, followed by stillness inside, being *looked at*, in Hardy's *The Fallow Deer at the Lonely House*:

> One without looks in to-night
> Through the curtain-chink
> From the sheet of glistening white;
> One without looks in to-night
> As we sit and think
> By the fender-brink.

One can give children themes or let them suggest their own and then prepare in groups to entertain the others, which they always love doing. These are simply a few suggestions of possibilities in what must be an essentially personal and individual sphere.

As soon as children accept poetry as natural and entertaining they will settle into a quiet expectancy for it. It is all important then to *let the poetry work*. This usually means no preliminaries of any kind – no writing up of difficult words on the board with injunctions to watch out for them; no questions about poems read last week, nor asking a class if they remember reading such and such a poem, by so and so, no matter how relevant ultimately to the poem about to be read; no talk about the poet, however useful and interesting in itself and generally instructive. One is about to read *Cargoes*, say, and cannot resist mentioning that John Masefield is our poet laureate. What does that mean? Does anyone know another poet who was once poet laureate? We read a poem by him last Thursday. Tennyson, that's right, good boy, Peter. I exaggerate deliberately but it is very easy to slip into some form of seemingly helpful 'introduction'. Yet at this point questioning *of any kind* focuses interest in the wrong place, alerts the intellect whereas one wants children simply to wait and then to listen, with mind and imagination, intellect and feeling, working together. Sometimes it helps this response to ask them to put themselves in the opening *situation* of the poem, to *imagine* that it is a winter's evening, for instance, they are by the fire with curtains drawn, no television for the moment, just sitting together. Then they are in a sympathetic receptive mood for Hardy's *The Fallow Deer at the Lonely House* I quoted earlier. This of course is what some poems actually ask children to do. Vernon Scannell's *Hide and Seek*, for instance, given in *Happenings*:

The sacks in the toolshed smell like the seaside.
You make yourself little in the salty dark,
Close your eyes tight and hope your feet aren't showing.
Better not risk another call, they might be close.

Where they enter a poem as immediately as this, they will probably need no help to understanding and enjoyment but, whether they do or not, the poem must first of all be allowed to make its own impact unaided. Help comes afterwards. Children quickly realise the need to concentrate, not in any kind of intellectual anxiety as to whether they will understand, but in readiness to respond to what they see and hear and feel in their minds. It is well, I think, that a strange puzzlement should sometimes be associated for them with poetry.

Then one should read the poem to the best of one's ability. One has chosen it, one thinks it worth reading, one must now make it live by the reading. Any poem with a rhythm one cannot give oneself to or needing an accent one cannot make the effort to imitate, had better not be read. Ballads, for instance, should have some approximation to a Scots accent. *Casey Jones* or *The Big Rock Candy Mountains* need an American accent, however generalised this may be. Obviously, though, if one's accent is so unsure (or even brilliant) as to distract, it is better to keep such poems for the occasions when one uses recordings and music.

Response to this first reading will vary according to the nature of the poem and one works from this. Often it helps to read a poem twice before saying anything about it. With other poems, some talk and a very little questioning may be better before a second reading.

Some teachers will say, no questioning, and they may well be right. Certainly none is better than too much. Ideally, I would say, it is best to have as little questioning as compatible with most children coming quite close to the experience in the poem. How much this means will vary from poem to poem but the important thing is to know when to stop. It may help to realise that there are two kinds of questioning. First, that directed at removing surface intellectual difficulty (a different thing from difficulty in the idea behind a poem which would make it beyond children): a word like *discern* for instance in the Hardy, or *fender*, since these now are rare, or *transmogrify* in *Janet Waking*. Teachers, though, are often over-anxious to explain. One should always remember that all of us have an idea of the meaning of many more words in a context than without one. The understanding of the poem *as a whole* is what one is concerned with, is what matters, and one should never forget the strong power of suggestion in good poetry. One should never try to improve the shining hour with any kind of related word testing. I have seen students with an interested class after a good reading ask who knows what a certain word means and then, because only one child puts his hand up, let interest evaporate while they wait for a better show of hands, telling the class they can do better. This of course is mainly the fault of inexperience but not all teachers, I think, are clear in their own minds about the *direction of talk* about a poem. It should never be to *test* existing knowledge but to bring children more fully *to possess the poem*. So ask whoever thinks he knows what a particular word means. If he is wrong and the word unusual, forestall any guessing by giving the meaning. That an *angle-worm* is a worm used by anglers, a *cat-a-mountain*, a wild cat, this kind of information can be quickly provided as one looks more closely at a poem.

The second, more important aim of questioning is to sharpen apprehension, to lead the children to explore the feeling in the poem more acutely. But one should always remember Words-worth's warning that 'we *murder* to dissect'. One should always be trying to *create* something for the child in the mind. On *Snail*, for instance, one could ask a class where they *imagine* the poet standing, and watching. What does he see first? The snail *clambers* down. What kind of movement is that? Why *topple* at the end? Why does she wait for the dark before venturing out? This takes very little time, especially if one presses the question-ing and avoids digressions unless they seem really fruitful. One needs a certain intentness in tune with the mood of the poem. Then one is ready to read the poem again. Sometimes before this one may want the children to read it quietly to themselves if they have copies and to brood on it individually for a short time. Other poems invite speech, demand to be chanted, and this is to be encouraged for the poem will live more fully because of it.

One should never question about techniques, unless very occasionally it helps reveal meaning more fully. For instance, in James Reeves's poem, *Cows*, it helps children to think for a moment why the poet used long lines at the beginning and such short ones when the cows talk. In practice one does not neces-sarily treat different kinds of questioning separately but I think

it helps to be aware of them. Some text-books still give questions
on poems, which I would never make use of. However perceptive they are (and the fact that a compiler has brought himself
to use them argues for me against his perceptiveness to poetry)
they must intrude between the shared experience of teacher
and class. They must destroy a teacher's pleasure as much as
the children's and anyway they are surely unnecessary. For if
one's choice has sprung from interest and concern and one's
reading has been intelligent, one must have given a little time
at least to possessing oneself of the poem. One must have understood it and felt it, which means pausing over certain words and
images, responding to the rhythm, enjoying the sound. One
may be inadequate in one's appreciation here but questions in
anthologies are often grossly so and at least one will have made
a personal response, which is worth more to children than any
written questioning. I would also strongly urge that one does
not make children write answers to 'comprehension' questions
on poetry. If some external test they have to take demands this,
I would do a minimum of written preparation for it based on
prose passages, leaving until the last minute that seems practicable the slight change of technique needed for poetry. This
kind of test kills the life of a poem save for very intelligent
children and very often for them too.

Poetry, especially for children, must first be listened to. Its
main life is always its spoken life. Yet one wants children to feel
at home with poetry books, either having one of their own in
school that is attractive and stimulating or having access to a
library that has many, or ideally both. They should always be
given opportunities to build up their own anthologies. The
consistently hard things I have said about many printed ones
refer mainly to the nondescript, low-priced, limp-covered
collections I have found in use in many first- and second-year
classes or at least in the children's desks; and to certain traditional anthologies fast being superseded. I have already mentioned several modern ones I think are good and I give details
of these and others in Appendix II and III. I also make a few
suggestions of poets not usually thought of as suitable for children
yet worth some exploration; and of books and articles about
teaching poetry for children which I have found helpful.

3

STORY

IF poetry intensifies experience for children, stories extend it
— into regions that are fascinating and exciting and, above all,
personal and important to them. It is a world of far and near,
with no middle distance. Far off the magical, the supernatural,
the marvellous abound. So increasingly do the heroic, the
adventurous, the stirring. There is cruelty, sadness, injustice
but always hope, never bleakness. Near at hand there is vivid
concern with the human relations most precious to a child,
those within the family, and with the intense everyday extremes
of childhood, as well as with ordinary activities and reactions.
All this is at once strange and familiar, provoking secret
recognition, horror and delight. Stories are not something a
child grows out of (although he grows out of childish stories)
but something that he grows up through. They reveal human
life to him in ways he can feel and understand and, according to
their quality, develop his power of understanding human life.

This is an exciting challenge for junior school teachers for
they have a tremendous opportunity where a child's experience
of story is concerned. More than anyone except parents, who
often do not trouble, they can make it varied, full and memorable. But teachers will not do this unless they believe in story
themselves. Many see it as inferior and opposed to what children
learn in other lessons. It is all right in the infant school for no
one suggests that children there do not think and feel as children,
and it is still usually accepted as valuable for the next two years,
but not always. After that one is less likely to find the regular
reading aloud of stories by the class teacher looked forward to
as natural and rewarding. The implication often seems to be
that 'childish' things must now be put away, especially if the
school prides itself on its eleven plus results. All teachers want
children to read as much as possible, recognising the unique
value of this in educational 'success'. Many fail to realise that
the best way to encourage private reading is for the appetite to
be whetted in class; for stories to matter there, to be enjoyed,
talked about, looked forward to.

Some of those teachers who do advocate reading stories are depressingly apologetic, as if fiction today were a kind of pill needing jam before a highly informed junior school child will swallow it. 'It is *possible* to interest children in fiction' (my italics) writes a teacher in the Schools Library Association handbook, *Using Books in the Primary School.* 'What will they want to read?' asks Rowland Purton in the brief, statistics-laden chapter on 'Reading for Pleasure' in his *Surrounded by Books.* He goes on: 'In the past it was the custom to offer some good story books and a number of readers. It may be easy *to fall into the same trap again* (again my italics). The fact is, however, that when children read for pleasure, there will be many who prefer to read a non-fiction book rather than a fiction one'. He admits that this may be due to the fact that all the new well-illustrated books are the non-fiction ones, but this must in turn be due to the bias of teacher or school librarian, for children's publishing has much to offer in every field. Instead of fact and fiction being seen as complementary for children, both in different ways feeding their sense of wonder, opposed categories loom in the background: true for fact, false for fiction.

Mr. Purton quotes evidence of a questionnaire about their reading filled in by junior school children. They were asked what kind of books they liked reading best, with the categories on the board in case they forgot them: Fairy Tales, Legends, Bible Stories, History, Travel, True Adventure, Nature, Science, Transport, Sport, Hobbies, Music, Poetry, Plays. What would one say to the intelligent child who asked where to put *Tom Sawyer,* or *The Secret Garden,* or *Moonfleet?* In all this passionate categorising there is no room simply for the story, which for the adult becomes the novel.

It is false and harmful to make children think in categories here. For there are as many kinds of story as there are kinds of people, settings and ways of life. What makes them true or false is the quality of imagination in their writers, the degree of their imaginative honesty. It is always individual books that live in one's mind and sometimes affect one's life, not categories. It is those composed to a formula, with predictable ingredients, that are indistinguishable from each other. One wants children to read books like *The Kontiki Expedition* or *The Ascent of Everest,* but won't label them 'True Adventure', thus implying that *The Call of the Wild* or Van der Loeff's *They're Drowning Our Village,* are false. One will not actively encourage them to read the sensationalised 'Real Life' stories that abound in boys'

comics and magazines, just as one will not thrust Biggles or
Enid Blyton into their hands. These are all churned out to a
formula. Yet one will recognise the genuine satisfactions that
they offer many children, who long for action and suspense and
to identify with children who, as one put it, 'do all kinds of
exciting things that I never do'. Children of junior school age
devour and are quite unharmed by many books that are not
imaginative at all. One must accept and build on this, not
deplore it and so develop two further opposed false categories
in their minds: good books – those I *ought* to read; bad books
– those I *enjoy* reading. *Surround* children with books, certainly,
but find room for a full complement of story, both valid and
exciting, so that unconsciously they begin to reject the secondhand and repetitive for themselves.

Junior school teachers have two related concerns here: what
to choose to read to children in class and what to recommend
and provide for children to read to themselves. In both spheres
they must be alive to children's basic expectations and satisfactions from story, without a static preconceived conception of
'good literature'.

There are always important individual differences in children's
tastes, but there are also some important differences between
boys and girls which need to be taken into account. Most boys
place more stress on suspense and physically violent action, and
enjoy being involved in this. They like the actual fighting. What
a friend wrote about her eight-year-old son strikes me as
typical, although many boys will have a much narrower range
of actual reading through lack of opportunity and home encouragement: Paul, she wrote, 'likes adventure, atavism, magic
and myth. Fights, pirates, naughty boys like Tom Sawyer,
dragons, evil magicians. Heroes and kings – hotted-up history,
the legends of King Arthur, of Troy, of Ancient Greece and
Rome. Currently listening to Tolkien and enjoying it hugely.
He says he likes nice long stories that go on, rather than short
ones that you finish at a sitting.' He dislikes being 'subjected to
a nice book for nice boys and girls. In fact, loathes anything of
an introspective or self-conscious bent.' It is worth noticing that
this boy likes 'bald information – lists of places, populations,
maps, short articles in encyclopedias. In fact,' his mother con-
cluded, 'he appears to be mad for information and action chiefly.
Boys of his age seem to live rather in a sort of classical/medieval
world, obsessed with fights, fair play and prowess.'

Many girls also like vigorous action, and dislike introspective-

ness but they are usually more romantic, in the conventional
sense, than boys, and have a smaller appetite for information
and violence. The latter they often positively dislike. Action
implies achievement, and achievement for most girls means
something different from what it means to boys. They do not
yearn, as boys do, to prove themselves by heroic deeds, but
probably to prove worthy of some hero. Boys have no time for
fairies (although evil magicians and dragons are another matter),
but want stories crammed with apparently realistic detail. This
last element is particularly important at eight and nine, when
they lap up fast moving stories about spacemen, deepsea divers
and racing motorists, full of convincing know-how, while girls
of the same age are eager for pony trekking and camping or the
backstage glamour of the stage.

As boys and girls grow older, their preferences grow more
markedly individual, and good teachers recognise this when
recommending books for private reading. However, the differences between the sexes go deep enough to need to be ever-
present in teachers' minds, and to suggest that the imaginative
experience one presents in class, particularly to boys, should be
outward-looking and realistic, and that one should present facts,
particularly to girls, in a way that allows scope for feeling. At
no point in the junior school does intellectual ability divide
children in what they enjoy and respond to in story, although
it conditions what they can read to themselves, which in turn
conditions appetite.

On the basic issues, children are at one. All children demand
action in their stories, and action that is interesting and un-
flagging, not as with some adults to stimulate a jaded appetite
or prevent boredom, but because everything still matters. This
means that the whole must always have some completeness and
point, some suggestion of total significance. An action so like
life that it peters out has no appeal for children. They love
most of all an action that involves some quest, journey or
adventure that carries them away from the here and now, lets
them take part in some testing experience and brings them
back invigorated at the end. Action in this context may be no
more than a holiday with comfortable familiarity in companions;
what they do not care for is any attempt by an author to make
them more vividly aware of their own environment and circumstance. The action must be straightforwardly presented, with
description emerging vividly from it, never indulged in for its
own sake. To grip children, characters must be sharply defined

and simply motivated. They must be directly and objectively presented, not psychologised in any way. The writer must believe intensely in his created world. If this has, as it well may, strong elements of fantasy, there will be no repudiation of this when one returns to the everyday. For the child fantasy is a kind of realism and in the good writer for children there will be some approximation to the child's vision at the heart of his story. In books that children enjoy most in private reading, there is always a central child or adolescent character through whom they enter into the action. This is not necessarily so when a teacher reads to them, when they tend to project themselves into more varied experience.

Fact and fiction will only truly nourish each other for the teacher who feels their complementary overlapping quality for children of junior school age and rejoices in this, rather than deploring it. It is the marvellous in both that draws and holds the child. As he grows older, what he learns in history, geography, science, number, deepens his conception of the marvels of fact. It begins to be grounded in some knowledge of what there is to be marvelled at. But story is still vital, whether read aloud from a book or in a teacher's creative 'story telling', which is what he is doing whenever he brings to life a past age or another country for a class. It is this power of making facts and information live in the mind which helps turn knowledge into experience for the child. As his intellect and command of language grow, a child is trained to consider an ever increasing range of knowledge from a more general and impersonal point of view, and there will be to some extent less need of story as an adjunct. The experience of story remains important, however, in its own right, as it has been since he could be read to. For good stories help children both to lose and find themselves. Describing his own development at this stage, Wordsworth speaks in *The Prelude* of the power of story books in letting a child 'forget himself'. Children need this self-forgetting, this extended absorption, this imaginative experience, as they need love and food and sleep. Their whole beings are fed by it. It is not the opposite for them of the 'real' experience of geography and history but often more 'real' in that they are often more vividly aware of it. The important thing for teachers is to see that the life children drink in from fiction is genuine; that it has its own imaginative reality. This is why it is so essential that teachers should realise what this is and believe in its value.

Justice to both fact and fiction must not only be done but be seen and heard to be done. Children are affected by distinctions in a teacher's attitude, besides obviously being much more interested in a vigorous and imaginative presentation of fact than half-hearted story reading. This applies just as much the other way about. Nothing is more unimaginative than the superior attitude towards science of some literary people. We expect junior teachers to be specialists in everything but for all of them one or two subjects must mean much more than the others. One would be suspicious of their teaching if this were not so. But teachers should let their involvement in the subjects they care more about *open* rather than close their eyes to the imaginative possibilities in others. Then it will not matter if their ability in these other subjects makes them unable entirely to match their practice with their vision.

As with poetry, children should be accustomed to listen regularly to stories in class; to talk about them naturally and sensibly, relating doings and people to their own experience, sometimes writing stories themselves as a follow-up or engaging in some other piece of personal writing that springs direct from a significant experience in the story. This gives them pleasure, has a memorable effect on them as people and undoubtedly benefits their English enormously. They write better in every way.

Most children are ardent listeners – to a story, that is – but they are not usually rapid silent readers and it is quite misguided to imagine that they cease to enjoy being read to as they grow older. Provided one has chosen well and is absorbed oneself, it never fails. Even at secondary level, teachers could make much more use of it. Edward Blishen in his book, *Roaring Boys*, wrote: 'I never knew if I read to them too much. . . . With some classes it would have been as easy for me to stop reading as it would be for a music-hall entertainer to deviate into reading Wordsworth. And I didn't really want to give it up. Even when I no longer used literature as a snake-charmer uses his pipe I wanted to go on reading aloud. . . . I felt sure that it was not a waste of time.'

In the infant school story *telling* by the teacher, as opposed to reading, is important but in the junior school I am sure that emphasis from the beginning should be on reading and on the original text as the source of pleasure. Teachers must not only be alive to the power of story but have the power to bring story to life. One needs to adapt or condense in places and also sometimes to modernise and simplify. For the rest, one's powers as a reader should be at the service of the author or the best translation that one knows. A paraphrase rarely does justice to a good original. Children, no matter how unbookish, have a tremendously literal, almost magical respect for the printed word. Their respect for story books and interest in them will be unconsciously strengthened by seeing their teacher care for them.

One will not want to read for very long at a time – fifteen to twenty minutes is enough for many tales, or one or two chapters from a book, which is not long to ask out of the lengthy school day we impose on seven and eight year olds (longer, it is worth recalling, than in any European country). For nine or ten year olds half an hour is about the right length of time. The important thing is to have regularity so that continuity and interest are maintained. A child reads the average adventure story to himself at a low pitch of imaginative concentration. Listening regularly to a story that moves steadily but in which nevertheless the language and feeling matter more, gives opportunities for something fuller. The child's faculties are alert, his power to recreate what he is listening to for himself, through his imagination, is strengthened. He becomes more likely to read *to* himself with greater concentration. One last point here, teachers should not confuse the experience of listening to a good adult reading, with recollections of boredom from schooldays, when they had to wait their turn through the halting efforts of others in the class. There are innumerable other ways in which one can give junior school children practice in reading aloud with a genuine incentive to do this well: in poetry programmes, presenting reports, talking about hobbies and other personal interests, reading to be recorded on tape. Story should always be read by the teacher, and always as well as possible.

The most important value of reading aloud regularly to junior children, however, is that it gives them access to so much peculiarly suited to them that is nevertheless too difficult for most children to read to themselves. This applies to a number of very good historical novels for children, which can be the centre of exciting project work, and I discuss these in a later chapter. It also applies to one or two great writers like Chaucer and Dickens, some of whose work is highly enjoyable to children. Above all it applies to a whole range of traditional literature, inspired by the full strength of adult imagination but peculiarly satisfying to children. Most epics, sagas, folk-tales and early fairy stories are full of mystery and supernaturalism, heroism and roguery. They also usually have the qualities of strong action, sharp definition of character and vivid objective presentation that children demand from a good story. This is not simply a happy accident but due to genuine affinity between primitive and childlike ways of looking at the world, between some aspects of primitive and childlike imaginations. It is no accident, I think, that there is something childlike and primitive about the imagination of Dickens and Kipling, our last truly popular writers, who always had a vivid sense of, and need for, a living audience. Most primitive literature was written to be listened to, not read.

Many junior teachers already make creative use of traditional sources but others would probably explore more adventurously if they were aware more fully of what is there, of its relatedness to different aspects of human imagination and of the kind of release and pleasure it offers children. Although there is much overlapping, I think that there are three main streams: the heroic and legendary; the fantastic and fairy tale; the fable and folk-tale; and although categories are dangerous I think that these represent meaningful divisions still in modern children's literature.

Broadly speaking, the heroic and legendary looks outward, is objective, concerned with actual people: Greeks, Norsemen, Charlemagne's Knights, Robin Hood and his men, or to take the last body of 'heroic' story created, one notes, by a people in a comparatively primitive stage of nationhood, the pioneers of the American West. All went forth to face dangers and create legends and myths. Stories about them are rooted in actual civilisations and ways of life. The actions involve us in moral issues and bring out certain values. Where supernatural events occur, these are because gods intervene, who are believed in by the mortals in the story and are expected to indulge their powers in this way. Many early heroes have gods or goddesses for parents, others are credited with almost godlike powers. Their actions fill listeners with an enlarged sense of human potentiality. One is invigorated but not consoled.

Fantasy and fairy story look inward. We enter a dark forest, a hinterland of the human mind, where urges towards cruelty are allowed free play, as well as dreams and romantic longings. The actions are usually of 'life and death', there is a constant struggle between good and evil, the latter, potent and fascinating but doomed beforehand to be overthrown. For our wishful thinking comes true: everyone lives happily ever after. Above all, this is the world of magic, embodying man's deep craving for unlimited power over the elements, the laws of nature, time, other human beings. To be under someone's spell – the words still work.

In essence subjective, bearing no relation to the *actual* world, but symbolic of much in man's imagination, all this is presented with vivid objectivity which grips children. 'Grannie, what big eyes you've got!' exclaims the innocent vulnerable Red Riding Hood, and they partly enjoy the prospect of a satisfying meal to come, as well as being terrified by it. Not consciously of course, but as part of an absorbed response. Witches, jealous stepmothers, terrifying dragons, all are there with intense reality and children enjoy the fear and fascination they arouse, secure in the knowledge that the dragon will be slain, the spell broken, Beauty freed and the Beast discovered to be a prince in disguise. After which, as so often in their own fantasy, everyone can go home for tea.

Most countries have a body of fables and tales that embody folk insight, rather than folk heroism, that express a kind of folk intellect, rather than offering an outlet for folk psyche. For most have a central point, or illuminate some aspect of human behaviour in a telling way. This insight is usually a combination of shrewdness and simplicity, in many ways a kind of childlike wisdom that sees through all adult pretentiousness. This is why so many of these tales are intensely pleasurable to children, who invariably see through adults who pretend to them.

Many fables illustrate their point about human nature by isolating the aspect they are concerned with in an animal traditionally thought to embody this; and we still often instinctively use animal metaphors and similes when describing people. Young children of five and six seem to see animals as the fables do, as kinds of human being, and by far the commonest and most popular stories for them are about 'animals who talk'. This is quite different from the deep relationship of older children with animals, through which they frequently explore feelings of love and tenderness.

Allegory, or extended parable, has a rather special place in the tradition. Here heroic and magical combine in surface adventure, to illustrate an underlying moral or religious truth. Stories were expected to teach or reveal and longer works to offer men a pattern for their aspiration. Story tellers were not concerned with documentary accuracy, but in the immediate event to move their audience to wonder. In any case life here was only a shadow, its 'reality' to be revealed after death. It was usually seen as a journey, a metaphor we still use. The Knights in the *Morte D'Arthur*, and later in the *Faerie Queen*, go forth to prove themselves morally and spiritually, just as Christian does later still. The dangers they encounter are not living enemies like the Trojans, or Berserks, or Saracens, or a sheriff's posse, but moral and spiritual ones. These are nevertheless tremendously real in the intensity of their conceiving and presentation, for the actual medieval world provided plenty of material from which to create danger and insecurity. So some terrible giant-like knight charges at one, an old hag called Slander drips filth, the foul fiend, Apollyon, straddles Christian's path. They are there vividly in the foreground, which makes children enjoy some incidental adventures in allegory very much, particularly at seven or eight, when they disregard the moral. Later they tend to find the adventures too unrealistic, although the total significance will mean more.

I have only divided traditional literature in this way to urge teachers to put it together creatively, for children need the heroic and the fantastic, the release outward and within, and hunger for some kind of moral significance. There is, of course, constant overlapping. In legends about heroes there is often much that is fantastic; in fantasy there is always vivid realism in the foreground. All offer at times the kind of physical release that is right for children, the release of burlesque comedy, such as abounds when giants fight each other or Thor lays about him with his hammer.

The emphasis will differ with individual children, and quite largely between boys and girls, but in general from nine onwards children need and enjoy the realistic and heroic most. Certainly this is the most profitable for reading aloud, because of its links with actual life and other work. But any timetabling can only be approximate and no substitute for the perception of individual teachers. I venture all the same to make some suggestions, without keeping to any strict divisions.

In the first and second years junior children are not ready for the sternest achievements of the heroic, for the *Iliad* or Norse Sagas, but they delight in tales about Greek and Norse gods and goddesses. They are not ready for the *Odyssey* as a whole; they delight in wondrous incidents from it. They also enjoy tales about mischievous folk heroes like Till Eulenspiegel or Robin Goodfellow. Many teachers make use of the attractively produced Oxford University Press collections of folk-tales of

E

different countries, particularly the Celtic ones. There are other good collections like Arthur Ransome's *Old Peter's Russian Tales*, and some of those in Muller's *Legacy Library*. Before reading extensively from a particular collection, one would probably want to have considerable interest in the mythology concerned or wish to give children stories from a country they are learning about in other lessons. It is probably wise not to switch rapidly from one mythology to another but to give children time to feel at home and allow time also for coming back to favourite stories.

The first two years are probably the best time also for reading the various adventures of Robin Hood. These tales are straight-forward and appeal to the developing gang instinct of children who in private reading are probably devouring the exploits of the Secret Seven or Biggles. Robin Hood offers exploits but there is no profound conception behind them worth waiting for children to respond to more fully when older. Like Dick Turpin or Ned Kelly, he appeals to the strong radicalism of children, which rarely at this stage finds legitimate outlet. Many teachers prefer to introduce Robin Hood through ballads and play-making but the prose versions of Roger Lancelyn Green in the Puffin edition and Rosemary Sutcliff's *Chronicles of Robin Hood* are to be recommended, if one wants to read the stories first.

The *Morte D'Arthur* is far from radical in its attitude to authority. The central chivalric ideal is not much admired or understood today, rooted as it is in lost ways of thought and feeling about love and courtesy. Some teachers question the value for children of these stories, arguing that they are suspect in their moralty with their Tweedledum/Tweedledee attitude to battles, reactionary in their social attitudes and above all anti-scientific, with their perpetual wizardry and magic. Teachers who feel this are sensible not to bother with them but they then cut children off from our only approach to a native mythology and also from a certain poetic kind of wonder and excitement not found elsewhere in adventure at this stage.

For children of eight these stories are a natural extension of fairy stories, with the same landscape of forests, castles and imprisoned damsels and the same powerful element of magic. Sudden marvels constantly occur. *Suddenly, of a sudden*, the words spring up on every page. A strong appeal lies in their colours, brilliant primary colours, frequently symbolic. Everything has a strange vividness, to be apprehended immediately but with the accompanying sense, as in a dream, that it means something else at the same time. 'And at last they came to a narrow pass in the rocks, and beyond it, in a cup in the mountains, Arthur saw a strange lake. All round it the hills rose darkly and desolately, but the lake water was of the clearest, sunniest blue, and the shore was covered thickly in fresh green grass and flowers.' The battles are marvellously realistic at a child's level, which boys love. On every other page, one meets this kind of thing: 'Then began a fierce battle, with many great strokes; they hacked and hewed at one another, cutting pieces off their shields and armour, and suffering each of them so many wounds that the trampled grass in front of the pavilion was stained with red. They rested once, and then charged each other again: but their swords met together with so mighty a crash that Arthur's broke in two, leaving him with the useless hilt in his hand.' This offers a harmless outlet for aggressive instincts, the kind of controlled emotional release that children need. It is not violence that they ever interpret in terms of their own lives. In the same way they delight in the marvels, without their having any adverse effect on what they are beginning to learn in science about the real nature of things. They make no connection between the two worlds. In some ways of course wizardry then, far from being against science, was the poor attempt at science of its time, man's attempt through secret knowledge and spells to exert some measure of control over hostile elements.

The actual presentation of action in the stories is always vivid and real, and imprints itself on children's imaginations. For instance, Arthur and Gawain suddenly meet a bejewelled lady riding towards them on a great white horse. As he looks at her, though, Gawain turns pale, and Arthur crosses himself, 'For she was the loathliest lady that ever the eye of man rested upon: her face was as red as the sinking sun, and long yellow teeth showed between wide, weak lips; her head was set upon a great, thick neck, and she herself was fat and unshapely as a barrel. Yet the horror of her seemed to lie in something more than the hideousness of her looks, for in her great, squinting, red-rimmed eyes there lurked a strange and terrifying shadow of fear and suffering.' Here is one original of the fairy story of Beauty and the Beast, though in reverse. Chaucer's Wife of Bath's Tale gives a more comic variant. Gawain marries the hag to save the life of his uncle, King Arthur, there is a ghastly wedding feast at which she guzzles wine and slobbers over the food and then, when he has taken her to the bridal chamber, she demands a kiss. He gives it despite such repulsion as shakes his body with sobs, and instantly she is transformed into 'the loveliest maid that ever his eyes had seen.' The ending brings out something of the conception of 'courtesy' behind these tales. For she offers him a choice — that of having her fair by day and foul by night, or the other way about. Respecting her, Gawain says that she must choose, for either way it is she who will suffer most from the loathing she must call forth when foul, whether from the court by day, or from himself by night. This unselfishness breaks the spell, and she is free to be fair by day and night.

The best story for second or third years, though, is probably *Sir Gawain and the Green Knight*, not in Malory, but preserved in the great anonymous medieval poem. So far I have quoted from the Puffin, *King Arthur and His Knights of the Round Table*, by Roger Lancelyn Green, who gives a much abridged but fast-moving version of this story that arouses immediate interest:

The minstrels had stopped playing and the whole company sat quietly in the great hall, only the roar and crackle of the log fires in the side hearths breaking the silence — when suddenly there rang out the clash and clang of iron-shod hooves striking upon stone: the great doors flew open and into the hall strode a strange and terrible figure.

I would also recommend M. R. Ridley's full prose translation in the Golden Legend Series, strikingly illustrated by John G. Galsworthy, which gives detail that junior children enjoy. For instance, the knight is green all over, clothes, crupper, stirrups, all green and encrusted with green stones. He rides a huge green horse, has long waving green locks and a great green beard. His only weapon is a bunch of evergreen holly, and a prodigious battle-axe with a spike sticking out beyond the head, forged of green and gold steel. The head is more than a yard long and sharp as the keenest razor. He offers a free gift of his battle-axe and his defenceless neck to any knight, but claims the right in return of a free blow at the challenger a year and a day from then. Sir Gawain accepts the challenge and runs his finger along the edge of the axe. The Green Knight bares his neck, Gawain lifts the axe high above his head, and brings it down 'swiftly and surely on the bare flesh, so that the sharp steel shore clean through the flesh and bone and clove his neck in two, and the bright blade drove on and bit into the ground.

The fair head fell from the neck and rolled among the feasters, who pushed it away with their feet. The blood spurted from the body and shone bright on the green mantle. The Green Knight did not fall or even stagger, but strode firmly forward among the knights and laid hold of his fair head and lifted it up. Then he turned to his horse, gathered the reins, put his foot in the stirrup-iron and swung himself into the saddle. He held his head by the hair, in his hand, and settled himself in his seat as calmly as though nothing had happened to him, though he sat there headless . . .'

Children love this combination of marvel and realism.

Children still respond to a simple conception of good fellowship and find the Round Table an easy symbol to grasp, as the outward social expression of inner trust. Arthur was young when he was called to lead. There was great need for unity and a central faith, both in fifth-century Britain when he almost certainly lived, with Rome crumbling, and Saxon threats increasing, and in the fifteenth century when Malory wrote. His *Morte D'Arthur* gave expression to an ideal of chivalry already murdered by the Wars of the Roses and profound economic change. Something of value, the tales suggest, was built up by Arthur. It was destroyed from within. Roger Lancelyn Green makes full use of the loose pattern of the original, adding some stories not in Malory, while preserving Malory's underlying coherence by giving complete the last tragic section, when the sin of Lancelot and Guinevere destroys the fellowship for ever. Children do not fully grasp the sin but feel the sadness, especially as brought out in the story of the return of Excalibur. There is no 'happy ever after' ending but a real sense that something of goodness and value has had its day. There is no link with ordinary life in the Middle Ages, for that we must turn to Chaucer, but for a few weeks' reading these tales are wonderfully self-sufficient, provided that the reader is moved by their beauty and strangeness and excitement. One can also give them a valuably realistic setting by linking one's reading with project work based on Cynthia Harnett's *Load of Unicorn*, which I discuss in more detail in the chapter on projects. This is about the rise of printing in the fifteenth century, and the attempts of the boy hero, Bendy, to track down some of the lost manuscripts of the *Morte D'Arthur* and vindicate its author, who died disgraced in Newgate. Bendy knows some of the tales and has a passion for them, which adds to their interest and gives greater reality to them in the eyes of a class.

Chaucer takes us straight into the actual medieval world. His *Prologue* to the *Canterbury Tales* gives us a wonderfully clear and detailed picture of ordinary fourteenth-century men and women, full of life and interest to ten year olds. They are immediately transported in time to April 1387, or thereabouts. The world is waking up after the long rigour of winter. All over Europe people long to go on pilgrimages, for the change of scene and company as much as the spiritual exercise. In Southwark at the Tabard Inn Chaucer meets twenty-nine such people, about to set off down the Dover Road to visit Becket's shrine at Canterbury. He decides to go with them, decides to tell us something of them first. It is quiet and documentary in approach and tone but one quickly discovers that Chaucer's powers of observation and insight are unusually wide-ranging and exact. His device of a story telling competition to pass the time by the way might have been devised with ten year olds in mind. In making a selection from the tales to read a class, one has a very good opportunity to try out their response to the varied kinds of traditional tale I spoke of earlier, for most are represented: fairy tale, moral tale, animal fable, romance. Of translations and adaptions for children I recommend Eleanor Farjeon's, published by Oxford University Press, which keeps close to the language and spirit of the original, while skilfully doctoring the content. I also recommend a selection and adaptation by Kent and Constance Hieatt, illustrated by Gustaf Tenggren. The *Prologue* in this is only a summary but the tales read well and children are very attracted by the book itself, its colour reproduction of a facsimile of a medieval manuscript and its striking illustrations. Teachers will also probably want to explore Nevill Coghill's complete verse translation.

Work in other subjects combines naturally, social history playing the largest part. Children may make a model or a frieze of the characters, contributing one that interests them particularly, having found out from coloured illustrations in costume books how their pilgrim would dress. Film strip of the illustrations in the Ellesmere manuscript is available, as are poster-size enlargements of some pilgrims, while one may be able to lay hands on a brass rubbing of a knight. They enjoy too illustrating the stories.

Children are interested in Chaucer himself, educated as a page in a royal household, serving the king's son, Lionel, in his wars in Flanders and then travelling in France, Flanders and Italy on various diplomatic and economic missions. Later he was an

important civil servant in London, first as Controller of Customs
in the Port of London, then Clerk of the King's Works, a job
involving him in duties like the upkeep of the Tower, repairs to
St. George's Chapel, Windsor, the erection of scaffolding for
tournaments at Smithfield. He certainly had cause to know
the route to Canterbury well for he was once on a commission
supervising its upkeep between Greenwich and Woolwich, and
was assaulted and robbed more than once in carrying out these
duties. He had every opportunity to know men and women of
all kinds yet he never speaks of himself as a busy experienced
man of affairs but always slightly mockingly of the quiet on-
looker, the dreamer, the devourer of books, who hurries home
to his house above Aldgate where, as he chides himself,

> . . . dumb as any stoon
> Thou sittest at another book
> Tyl fully daswed (dazed) is thy look . . .

With *The Prologue* children respond immediately to the
objective detail, particularly physical detail: the soft white neck
of the Friar, the open sore on the Cook's leg, the Summoner's
flaming carbuncles, the wart on the end of the Miller's nose,
tufted with hairs 'red as the bristles of a sowes ear'. They
remember the Wife of Bath, with her broad hat, her easy seat
upon a horse, her 'footmantel about her hipes large', five hus-
bands to her credit already, as well as 'oother companye in
youthe' and now on the lookout for a sixth. Children miss many
of the social and moral implications yet one can be vividly
aware of people without understanding them and they quickly
get the feel of Chaucer's characters. Then they are eager to be
off on the journey, whereas with too much teaching at higher
levels the implications are understood but one may never leave
Southwark.

These people are setting out on a sort of quest, even though
its spiritual significance is not uppermost in many of their minds.
An *ad hoc* fellowship is created by the journey, intimate while it
lasts, and in Harry Bailey, the Host, they have a born organiser.
The journey reveals character as party travel always does. The
interchanges on the road and the stories themselves sometimes
show this. The drunken Miller tells a tale against a carpenter;
the Reeve, himself a carpenter before he took to managing his
Lord's estate, replies with one against the Miller. The same
thing happens with the Friar and the Summoner, so effectively

that the latter rises up in his stirrups shaking with rage 'like an aspen leaf' before launching his crude rejoinder.

There are a number of tales that one cannot read to children but a variety remain. Apart from other qualities Chaucer is a superb story teller, and time has not lessened the continuing power of 'Once upon a time' to entice one to read on. To consider a few of the openings quickly suggests his range, his power to set a scene, compress detail, arouse interest.

Romantic ones, for instance:

At Sarray, in Tartary, there lived a famous King who was for ever harrying Russia, and killing Russians. His name was Cambuskan, and he was everything that a King should be, brave, wise and rich, merciful and just, true to his word, and honourable in all things.

Or:

There was once a knight who lived and loved in Armorica, which we call Brittany. He loved a lady, and performed many a labour before he won her. She was the fairest under the sun, and came of a noble family, so that he lacked the courage to tell her how he loved her. But her eye had fallen on him, and she had determined secretly to take him for her lord and master – or such mastery as men may have over their wives!

More realistic, when one senses that some agreeable rogue is going to be exposed:

A Merchant once lived in Saint Denis, who was so rich that he was held to be wise. And he had a most companionable wife of excellent beauty; but so fond of feasting, dancing, and fine clothes, that she cost him a great deal. Because he was generous and his wife was fair, the Merchant's house was much frequented by guests, amongst whom there was a Monk, a handsome man of about thirty winters . . .

Or:

There was once a priest in London ,who had lived there many years, and made himself so pleasant to the wives of the houses he called at, that none of them charged him for board or lodging, and he always went well-dressed and had plenty of silver to spend. And my tale is about a Canon who brought this priest to confusion.

Some equally realistic sound a familiar pulpit note of warning:

> There was once in Flanders a company of young people who lived
> a riotous life, gaming, and eating, and drinking, and dancing, and
> dicing to excess, both day and night; and swearing most abominable
> oaths.

All the tales have Chaucer's delight in people and human
behaviour, a fresh objective quality that holds children. Of the
many romantic tales, the Wife of Bath, surprisingly perhaps,
tells a fairy story with the same theme, but not the same tone,
as that of Sir Gawain and the Lady Ragnell; the Squire begins
a tale of wonder about King Cambuskan that children enjoy
trying their hand at finishing; the Franklin, with his tale of the
'knight who lived and loved in Armorica', vindicates true love
between husband and wife, in contrast to the conventional
courtly mocking of it; the Prioress tells a touching tale based on
the story of little Sir Hugh of Lincoln, murdered supposedly by
the Jews on his way home from school. The most beautiful and
moving tale is the first, opening the debate on love which is the
central theme of *The Canterbury Tales*. Children enjoy the
Knight's Tale very much. They laugh at the ridiculous plight of
the imprisoned princes, both equally smitten with love for the
unattainable Emily but follow with interest the course of their
prolonged attempts to win her. 'Emilye the shene', Chaucer
calls her and this bright shining quality is everywhere: with
Emily walking in her garden, with the court riding forth to
keep the rites of May morning, in the preparations for the joust,
in the colour and ceremony of the life represented. The climax
comes with Theseus's judgement for Arcite, to be followed immediately by his tragic accident and death.

> Now with his love, now in his colde grave
> Allone, withouten any companye

is Chaucer's comment although he wisely suggests that Emily
and the now successful rival Palamon will be very happy together, and that there is something amiss with the conception
of courtly love as a religion, which was what caused the tragedy.
    The bawdy anecdotes of the Reeve and the Miller, each told
against the other, and each depending for its point on some
form of sexual deception, have been skilfully adapted by Eleanor
Farjeon, retaining enough comic neatness of plot to be quite

entertaining to children. They are amused for the moment but as a nine-year-old boy put it, who had loved *The Knight's Tale*, 'they don't leave you with anything'. *The Canon Yeoman's Tale*, whose opening I quoted just now, offers more for this exposes a rascally alchemist-cum-Canon and this kind of confidence trickster has plenty of descendants, particularly in the advertising world. *The Parson's Tale*, an ordered sermon against the seven deadly sins, is not for children, although it is worth telling them how Chaucer chose to round off the whole, especially as they will have realised in talking about the other characters the importance of the church in people's lives. There is no point in boring them with *The Monk's Tale*, a catalogue of tragedies according to the conception of the time, stories of great men brought low by the turning of Fortune's Wheel. But they love *The Nun's Priest's Tale*, an animal fable of the overproud Cock and sly Fox, especially its noisy climax; and also the macabre neatness of the Pardoner's grim story of the three revellers who go in search of the thief, Death, and are themselves his victims. 'I get it', I remember one ten year old calling out excitedly, as the last lap of the race opened with the third reveller going into the apothecary's to buy poison, to kill the friends who at that very moment were plotting to stab him.

Sometimes the moral tale becomes true fiction, and will not be put in any category.

There was once a good old knight dwelling in Pavia, in Lombardy, where he had long lived in great prosperity. After having lived out the better part of his life as a jolly bachelor he began to long to be married, and know for once the blissful life shared by husband and wife. 'No other life is worth a bean,' he said. 'I understand that wedlock is paradise on earth.' So said this wise old knight, whose name was January.

One can read on to children in Eleanor Farjeon's adaptation and have no idea of Chaucer's full insight and power, not surprisingly, because the feeling and action are outside the world of children. There is a scene in the original when, after marrying a young wife, hustling off the rowdy wedding guests, fortifying himself with wine and hot spices, old January rubs his wife's tender face with his bristly dogfish-sharp beard and eagerly sets forth on his licensed pleasure. In the morning he sits up in bed and crows with delight while 'the slakke skin aboute his nekke shakyth'. God knows, adds Chaucer,

what that May thoughte in hir herte,
Whan she hym saugh up syttinge in his sherte,
In his night-cappe, and with his nekke lene.

Yet one is left also with some sympathy for the pathetic old lecher. One cannot read this to children but one is more likely to be drawn into Chaucer's world and to realise what it *can* offer children, if one has some measure of its adultness also.

An important aspect of this work, once children feel the aliveness of Chaucer's characters, and are involved in finding out something of their social setting, is to let them create modern counterparts and modern tales. I did this recently with a class of third-year juniors, working in four groups. Each travelled by different means so that we had *Tales of a Voyage*, told on an ocean cruise, which it was felt gave plenty of time for story telling; *Camping Tales*, from a group of hikers exploring the Pilgrims' Way to Canterbury (the school was very close to the A2); *Tales from a Forced Landing*, when story telling would possibly keep one's mind off the danger of such a situation; finally, from a group travelling by coach, *Kidbrooke Chronicles*. Of course not all the stories were in character, but many were, as well as frequently being told with great drive and economy of language; while the character sketches were full of sharp observation, simply and directly presented. We had talked about the kinds of detail that Chaucer noticed and of the sort of people one would find today on a hike or cruise or long-distance air trip. Eventually the groups assembled their characters and stories, mounting them on different coloured sugar paper in book form, producing delightful surrounding designs and in some instances illuminated capitals. In between, each group had the chance to present themselves in character to the rest of the class and, if they wanted to, to tell their story. Most were eager to do this and just as Chaucer's pilgrims commented in varying fashion on each tale, the audience was allowed to question and comment here. Most questions were very searching and literal, seizing on impossibilities in the action and forcing many story tellers to realise that 'imagining' in this context demands much more regard for probability and exactness of recollection than they had supposed. This led to some alterations and additions to the stories and characters before they were put in their books.

The following sketches and tales give some idea of the results, although the longer, more adventurous stories have had to be excluded:

A Country Nurse

A nurse was rideing along a road on a bicycle, but the chain broke, and the nurse was no engineer so it had to go to the garage. That was why she was on the coach.

She had blue eyes, a kindly face, dark skin and nice curly hair. She was not at all 'prim and proper', but amused her patients a lot. Her finger-nails were short, and her hands looked clean and soft. The nurse's name was Miss Chapman, but her patients called her 'Chappie'.

She liked pop stars and music, for she was a child nurse.

The Nurse's Tale

A long time ago, when I was a student, the head docter was going to see a patient. I was supposed to go and get the patient ready, which I didn't do. Sister told me off, and I was so red (because it was in front of the other patients), that it was as bad as my face and neck being covered in blood.

I was so ashamed that I didn't hear the engine running in a closed garage, and it was my colleague, Betty who heard it. 'Car engine running in a closed garage,' she said. So we ran and opened the garage door, and, slumped over the engine, was a boy, Sister's nephew. 'Carbon Monoxide poisoning,' said Betty. 'Oxygen needed,' she added.

I waited about 2 mins, but Betty didn't come. As the boy still wasn't breathing I got a mat from the back of the car, and pulled the boy on it, then I pulled the mat over to the door and gave him artifichal respiration. He started breathing just as Sister and Betty arrived.

(Kathryn)

The Seargent Major

There was one single man on the coach. He was a seargent major with a bent nose. He wore an army cap that was low down on his thin head. He also held a stick under his arm with determination. He wore an army uniform with rows of medal ribbons. He was thin and wiry with a battle scarred weather beaten face. Beneath his nose was a tiny moustache that went about $\frac{3}{4}''$ of an inch each way. He was a scornful man and had no sympathy for weaklings as I soon discovered when a little man very thin and bony looked at him.

He looked at him as if he might tred on him like an ant. For this reason I was frightened also because he shot a piercing look at everyone that made him seem cruel.

(Brian)

Mr. Morris

There was a person on the ship whom we all disliked. She was always telling us what to do and what not to do, it was very irritating. She had had her hair dyed several times. It was now a bright red. We were all glad that there was not a women's hairdressing salon on the ship for fear that her hair would be yet a different colour when we reached our destination which was a long way off.

She was rather fat especially when compared with her husband who was rather thin.

We usually talked about her as 'that busybody'. It was unkind but the name suited her so well that we hardly realised that it was unkind.

Her clothes were rather expensive and in a size bigger than most peoples. She wore a very tight skirt of scotch tweed and a very chunky cardigan. She was never seen without her stockings which were black with a criss cross pattern on. She wore pointed high-heels so that she was always stumbly or almost falling over-board.

Mrs. Morris told a story which none of us quite belived. Once her husband was going on a cruise and the weather turned bad. Most people fell sick and her husband was among them. After many storms and hardships the cruiser reached England. Most of the people were so sick they had to go to hospital. Mrs. Morris's husband happened to go to the hospital where Mrs. Morris was a nurse, for she was not yet married.

After a few days in hospital Mr. Morris was the only one of the people on the cruise still in hospital. All the nurses and doctors could do nothing for him untill Mrs. Morris heard about him. She was sure she would make him better. Under her care he got better and was soon out of hospital. Soon they were married.

(Anne)

The Park Keeper's Tale

The park keeper was a bad temperd old man. He had a bald head, but he usually wore a wig, this is how he told his tale. Once upon a time in the park where I work, there was a fire which destroyed nine oak trees and three bushes. I did not know what started the fire but I would have liked to find out. The only witness I could find was a lady called Miss Penge and all-she saw was three youths with matches and cans of Paraffin. Well on the very same day, the same lot of youths came and they started to pull up the flowers. So I began to chase them. I finally caught up with them and I got hold of one of them by the ear. I could see he was in pain but I did not care. I took the boy to the police and told them where the other boys were and that is the end of my story.

(Jacqueline)

The Pop Singer

On the aeroplane was a pop singer. He was 19 and had black hair. His eyes were hazel and he wore black rocker boots. He wore a black suit and had a fringe his voice was deep and romantic and his name was Paul Templar. The group he was in was called The Paul Templar Four, he was the leader. On the journey he sang us a few songs. He did not have his group with him, he was very jazzy.

On top of his black suit he wore a suede jacket.

The Pop Star's Tale

Once when I was on stage I had to do an act with a lovely girl. At once I fell in love with her. After a few kisses I asked her to marry me. She had lovely blue eyes and lovely black hair. Her name was Juanite, she was Spainish. Once we were married we lived happily for four years, then I took her to a ball and she saw another man, then she ran off with him that night. Now I am out to seek another girl.

(Marisha)

The Butcher

On the ship to New Zealand there were many pepole. There was one person that I noticed particularly. He was a butcher. He was about five foot tall and I should think that he weighed about twelve stone. He was very fat. He had straight jet black hair. He had blue eyes and a mouth which curled down at the ends. Sometimes he smoked a pipe it smelt a lot. It was an old pipe. The pipe curled down then up again. His overcoat was dark blue. His trousers were blue with black stripes. His shoes were a very shiny black. On his wrist he had a scar.

The Butcher's Story

Before I was a butcher I was a gunner of a tank. It was in the first world war. The tanks then were ancient old crates against what they

are now. Part of the German infantry had invaded France. Our
tank and forty nine other tanks were told to patrol the Western
Front so we did. When we had gone twenty five and a half miles we
ran into some German tanks. There were about a hundred of them
against fivty of us. After about five minutes our tank backfired and
caught fire. In about one and a half hours there were only about
seventy five tanks left. It was then that we discovered that the
German tanks were really a hundred English tanks camouflaged as
German tanks to confuse the Germans.

(Ian)

And to end with, a very moral tale indeed!

A Doctor

This young doctor was quite plump with very dark red hair. He
had a case containing instruments. He was a londoner and had
obviously come from a hospital, for he had a white overal over his
arm. He said he had come from Kings college london and was going
to Folkston to pass his second exam and then to become a proffes-
sional doctor.

The Doctor's Tale

Once, he began, where I used to work lived a very sensible and
inteligent young student who one day was baby sitting a young
child on fireworks night. Although he had been told by the mother
'no friends are to come in.' But this young boy was disobedient and
did have friends in and he put some fireworks underneath the babys
bed then by accident, dropped a match and it happened that under
the cot were bangers, rokets and screamers in fact all the rokets and
fireworks went up killed himself and the baby and burnt the house
down, perhaps you will not disobey now!

(Hilary)

Throughout this work, which was spread over nine or ten
weeks, the children showed great interest in Chaucer, his time
and how people lived then, as well as in the six or seven tales
that we read. They were particularly interested whenever there
was a direct modern link. For instance the poor scholar, although
not at all a lively person, excited much interest because of his
connection with Oxford and caused a long digression about
modern students and colleges, ancient and modern. Some children got out the books I was using from their libraries and read

other tales for themselves. One or two looked at an original text possessed by their parents. All stimulated by the imagination and skill of their class teacher worked on a delightfully expressive frieze of the characters, as fresh and bright coloured as the Squire's clothes. Chaucer will be more than a name to them, even if they never read another word he wrote.

Norse civilisation is much simpler than medieval and so is our reaction to it. There is less divorce between realism and wonder and the wonder is primarily in what happened, in the extraordinary range of the Viking raids, and the extraordinary adventuring spirit that inspired them. To go a-viking was a kind of heroic piracy. Children respond excitedly to this, especially boys. They can trace the voyages on their atlases; grasp in detail the appearance of the long ships, especially if one gets hold of photographs of Scandinavian reconstructions; find out about their burial chambers, in this country as well as Scandinavia. There is one in the Hebrides, for instance, where a pair of scales was unearthed beside a battle-axe. Their gods, still commemorated in our days of the week, embody stern and simple beliefs and noble if limited ideals of courage and loyalty. There is no trace of puritan conscience, neither are there any profound spiritual conceptions. Instead, a free independent form of society, in which fellowship is very strong but without the hierarchy of feudalism.

Norse literature mingles folk-tale with a grim sense of destiny, burlesque with epic, myth with heroic action. Children respond most immediately to the latter when it has the vivid economical power of the following in creating the men and ships they have been learning about:

Hrothgar's Coast Warden, sitting his horse on the cliff top northward of Heorot, saw a strange vessel running in from the open sea, between the high headlands at the mouth of the fjord. A war-galley, long and slim and swift; and the light blinked on the painted shields hung along her bulwarks and the grey battlegear of the men who swung to her oars. The square striped sail fell slack as the headland took the wind from it, and then came rattling down, and urged by her rowers she headed like some eager many-legged sea creature for the low shelving beach where the cliffs dropped at the head of the fjord. ...

A little earlier in the opening scene of this, which is from Rosemary Sutcliff's fine modern prose version of the Anglo

Saxon epic poem, *Beowulf*, they will have met the hero, sitting
among the thanes in the great mead-hall of Hygelac, King of
the Geats, a race of Southern Sweden:

A young man, fair-headed and grey-eyed as most of his fellows
were, but taller than they by half a head, and with strength that
could out-wrestle the great Northern bear showing in the quiet
muscles of his neck and shoulders. He sat in a place that was not
particularly high nor yet particularly lowly; indeed he was one who
seldom cared about his rightful place unless another man thought to
deny it him. Yet there was something in his face and his whole
bearing that would have marked him for who he was, even to the
passing glance of a stranger.

He is nephew to the king and foremost among his warriors. At
this moment he listens, as all the others listen and as the children
themselves are listening in the long oral tradition to someone
telling a story. It is not Angelm, the usual harpist, singer and
story teller, but a stranger, a Sea Captain, welcome with his
men as bringers of news after the long frozen isolation of winter.
He contrasts the good-fellowship and hospitality of their surroundings with the terror reigning in the hall of the Danish
King, brought by Grendel, the Man-Wolf, the Death-Shadow,
who comes nightly from his lair among the sea inlets and coastal
marshes, snuffing round the porch, 'hating all men, and all joy,
and hungry for human life'. Even as the tale is being told, the
listeners huddle forward towards the log fires, with here and
there a glance behind into the shadows; for they know bolts and
bars will not keep the Troll-kind out. Grendel's attacks are so
swift that he has seized his victims from among the noblest
thanes and gone, before a cry can be heard outside, and in the
morning 'only blood splashed on walls and floor and the
monster's footprints remained to tell their fate'.

Here is a quest crying out to be undertaken. Beowulf offers
himself, partly because he had been brought up in the Danish
court and owes the king much, but more because the longing
for adventure is stirring in his blood, as it does every spring
when his war-boat waits in its shed, freshly caulked and painted
and like a mare expecting her rider. His companions, his
'shoulder-to-shoulder' men of other journeyings, share his feelings as they listen and watch him in the firelight and the flare
of torches. So they go forth to rid Denmark of this monster,
are seen by the Coast Warden and led to the king's hall

F

where they are feasted and much welcomed, though with no optimism.

At length all the Danes depart for none will sleep in the hall; but Beowulf and his fourteen shoulder-to-shoulder men lie down on straw-filled bolsters and warm wolfskin rugs, to wait. Grendel comes, a shadow first, lit only by green phosphorescent eyes. Then, tangible, he seizes the young warrior Hondscio, tears him apart and drinks his blood. A long fight with Beowulf follows, that seems to end in victory for the man, for Grendel flees, leaving his hairy arm behind, wrenched from its socket in the struggle.

Fear has gone, all day and evening there is feasting and rejoicing in the great hall but next morning Hrothgar, the King, has a face as set as stone. He had felt deeply for Hondscio, the newly arrived young warrior who died. But now his grief is deeper, for his dearest counsellor and close friend, Aschere, has been carried off by Grendel's avenging mother and his head found 'lying abandoned like some fragment of a mouse that a great cat has dropped from its jaws . . . where Grendel's dam had torn it off before she plunged down to her lair'.

The old king and the young hero, Beowulf, ride forth to face the new danger. At the cliff top they leave their horses and climb down the steep chill gorge until emerging from the trees they come to the inlet where waters churn and lash the rocks and are sucked down the monster's sea-hole. Here no sea birds cry, there are only seals and tusked walruses basking on the ledges. Armed with a special sword from the king's jester, Hunferth, envious when Beowulf arrived but won to admiration since, the hero plunges down into an undersea world very different from the Little Mermaid's and is clasped by the monster and locked in struggle with her until Beowulf finally triumphs.

He returns to Sweden, years pass, he is made king through failure in the direct succession and rules nobly until the fiftieth year of his reign when horror strikes the land. This time a fire-dragon so terrible that no thane will approach it with Beowulf except the youngest, Wiglaf, whose grandfather, Waegmund, sailed in the original long ship fifty years before. In overcoming the dragon and winning its treasure for his people, Beowulf is killed. Children are not moved by the sadness of age so that for many young listeners the story does not develop but repeats itself, with another long gripping fight. Yet all are held and moved by the ritual of the close.

I know no other story of Norsemen that has so much to offer children in its own right. The successive stages of the action are presented with controlled suspense and with precision and power as well as great beauty of language. There is great violence but there is human dignity in face of it and no trace of sensationalism. The sway of emotion is extreme but is never manipulated to provide some new twist or add sauce for tired appetites.

One may well want to make *Beowulf* the imaginative centre of a project on the Vikings. Some of the stories of Henry Treece are valuable here, the *Horned Helmet, Viking's Dawn, The Last of the Vikings,* for these take children into the Viking world through the mind and feeling of a boy. They are brought into intimate contact with life on board a long ship, its practical details, the fellowship and rivalry among a crew, as well as with the danger and splendour of the sea. There is also an exciting chapter in Kipling's *Puck of Pook's Hill*, aptly called 'Joyous Venture', when the Norman story teller is captured by Danish pirates in mid-channel and taken by them to Africa, where they are attacked by gorillas.

The Icelandic Saga of *Grettir the Strong*, which Bodley Head publish in a good modern translation by Allen French, is worth reading to top juniors, although it appeals to a rather narrow range of emotion. Grettir was a real person, born just before the end of the tenth century when Iceland was converted to Christianity. The mythical and the actual no longer merge. Trolls, ghosts and hauntings abound as one would expect in such early times and in so grim a natural setting, but gods no longer come in person into the story. A harsh 'ordinary' life goes on, on farms and in small communities. Shepherds need hiring, kin must be visited, there is the new festival of Christmas to be celebrated with the continuance of many Yuletide traditions. Above all, the frequent mention of lawsuits and of disputes being raised and settled at the local Althings, or moots, reminds us that Iceland's parliamentary tradition is older than our own. This is already a shrewd legalistic society in which ordinary men and women act as warriors only when forced to because there is no police force. Those wanting more continuous adventure seek it abroad.

Grettir is an early outsider, not a merry outlaw like Robin Hood but an ill-fated man, with strength like Samson's, a sarcastic tongue and a cunning brain. Fundamentally, though, by the standards of this society he is a generous man and unhappy in his enforced loneliness. He is outlawed first for three years while barely more than a boy, for killing a man in self-defence, and there are a number of episodes from this period of his life which children find very exciting. For instance, when he climbs down a haunted barrow to rob it of its buried treasure and is suddenly gripped from behind by the unlaid ghost of the dead man. On another occasion he outwits some marauding baresarks who raid the farm when he is being grudgingly sheltered, while still more exciting is his fight with the ghost of the shepherd, Glam, who was struck dead for eating meat on Christmas Eve and returns to haunt and terrorise the neighbourhood. Ghosts in this world are as substantial as men, which takes some explaining to children, but usually their appearance heralds a gripping fight and so the questions about them are not pressed. In the end, through acting unselfishly, Grettir is outlawed for life, and wherever he goes he is a source of danger to those who shelter him and has to move on. He endures a Crusoe-like existence in the mountains, which are dark and hateful to him. 'I must be somewhere,' he says on one occasion and this seems to sum up his predicament. Needless to say he comes to a violent end.

Once upon a time, before ever this world was made, there was neither earth nor sea, nor air, nor light, but only a great yawning gulf, full of twilight, where these things should be.

To the north of this gulf lay the Home of Mist, a dark and dreary land, out of which flowed a river of water from a spring that never ran dry. As the water in its onward course met the bitter blasts of wind from the yawning gulf, it hardened into great blocks of ice, which rolled far down into the abyss with a thunderous roar and piled themselves one on another until they formed mountains of glistening ice.

To seven and eight year olds this is the opening of a fascinating story, which comes best then, so that it is to some extent part of their experience when they meet Beowulf later. At ten or eleven children would want to discuss the story in relation to Genesis, which may or may not suit one's purpose, or be inappropriate because one wants at that time to fire their imaginations with some simplified astronomical knowledge of the universe.

If one reads young children Norse stories of creation, it is much better to read a full version, such as Miss E. M. Wilmot-

Buxton's *Tales from the Eddas*, which I quote from, than briefer
summaries, for children need time to enter a new imaginative
world and to begin to feel at home there. Miss Wilmot-Buxton
is a particularly good story teller for younger children. For
second and third years, Roger Lancelyn Green's *Myths of the
Norsemen*, attractively published by Bodley Head, and available
also under its original title, *The Saga of Asgard*, is quite good,
but I prefer Barbara Leonie Picard's *Tales of the Norse Gods*,
published by Oxford University Press. There is less compression,
the stories flow in a more compelling way, and hold children's
interest better. The classic Victorian version, A. and E. Keary's
The Heroes of Asgard, through emphasis, and above all its
language, gives a gentler, more romantic picture.

Norse mythology has great vitality, a strongly grotesque
quality and much burlesque comedy, which juniors love. When
Thor visits the giants, for instance, and swings his great hammer
at the mighty Skrymir, who is snoring like a thunderstorm, the
blow simply makes the giant roll over, open his eyes and ask
sleepily, 'What's the matter, Thor? It seems to me as though a
leaf has fallen on my head and woken me.' At the next tremendous crack, he thinks it is an acorn, the third time a twig.
Another time, when Thor is visiting Geirrodur, the crafty Troll
king, he strides warily up the hall, with big fires burning down
each side, to where Geirrodur stands beside the hottest fire of
all, '. . . and when he drew near the Troll king, Geirrodur
suddenly drew a bar of white-hot metal out of the fire with a
huge pair of tongs and flung it at him.' But Thor is match for
him, catches it in his iron gloves, whirls it round his head, and
hurls it back. This is thoroughly satisfactory behaviour in
juniors' eyes. Some of them will have met trolls in J. R. Tolkien's
The Hobbit, which is steeped in Norse mythology. These strange
misshapen creatures, related to dwarfs and giants, living under
low hills in a kind of luxuriant squalor, intrigue as well as rather
frighten them.

There is also a kind of poetry that children respond to in the
strange fine-sounding Norse names. What could be more wrig-
glingly expressive than *Yggdrasil* for the great World tree, or more
brutish than *Nid Hog* for the name of the creature gnawing at
its lowest roots? What more echoing and empty than *Ginnun-
gagap* for the Yawning Void, the Norse counterpart of the
Greek *Chaos* and our *Nothingness*?

There is much less variety and human interest for children
in the Norse world than in the Greek, and a bleakness and sad

ferocity about a realistic story like *Grettir the Strong*, or the story of *Völund the Smith*, which makes one hesitate to read them even to fourth-year juniors. Boys enjoy the Norse world much more than girls and one must guard against reading stories of violence simply to meet and feed aggressive instincts. One must be moved, oneself, I think, by the strong positive values of the Vikings, and also see that in one's total pattern of story for a class these tales are balanced by others closer to their own lives and experience.

Greek literature and mythology has marvellous richness, beauty and interest for children. Seven and eight year olds delight in stories about the Minotaur, Persephone, King Midas, Orpheus and Eurydice, the Golden Fleece, for their excitement and suspense as well as their wonder. There are many retellings of these stories for children, from Kingsley's *Heroes* and Hawthorne's *Tanglewood Tales*, to modern ones by Robert Graves and Rex Warner, Robert Penn Warren and René Guillot. It is worth exploring several before deciding which one likes best, and, equally important, thinks will appeal most strongly to a particular class. Children enjoy retelling the stories in their own words and especially improvising from them in drama.

If one wants even so early to give more than a random selection, Roger Lancelyn Green in his *Tales of the Greek Heroes*, available in Puffin Books, expressly sets out to show the tales as an evolving sequence, the history of the Greek Heroic Age, which was how the Greeks themselves saw them. Beginning with the war between the giant offspring of Earth and Sky and the final victory of Zeus, they then tell of Zeus sending Prometheus to create Man from clay and of Prometheus's own rebellion against divine authority when he steals fire to give to Man. The first great semi-divine hero is Perseus, his greatest successor, his great-grandson, Hercules, to be followed by Theseus. Lightly stressed, this sense of continuity adds interest although one can omit some stories if one wishes. The Heroic Age is ended by the ten-year Trojan War, which Roger Lancelyn Green does not write about here, but in his other book, *The Tale of Troy*.

However, I would not rely too heavily on this author. His attitude to the Greek world tends to be nostalgic, in the romantic late nineteenth-century tradition kept alive by scholars like Gilbert Murray. He softens, as he must, the true nature of the satyrs but his prose is simple and effective for young readers and his opening chapter helpful in its exposition of how the

Greeks looked at the natural world, and of how they regarded
their gods. For they saw them as very like themselves, only
more powerful, beautiful and free; and capable of cruelty,
deceit and selfishness which in human beings they would have
condemned.

Andrew Lang's classic version, *The Adventures of Odysseus*, still
has much to recommend it for children, having a single focus
of human interest, and combining the matter of both *Iliad* and
Odyssey, with popular additions at the end, into one enthralling
story. Particularly he brings alive the hero's boyhood in Ithaca,
the beauty of the Greek islands and the simple graciousness of
Greek life. A child can identify himself with Odysseus in a way
he never would if he met him first as a cunning adult. But Lang
is romantic in a way the originals never are, particularly in
idealising the 'Lady Helen'. Many descriptions of the fighting
are sheathed in a gleaming nineteenth-century conception of
courtliness of which this is a fair example: 'Then they fought a
gentle passage of arms and took courteous farewell of each
other.' But his description of the Wooden Horse (not in the
Iliad at all, and described after the event in the *Odyssey*) is full
of suspense and excitement. Children love the kind of detail
that he gives here: the Greeks, for instance, swathing themselves
in soft silks in case their armour should clash when the Horse
is dragged inside the city. Excitement for children is at full
pitch throughout, with the fake departure of the Greeks, who
burn their huts and launch their ships to give the Trojans a
false sense of security. There is drunkenness among the Trojan
sentinels and wild rejoicing as the Horse is dragged in to the
city; fear follows when Helen comes and underneath the belly
of the Horse uses all her famous powers of mimicry to make the
men inside believe their wives were talking down below. Only
Odysseus's insight, who whispers 'Echo' to the waiting men to
remind them of Helen's gift, saves them from betrayal. 'Mean-
while the Greek ships were returning from behind Tenedos as
fast as the oarsmen could row them.' Ultimately when 'the
grey city fell, that had lorded it for centuries', Andrew Lang
provides an exciting link for children with the present by speaking of the great treasure, mostly divided among the victors but
part hidden in the hollow of the wall; for it was this treasure,
he writes, which was 'found not very many years ago by men
digging deep on the hill where Troy once stood'.

He refers, of course, to the discoveries in the 1870's of the
remarkable Heinrich Schliemann, who had made a business

fortune in his twenties and gave up everything to his pursuit of
archaeology. He has recorded how this passion dated from
Christmas, 1829, when at the age of seven he was given Jerrer's
Universal History for a present. An engraving of Aeneas carrying
his father, Anchises, from the burning Troy convinced him that
Jerrer must have seen Troy to draw it, and he would not accept
his father's explanation that it is only a fanciful picture. In his
book, *Ilios*, he records the conversation that followed:

'Father, did Troy have great walls like these in the picture?'
'Probably.'
'Then, they can't *all* have gone. Some must still be there, hidden
under the ground. I'd love to dig them up. Father, some day shall
I go and dig them up?'
'I shouldn't be surprised. And now be quiet. I want to sleep.'

Modern children are still passionately literal. They want
maps to find where Troy was, near the modern Hissarlik and
the mouth of the Dardanelles, and to trace the many voyages.
To them, the *Argo* of the Argonauts seems very like a Norse
long ship, especially when they read of its crew resting their
round shields on a shield rack along its side. The Argonauts
went far north, to a strange land of ice, where when they landed
they saw great white bears and wild men clad in skins, who
foamed at the mouth when they fought. Odysseus, too, came
to the land of the Laestrygonians – 'huge fellows, more like
giants than men', Homer wrote – who pelted his fleet with
rocks as it lay in harbour surrounded by steep cliffs. Here,
according to Odysseus, 'shepherds bringing in their flocks at
night hail and are answered by their fellows driving out at
dawn'. Could it be that Greek and Norse worlds briefly touched
centuries before *Beowulf* and still longer before the Vikings sailed
to Athens? Children are excited by the possibility.

Before Schliemann Greek history was dated from about 770
B.C., Homer's heroes and the Trojan War being thought part
of a kind of classical fairyland. Schliemann's discoveries beneath
the Hill of Hissarlik, and his subsequent uncovering of the
great treasure-laden Shaft-Graves at Mycenae, Agamemnon's
'golden city', inspired the English archaeologist, Sir Arthur
Evans. His work and that of his successors at Knossos in Crete
revolutionised our knowledge. The most recent discovery of
importance in this romantic yet scientific pursuit of the past
came in 1952 when the young scholar, Michael Ventris, later

killed in a car crash, deciphered the writing known as Linear
B script found on clay tiles at Knossos and proved it to be
Greek. The early Mycenean civilisation was, it would seem,
Greek after all, occupying Greece for more than five hundred
years, in the end conquering and colonising Crete, not, as
Evans thought, the other way about. Its golden age was from
roughly 1200 to 1100 B.C., when the siege of Troy probably
took place. Homer himself wrote later, it is thought, around
900 B.C., after the Dorian invasion had driven many Greeks
into exile, who took with them lays and legends of the Mycenean
Age which Homer must have known.

There is a joyous irony in all this. It was the exactness of
Homer in his descriptions of Troy and of battle techniques not
known in classical Greece, such as fighting from chariots, and
using great shields as tall as fighting men, that caused the
excavations. Schliemann and other scholars were convinced that
Homer must have *seen* what he described, to create so concrete
a world. The excavations ultimately proved that after all Homer
was 'using his imagination', in that he wrote of a time several
centuries before his own but drew on his knowledge of human
nature and that of other poets as well as what he actually saw
around him as he wrote. Eye-witnesses of lesser genius would
undoubtedly have produced something that seemed less 'real'.
The imagination had then, as it has now, its own reality.

The early excavations have a gripping dramatic quality, and
buried treasure is so much at the heart of children's adventure
stories that it would be a pity to waste one of the most exciting
actual examples of it there has ever been. Leonard Cottrell's
Bull of Minos, of which there is a special children's edition, is an
inspiring introduction. Cottrell describes each stage in the
excavations, with Schliemann and his wife eagerly watching
their workmen and an ephor, or Greek Government official,
suspiciously watching them all. The first thrilling moment came
when the spades hit solid rock and the edge of a cutting was
revealed, the beginning of a vertical shaft going down into the
rock to an unknown depth. They had found the first of the
Shaft-Graves. From then on every shovelful of earth had to be
carefully examined. When the men were fifteen feet down,
Schliemann's wife saw a bright gleam in the soil and picked up
what proved to be a gold ring. After that the principals worked
alone with pocket knives because they dare not risk the carelessness of the workmen. In the first five of the six graves ultimately
discovered were the remains of nineteen people, men, women

and two small children, the men wearing golden masks and breastplates, two women golden frontlets and one a magnificent golden diadem. The two children were wrapped in sheet-gold. Buried with them were swords, daggers, gold and silver drinking cups, gold toilet boxes and precious dress ornaments. These details fascinate children as well as providing significant points of contrast and comparison for them with what they may have learned of Norse burial customs.

In the last grave were three male bodies, with golden breastplates, and golden masks. When these were removed, the skulls of the first two crumbled at once. Of the third, Schliemann wrote: 'the round face, with all its flesh, had been wonderfully preserved under its ponderous golden mask; there was no vestige of hair, but both eyes were perfectly visible, also the mouth, owing to the enormous weight that had pressed upon it, was wide open, and showed thirty-two beautiful teeth. From these, all the physicians who came to see the body were led to believe that the man must have died at the early age of thirty-five.' Schliemann lifted the golden mask, kissed it, then sent the King of Greece a telegram which read: 'I have gazed on the face of Agamemnon.' Subsequent research has shown that he had not but on that of some much earlier king, which adds rather then lessens the wonder of it.

The reality of this has a tremendously powerful imaginative appeal for children. The American writer, Henry Miller, puts it vividly in his *Books in my Life*, well worth teachers' reading in this context for its chapter on the books of childhood. 'Looking out over the plain of Argos from Mycenae I lived over again – and how vividly! – the tale of the Argonauts. Gazing upon the Cyclopean walls of Tiryns I recalled the tiny illustration of the wall in one of my wonder books – it corresponded exactly with the reality confronting me. Never in school had a history professor even attempted to make living for us these glorious epochs of the past which every child enters into naturally as soon as he is able to read. We learn nothing from the pedagogues. The true educators are the adventurers and wanderers, the men who plunge into the living plasm of history, legend, myth.'

Adventurers and wanderers – the more teachers approach story for juniors in this spirit, the more children will respond, enjoy, remember what is read to them. This is essentially the spirit of the *Odyssey*, an exciting novel with a close-knit plot but also with much fascinating incident in its distinct episodes.

There is much magic and the appeal of a quest while the last
section, when Odysseus returns in disguise to Ithaca and plots
to overthrow the idle suitors of his supposed widow, Penelope,
has the appeal of a powerful thriller. There is both variety and a
single goal, which holds third-year juniors. They love incidents
like the outwitting of the Cyclops and the sheer terror of the
passage between Scylla and Charybdis, not to mention the
temptations of the Sirens, Circe, Calypso, which add the underlying significance of moral allegory to romantic adventure.
There is much attractiveness also in young characters like the
beautiful and tender-minded Nausicaa and Odysseus's son,
Telemachus, whom we see grow in stature as a person as the
story advances; while even a monster like the blinded Cyclops
excites some sympathy when he talks affectionately to his favourite
ram. The only part one may want to omit is Odysseus's voyage
to the underworld, for this troubles some children a good deal.
Of the many retellings for young readers, I like Barbara Leonie
Picard's full version best. She simplifies the structure of the
original, taking children straightforwardly through Odysseus's
adventures in the first part and not showing us the sad state of
affairs on Ithaca, which Homer opens with, until Part II.

Most teachers are less adventurous where the *Iliad* as a whole
is concerned and yet it is a wonderfully absorbing and moving
drama. From the outset children can easily grasp the situation
and picture the scene: the Greeks led by Agamemnon encamped
on the edge of the Trojan plain besieging Troy, where Paris,
King Priam's son, has carried off Helen, wife of Menelaus,
Agamemnon's brother. The nine-year siege has never been
complete, the Trojans always being free to take in supplies from
the rear, the Greeks supplying themselves by sporadic raids on
coastal cities of the Eastern Aegean. Homer's detail is superb
and exactly suited to the children's imaginations. No matter
how literal their questions, he forestalls them; and children like
to know how the Greeks beached their ships, raising them up
on stone supports to prevent their keels from rotting, and how
the leaders lived, each with their men behind his own ships, in
huts of wood and earth well thatched with rushes, with shelters
for cattle and slaves and stabling for mules and horses. Still
more they like to know how they fought, each leader in a light
battle chariot, with a strong wooden and bronze frame, sides
of wicker work and, as a form of primitive suspension, a platform
of plaited strips beneath to lessen the jolting. His chosen warriors
ran beside the chariot, then lords and nobles in their own

chariots with their followers, and last the men who fought on foot.

Inside Troy we see the high citadel, the Pergamus, where Priam's palace was and the houses of Hector, and Paris and Helen. From there a broad paved way ran down to the Scaean Gate, with a near-by tower, from which the battle on the plain could be watched. Outside was a burial mound to Ilus, an ancient Trojan king, and a sacred oak on which, in likeness of two vultures, Athene and Aphrodite sat to watch the combat with far-seeing eyes. (There were also two gushing springs, one hot, one cold, and so convincingly literal was Homer's description that long before Schliemann came to excavate erudite European scholars had gone over the whole area armed with thermometers.) The gods take sides in this war and interfere at crucial points in the action, which although unfair is acceptable to children when they realise how powerful feelings are involved. Athene, for instance, goddess particularly of Athens and the Greeks, was scorned by Trojan Paris in the contest of the Golden Apples, when he favoured Aphrodite, so she is naturally for the Greeks and Aphrodite for the Trojans. Agamemnon slights Chryses, whose daughter he takes as a special prize of war, Chryses is priest to Apollo, and so Apollo also supports Troy. Thetis, on the other hand, is Achilles' mother and supports the Greeks. All these save Thetis are children of Zeus but Athene is his favourite daughter and ultimately, one knows, the Greeks must win. But although the dice are loaded in this way, and although Homer reveres the gods and shows them to be formidable, this never for a moment makes the human characters puppets. Significantly the one god he does not respect is Ares, or Mars, the god of war, who always seems an ugly bully. There is no need to go into great detail over all this, although ten and eleven year olds are great ones for detail. Most of the time, however, they are oblivious of the gods, because Homer is so supremely concerned throughout with human beings and human values.

Description for its own sake soon bores children but all Homer's detail is conveyed in direct presentation of action, as is our vivid full awareness of the characters. The action starts at once, with the great quarrel between Agamemnon and Achilles. Agamemnon has no absolute authority, only a loose overlordship. In the intermittent fighting and foraging for supplies, Achilles, youngest, most beautiful of the Greek kings and their greatest warrior, has been far more active but it is

Agamemnon who has always taken the richest share of the
spoils. Now because he has taken the daughter of Chryses,
Apollo's priest, the god has sent a plague to punish the Greeks
and he is forced to return his prize. In revenge and to assert
his authority, he takes the slave girl of Achilles. In his wrath
Achilles is tempted to kill Agamemnon but Athene persuades
him not to precipitate civil war among the Greeks. He retires to
his hut, vowing to take no more part in the fighting, and continues to sulk there, with his great friend, Patroclus. Much of this
may seem too adult for children yet the passions involved are
not primarily sexual. Children understand the main issue of
hurt pride well enough and know from experience how this
leads to selfish self-assertive behaviour. They are quick, too, to
see how both Achilles and Agamemnon are at fault.

One could continue summarising and at every point find the
line of action clear and compelling, the suspense great, the
interest sustained; but no summary can give any idea of Homer's
power to involve and divide our sympathies. At a tremendous
disadvantage without Achilles, the Greeks build a wall to pro-
tect their camp and ships but the Trojans break through and
there is vivid description of the fighting at the ships, with Ajax
leaping from stern to stern, thrusting down with his grappling
iron any Trojan who tries to climb on deck, shouting all the
while to hearten the Greeks fighting on foot between the ships.
Hector finally sets fire to one of the ships and the need for
Achilles grows imperative. But having already rebuffed un-
gracious overtures from Agamemnon, he still refuses to fight.
However he gives way to Patroclus's plea that he may be
allowed to fight in Achilles' armour.

From then on to the end there is no easy allegiance, as there
is in the fighting in *Beowulf*. Patroclus is killed and the great
and noble Hector does not emerge well, although the real villain
is Apollo, who causes Patroclus's helmet to roll off, his shield
strap to break and his spear to slip from his grasp. An unnamed
Trojan drives his spear between his shoulder blades and then,
as he stumbles back defenceless, Hector thrusts his spear into
his body and laughs in triumph. 'Patroclus, lying before him,
twisted on the ground, his hands scrabbling at the spearshaft,
looked up at him only through a mist of pain. "You need not
boast of having killed me, Hector," he said, "for you only
finished what others had begun. The immortal gods who took
away my strength and disarmed me, were before you, and the
man who struck me from behind."' Hector stows Achilles'

armour in his chariot as a spoil of war and wants Patroclus's head for the Trojan battlements. He lifts it by its long bright hair but Ajax leaps forward and saves the body.

Achilles' grief when he learns of Patroclus's death is terrible and excessive. He recognises his own responsibility for it and wants nothing but to kill Hector. He has to wait a day while his goddess mother fetches new armour for him, forged by Hephaestus, craftsman of the gods, and he spends it brooding, only at sunset appearing on the ramparts, where the Trojans see him godlike against the evening sky.

Yet, despite pity for Achilles, our sympathies are all with Hector in the final encounter between them especially when, having stabbed Hector through the one flaw in his armour, 'an opening at the gullet where the collar bones lead from the shoulders to the neck, the easiest place to kill a man',* and which he knew because Hector was wearing Achilles' armour, stolen from the dead Patroclus, he ignores Hector's pleas not to leave his body to the vultures. Instead, he pierces the sinews of Hector's feet from heel to ankle, binds them with a thong, fastens the body to the back rail of his chariot, so that the head trails in the dust, and drives in triumph round the stricken city. He later drives the body round the burial mound of Patroclus, then leaves it 'lying there, outstretched upon the ground, and returned once more to his hut in search of rest, his anger a little blunted but his heart uncomforted'.

At this point the involvement of children is partly resolved. Before, it has been almost unbearably intense. Majorie Hourd in her most valuable book, *The Education of the Poetic Spirit*, describing her work with first-year secondary girls, many still only ten, quotes one girl's exclaiming at the beginning of the final encounter: 'I don't know what to do, I like them both so much.' After Hector's body has been dishonoured, she had no doubts: 'Well, after that I don't mind that happens to Achilles, the brute!' Other comments made when they were asked which character they would like to be in their dramatisation reveal the degree of perception that children of this age are capable of. One girl of ten years eight months said of Achilles: 'it was babyish of him to sulk in his tent – and he really didn't love Patroclus right. He loved him too much really, because when he was killed he didn't know what to do. He was so upset. He couldn't believe it, so he just rushed into the battlefield and

*E. V. Rieu, *The Iliad*, Chap. 22, new translation, Penguin Classics, p. 405.

struck out at everybody. He wanted to hurt anybody who came near him, but it was death really and he just would not understand that.' Priam was chosen by another because 'he did not take sides like saying "My armies are better than the Greeks. We are sure to win." He praised up the armies of the Greeks, which I thought was very nice indeed.' Another said: 'I would like to be Agamemnon because I would like to be in the quarrel. Agamemnon is very kingly and great and thinks he is the only pebble on the beach.' The quarrel, verbal battle, not physical, offers great pleasure and release to children. One of Miss Hourd's girls, revealingly, did not mind whether she was Agamemnon or Achilles in the scene, for 'In it everybody is very sarcastic to everybody else. And whichever part I took of these two, I should enjoy taking very much.'

Homer resolves matters for us with the moving account of old Priam's journey to Achilles to beg for his son's body, and of Achilles' final act of generosity and respect. Like *Beowulf*, the *Iliad* ends with the description of funeral rites, those of Hector, whom in his last line Homer simply calls, 'tamer of horses'. Among other feelings one is left with an overwhelming sense of the ugliness and pointlessness of war.

I have quoted except where indicated from Barbara Leonie Picard's *Iliad*, which is the best I know for children. If one wants a more condensed version I prefer Rex Warner's *Greeks and Trojans* to Robert Graves's *The Siege and Fall of Troy*, excellent though the latter's prose is. Both condense too much for the real power of the story to come through. Ten pages in Robert Graves, for instance, covers the whole of the action of the *Iliad* from where Patroclus pleads with Achilles to be allowed to fight, to the sack of Troy, including several additional incidents which he chooses to use from later sources. This disturbs the full satisfaction of Homer's resolution of feeling at the close. Also Graves gives more weight than Homer, in relation to the rest of the action, to the interventions of the gods, so that the effect of his version is of some brilliant manipulation, lacking the moving complexity of feeling of the original. There does not seem adequate evidence, either, for his strong dislike of Odysseus while his marked anti-heroic tone strikes me as wrong for children.

If one decided to read one or other of these great epics to a class, one should allow plenty of time. I do not envisage any close-knit project, although there is plenty of scope for related work in history, geography, art and archaeology. Children love dramatising incidents, one will ask them to write sometimes in varying ways but the main value and deep interest, I am convinced, is in the experience of the stories. Just because this is a maturing and extended one, it should not be rushed and over-concentrated.

With later literature for children one is mostly concerned with individual writers who, despite differences in content, share a childlike quality of vision, an ability to see life vividly and immediately from a child's point of view. Sometimes, though, one may find rewarding autobiographical experience in adult writers as they remember childhood, school, growing up. The important thing in the junior school is to give children richness and variety. They should not automatically associate what their teacher reads to them with the past. One should read from modern writers as well, just as one should vary the emphasis between fantasy and realism, long epic or novel, and short story or excerpt.

Seven and eight year olds, boys as well as girls, love strange grotesque stories and magic of all kinds, provided it is compellingly created for them. One will banish all whimsical fairy story but many powerful traditional stories of Perrault, Grimm and Hans Andersen are wonderful material for playmaking, as I suggest in the next chapter.

Hans Andersen, I think, is an unexpectedly rewarding writer for there is a simple naturalism lacking in the brothers Grimm, as well as sharp fantasy. He is quite often sentimental but usually from a genuine sense of a child's isolation and capacity for suffering, and where this is true to his age, but false now, one can easily cut. Like Dickens he is much more compelling in his pictures of fear and terror, than in mawkish descriptions of the purely good. His imagination is always most powerfully stirred by what is pre-Christian in the Scandinavian world: the cold dark forests, the witch-like crones, the long winter nights broken only by short green summers. For English children now, his nineteenth-century Danish boys and girls are as distant as Red Riding Hood and so they are not fundamentally disturbed by the real unhappiness that he sometimes shows, as they would be by a powerful modern story about a deprived child. But, then, that would not be a story *for* children at all. He also has the value of presenting a tender, yet unsentimental picture of the relationship between childhood sweethearts, making us aware of feelings that exist but are rarely given expression in modern children's stories. In a story like *The Snow Queen*, or the

less well known, more naturalistic *Ib and Christine*, this is particularly so. Each is a kind of allegory, with values emerging still
important today.

In the former the cold distorting splinter of reason in Kay's
heart is not washed away until Gerda's love melts the ice that
grips it. In the second story the children, lost in a great forest,
are suddenly confronted by a tall old gypsy woman, with shining
black hair and gleaming eyes. She gives Ib three wishing nuts,
two promising carriages and fine clothes, which Christine takes.
The third, a little black thing, which the gypsy tells them
contains the best of all things, Christine graciously says that Ib
may keep. When he gets home he cracks it and finds that it has
only a little rich black earth in it. Christine goes off to Copenhagen into service, marries a rich spendthrift and forgets Ib,
who stays at home farming until one day his plough strikes a
great gold armlet from a Viking grave. The earth has yielded
riches after all and although too late for a happy ending with
Christine, he does discover her child, now orphaned, and is
transported to his own childhood again in caring for her.

The emphasis in both these stories is on the human feeling
involved and not the moral. Sometimes Andersen presents his
gentle criticism of the world's pretentiousness through fable-like
tales that illustrate a clearly defined idea. A point is proved
rather than a more complex and fully human morality hinted
at. Children are very clear-sighted in these matters and enjoy
this kind of tale. After all, in *The Emperor's Clothes* it is a child
who first cries out: 'But he has nothing on!' Children enjoy
this story and also *The Nightingale*, about an Emperor of China
who lives in a brittle palace of delicate beautiful porcelain, and
who hangs silver bells on the most beautiful flowers in his
gardens in case people should not notice them. Travellers and
visiting poets declare that the nightingale surpasses all the
flowers in beauty. The Emperor did not even know he had a
nightingale but now the bird has to be found and tethered to
a golden perch in court where he not only keeps a drowsy
Emperor awake but moves him to tears. Twice daily the bird is
taken out by twelve servants, each holding a silken string tied
to the bird's legs. One day the Emperor is sent a present of a
golden bird which can be wound up and made to sing a waltz.
The new bird is all the rage, the old one banished, for his song
is unpredictable and won't fit when the court music master
wants to arrange a duet with the golden bird. The latter could
be opened up and 'explained' so that people knew where the

G

waltzes came from. Of course in the end the mechanism breaks down and cannot be repaired. The Emperor is dying and, delirious, commands the golden bird to sing. But it is the live nightingale outside on the spray who restores his health. This time, however, the Emperor does not tether him but waits for the bird to come from his nest.

Europe was at this time highly interested in mechanical inventiveness. The possibility of creating a kind of life intrigued the imagination. One thinks of Collodi's charming tale of the puppet, Pinocchio, and E. T. A. Hoffman's story of the toy maker, Coppelius, both of which delight first-year juniors. But neither has that implicit direction of our sympathies that one finds in Andersen towards the natural, the created that cannot be 'explained'.

Many children undoubtedly delight in the quite different kind of fantasy in *Alice in Wonderland* and many teachers find pleasure in reading it to a class. These remain the best reasons for continuing but I think it is worth realising the arbitrary intellectual nature of Carroll's world and the more truly child-like fantasy of Hans Andersen. He was often sentimental when he contemplated innocence having to grow up into an unkind world but his sorrow was for the child. We know how sad Lewis Carroll was when the real Alice grew up and, in their turn, her several successors, but his sadness was for himself, deprived of a relationship that he needed. Fantasy for him was both escape and compensation. But it is a tribute to his quite remarkable minor genius that there is no trace of self-pity in the Alice books. Their fantasy is primarily logical, beautifully apt, intellectually satisfying. Like the nonsense poems of Edward Lear, they offer the release of laughter, and much pleasure in words, their sounds and expressiveness. But they do not excite much genuine wonder in a child; for they touch no deep personal feeling nor extend or intensify his awareness of the marvellous in the actual world. They offer a delightful freedom but journey nowhere. However, they dramatise delightfully and here I think lies their chief value for juniors.

There is a strong element of escape and compensation in the other classic fantasy for children of this age, Kenneth Grahame's *The Wind in the Willows*; and as with Carroll the emotional immaturity implied by this both accounts for his appeal to children, and qualifies his ultimate value *for* them. *The Wind in the Willows* strikes me as a delightful fable of arrested development, appealing – which probably explains why so many adults love it – to a peculiarly English tendency to perpetual boyishness, which makes many English fathers love to take over their sons' railway systems or sail their boats for them. But to be fair to Kenneth Grahame, he strikes a moving chord, for everyone often longs for freedom away from school, bank or office. Children of junior school age delight in *The Wind in the Willows*. It lives and will live, because of the endearing quality of its characters and the permanently satisfying attitude towards authority of Mr. Toad. Like *Alice* it provides splendid material for dramatisation. Also like *Alice* it arouses no wonder. It offers escape to a free ideal holiday world, to which children are also transported by non-fantasies like *Swallows and Amazons* and a host of lesser successors about ponies and sailing and camping of some kind. This world and these books play a major part for most children in their private reading. The books undoubtedly mean a great deal to many of them. But they are books to grow up with, not books one grows up through. They are books one wants children to read for themselves, not books to give overmuch time to in class.

Kipling is a writer of a quite different kind. His books for children are not an escape for him, so much as an extension into a child's world of important elements in his imagination. And it is worth remembering that he, like Dickens, was an essentially *popular* adult author, who also had a naïve immediacy of contact with his public. Apart from his *Just So Stories* for younger children, his *Jungle Books* and *Puck of Pook's Hill* offer junior children much that is both realistic and imaginative. The *Jungle Books* are fantasy only in the technical sense that he gives his animals powers of thought and speech which they do not actually have. Otherwise, they are vividly realistic but always from a child's point of view, especially where human relations with animals are concerned and the immediacy of awareness of the natural world. Everything registers sharply and closely as it does to a child.

For instance, we immediately sense the heat of India, its lazy agriculture, where 'cattle move and crunch, and lie down, and move on again, and do not even low', where 'the buffaloes very seldom say anything, but get down into the muddy pools one after another, and work their way into the mud till only their noses and staring china-blue eyes show above the surface, and then they lie like logs'. Mowgli's up-bringing by the wolves is fascinating to children, the boy learning the meaning of every sound in the jungle and acutely aware of all of them. His life as Kipling describes it is infinitely preferable to school, for 'When he was not learning he sat out in the sun and slept, and ate and went to sleep again; and when he felt dirty or hot he swam in forest pools; and when he wanted honey, he climbed up for it, and that Bagheera showed him how to do. Bagheera would lie out on a branch and call, "Come along, Little Brother," and at first Mowgli would cling like the sloth, but afterwards he would fling himself through the branches as boldly as the gray ape.'

Each of the animals who are Mowgli's companions is vividly presented so that the reader often senses an individual power and presence rather than a humanised character, although that element is there too, and brings the animals very close to children. For instance, Kaa, the Rock-Python, is first met 'stretched out on a warm ledge, admiring his beautiful new coat . . . and twisting the thirty feet of his body into fantastic knots and curves'. His main fighting power, which we see in action when he rescues Mowgli from the despised Bandar-Log or Monkey People, is 'in the driving blow of his head backed by all the strength and weight of his body. If you can imagine a lance, or a battering ram, or a hammer weighing nearly half a ton driven by a cool quiet mind living in the handle of it you can roughly imagine what Kaa was like when he fought. A python four or five feet long can knock a man down if he hits him fairly in the chest, and Kaa was thirty feet long . . .' Most children, especially boys, relish exactness in matters of this kind, just as they relish the excitement and terror of the fight of the mongoose, Rikki-Tikki-Tavi, with Nag, the cobra, in the bathroom of the bungalow where Rikki-Tikki is protector of the English family, but especially of the boy, Teddy, whose pet he is.

There is frequently this protectiveness and care for life in Kipling and it is aroused in children listening to the stories. Mowgli arouses the protective love of the Mother Wolf when he is threatened by Shere Khan, the mangy tiger; Rikki-Tikki is half choked by summer floods, wrapped in cotton wool and warmed over the fire, like any sick pet at home. Protectiveness is aroused particularly strongly in *The White Seal*, the only tale in the original *Jungle Book* not about India, for Kotick, who after he has seen how men drive off and kill droves of seals, determines to discover remoter safer islands for the seal nurseries. The men come every year, as set on profit and as callous and systematic in their methods as their modern successors at

Lindisfarne and elsewhere. At first Kotick cannot understand, for the rest of the seals play on and no one will tell him what is to happen to those driven off. Then he follows to see for himself. The seals are driven slowly because, if they get heated, their fur comes off in patches when skinned. Kotick follows, panting and wondering. Then Kerick, the man in charge of the operation, 'sat down on the moss and pulled out a heavy pewter watch and let the drove cool off for thirty minutes, and Kotick could hear the fog-dew dripping off the brim of his cap. Then ten or twelve men, each with an iron-bound club three or four feet long, came up, and Kerick pointed out one or two of the drove that were bitten by their companions or too hot, and the men kicked those aside with their heavy boots made of the skin of a walrus's throat, and then Kerick said: "Let go!" and then the men clubbed the seals on the head as fast as they could. Ten minutes later little Kotick did not recognise his friends any more, for their skins were ripped off from the nose to the hind-flippers, whipped off and thrown down on the ground in a pile. That was enough for Kotick. He turned and galloped (and a seal can gallop very swiftly for a short time) back to the sea; his little new moustache bristling with horror.'

Most children feel deeply about cruelty to animals, as their unfailingly strong response to Anna Sewell's *Black Beauty* shows. A story like *The White Seal*, that also calls forth strong moral indignation in a situation that genuinely demands it, and for which there are unpleasantly close modern parallels, is worth far more than the morally neutral outlet of much fantasy. Kipling may exceed scientific truth in giving thought processes and moral sense to Kotick and to other animals in his stories but he never overplays this; it is never a substitute way of saying things about human beings, as it is with lesser writers. When there is so much ambiguity in adult and adolescent attitudes to violence, teachers should take every opportunity of reading children stories that present it in a morally truthful and accessible way. Kipling makes *The Wind in the Willows* seem more than usually cosy and domestic.

It would be misleading, though, to suggest that his main impact on children in his Jungle stories is a moral one. He takes them into a fascinating and exciting world. This comes out very strongly in the story *Toomai of the Elephants*. A child identifies himself immediately with Toomai, the small son of a government-employed elephant driver. With his sunbleached hair flying loose, looking like a goblin in the torchlight, we first

meet him wriggling for joy on top of a stockade post while the
newly caught wild elephants are brought in. Later, full of pride
at having attracted favourable notice from Petersen Sahib, the
Englishman in charge of all elephant hunting activities in the
area, he 'sits down to a sort of revel all by himself', thumping
a tom-tom lent him by the camp sweetmeat seller. There is no
tune and no words but the thumping makes him happy; and
tired he falls asleep on the elephant fodder beside Kala Nag,
his father's great elephant, who after all the others have one by
one lain down to sleep stands 'rocking slowly from side to side,
his ears put forward to listen to the night wind as it blew very
slowly across the hills'. In the night Toomai wakens to see the
great elephant freed from his shackle moving off from the camp.
Instead of raising the alarm the child runs barefoot after Kala
Nag down the moonlit road, calling softly, 'Take me with you,
take me with you.' What follows would be particularly exciting
for a child, perhaps with memories of an elephant ride at the
zoo, for 'the elephant turned without a sound, took three strides
back to the boy in the moonlight, put down his trunk, swung
him up to his neck, and almost before Little Toomai had settled
his knees, slipped into the forest'. There is a marvellous description of the journey as experienced by Toomai, swishing through
the jungle, emerging to see the tops of the trees, speckled and
furry in the moonlight and a blue-white mist over the river in
the hollow, and vividly aware of the forest awake and alive
and crowded all around. Finally they join the wild elephants,
whose trumpetings had excited Kala Nag, and Toomai witnesses
their dance.

Puck of Pook's Hill shows us Kipling's powerful historical
imagination and his awareness of the past, of the continuity
existing in the measured pace of country life in a particular
place, and also all the 'joyous venture' of earlier periods. Puck
is credible enough, for Kipling himself is indignantly aware of
the modern debasement of fairies and recalls the earlier potent
reality for country people of goblins, leprechauns, giants, and
other People of the Hills. But he is only a device so that children
may walk back into the past and enter intimately into the lives
of Englishmen at earlier periods. A Sussex mason, for instance,
born in the late fifteenth century, when Henry VII was building
up a navy, recalls an exciting incident of attempted gun-running
by a Brightling foundry master, intended to aid a Scottish
nobleman-pirate. I discuss this side of Kipling's work for
children more fully in the chapter on 'Projects', for apart from its

intrinsic value as story these self-contained episodes have the added value for junior school children of associating fact with experience, and thus help teachers bring history to life. It is the kind of book that needs to be read aloud for the average child left alone with it would dismiss it as old-fashioned and difficult. The speech of past characters is sometimes rather phonily archaic, in a way that the nineteenth century admired, but a good teacher can easily make the necessary alterations.

Dickens always saw life as children do, vividly, in black and white, fairy story or nightmare. There are good fairies like Mr. Pickwick or the Cheeryble brothers; and far more potent ogres like Fagin and Quilp. Like children Dickens had an unerring eye when creating people for what makes everyone unique, no one ordinary. Usually when he conceives a character in a sup-posedly more mature way, with some conscious attempt at ex-planation, we get cardboard figures like Mr. Brownlow or Agnes Wickfield. Fagin, Scrooge, Uriah Heep are beings of a different kind. Dickens never explains them. They are, and their power of being has been sufficient to penetrate the popular imagination, for they still have some existence for people who have never read Dickens.

The child in all of us enters Dickens's world in an especially secret way for in almost all his books there is a lost child at the heart. One thinks of David, Pip, Little Nell, Oliver, Tiny Tim, Paul Dombey. Persistently through the child he seems to re-express his own deep sense of abandonment, when he was sent at twelve to work in the blacking factory, as he describes David Copperfield being sent. But David was an orphan. It was Dickens's parents who did this to him. He was taken away only because his father quarrelled with the manager. Of his mother he wrote years later: 'I never afterwards forgot, I never shall forget, I never can forget, that my mother was warm for my be-ing sent back.'

This means that there is much in Dickens which, brought alive by good reading, or enacted on television, will hold and move children strongly. He is also a superb entertainer, taking the same kind of creative relish in life and people as Chaucer. Take the scene, for instance, on the way to Yarmouth where dinner has been ordered in advance for David Copperfield and the waiter, 'a twinkling-eyed, pimple-faced man, with his hair standing upright all over his head', immediately marks down the child as fair game. First he embarrasses him by staring while he eats, then having poured out his glass of ale, he drinks

it down for him to save David from the fate of a certain Mr.
Topsawyer, who took a glass the day before and fell dead as a
result. Far from seeming the worse, as David notes he seemed
the fresher for it.

'What have we got here?' he said, putting a fork into my dish.
'Not chops?'

'Chops,' I said.

'Lord bless my soul!' exclaimed. 'I didn't know they were chops.
Why, a chop's the very thing to take off the bad effects of that beer.
Ain't it lucky?'

So he took a chop by the bone in one hand, and a potato in the
other, and ate away with a very good appetite, to my extreme satisfaction. He afterwards took another chop, and another potato;
and after that another chop and another potato. When he had done,
he brought me a pudding, and having set it before me, seemed to
ruminate, and to become absent in his mind for some moments.

'How's the pie?' he said, rousing himself.

'It's a pudding,' I made answer.

'Pudding!' he exclaimed. 'Why, bless me, so it is! What!' looking
at it nearer. 'You don't mean to say it's a batter-pudding!'

'Yes, it is indeed.'

'Why, a batter-pudding,' he said, taking up a tablespoon, 'is my
favourite pudding! Ain't that lucky? Come on, littl'un, and let's see
who'll get most.'

The waiter certainly got most. He entreated me more than once
to come in and win, but what with his tablespoon to my teaspoon,
his despatch to my despatch, and his appetite to my appetite I was
left far behind at the first mouthful, and had no chance with him. I
never saw anyone enjoy a pudding so much, I think: and he laughed,
when it was all gone, as if his enjoyment of it lasted still.

Dickens's canvases are far too wide and crowded, his designs
too adult, for anyone to advocate reading him extensively to
ten and eleven year olds. On the other hand, children have no
prejudices and a good teacher who loves him can give them
vivid and immediate pleasure at an impressionable age by
creative selection. Sequences such as the boyhood of David
Copperfield, Little Nell with Mrs. Jarley, Oliver with Fagin,
Squeers expounding his project system of education, can live
vividly for children; or a gallery of people in Dickens, for
instance, following an earlier gallery in Chaucer. The value in
addition to the immediate pleasure would be in giving them

like Oliver an appetite for more, and will lead some when older
to read for themselves because they want to. Many children of
junior age do actually read Dickens quite extensively already.

One book of Dickens works wonderfully as a whole with third
or fourth year juniors and dramatises wonderfully also. I mean,
of course, *Christmas Carol*, which has been brought out in several
attractive children's editions. As in other children's fantasies,
we are taken on a journey into past, present and future. Scrooge
must be made to *see*, to use his imagination, so that he *feels*
what a shrivelled ugliness he has so far made of his life and, by
looking into the future, what power he possesses to blight or
make fertile the lives of others. But first we are made to see the
actual Scrooge as he is, which never fails to grip a class, especially if the description is read by a good reader, with Christmas
only a few weeks away and afternoon fog possibly deepening
outside:

Oh! But he was a tight-fisted hand at the grindstone, Scrooge! a
squeezing, wrenching, grasping, scraping, clutching, covetous old
sinner! Hard and sharp as flint, from which no steel had ever struck
out generous fire; secret and self-contained as an oyster. The cold
within him froze his old features, nipped his pointed nose, shrivelled
his cheek, stiffened his gait; made his eyes red, his thin lips blue; and
spoke out shrewdly in his grating voice.

One could cut, of course, but there is no need. This will have
meant something to everyone. Everyone will have grasped the
main point although any teacher obtuse enough to start
questioning about the meaning of individual words deserves all
the frustration he will get. The story, anyway, begins immediately.

Once upon a time – of all the good days in the year, on Christmas
Eve – old Scrooge sat busy in his counting-house. It was cold, bleak,
biting weather; foggy withal: and he could hear the people in the
court outside, go wheezing up and down, beating their hands upon
their breasts, and stamping their feet upon the pavement stones to
warm them. The city clocks had only just gone three, but it was
quite dark already – it had not been light all day – and candles were
flaring in the windows of neighbouring offices, like ruddy smears
upon the palpable brown air.

Dickens's more elaborate descriptions, cut, certainly, but not
as some workmanlike abridged versions do the powerfully poetic

ones. The bitter irony of some of his social comment has to go but the essential drama is *enacted*, not described, and a teacher here has a wonderful opportunity to bring out character and significance, by tone of voice and contrast. Most terrifying and popular of all is Marley's ghost, clanking, first, deep in the cellar of the lonely, empty house; then

'much louder, on the floors below; then, coming up the stairs; then, coming straight towards his door. "It's humbug still!" said Scrooge. "I won't believe it." His colour changed though, when, without a pause, it came on through the heavy door, and passed into the room before his eyes.

. . . "How now!" said Scrooge, caustic and cold as ever. "What do you want with me?"

"Much!" — Marley's voice, no doubt about it.

"Who are you?"

"Ask me who I *was*." '

Throughout, the appeal to children's emotions is strong and on Tiny Tim's behalf almost too painfully so but there is release into a splendid boisterousness when Scrooge does reform. For like children Dickens is an optimist at heart. This is the kind of story that leaves children longing to do something about it and it never fails when they act it out, or some scenes from it.

Moral fables like this appeal strongly to children, most of whom are idealists, and are especially suitable to read aloud for the talk in class afterwards deepens a child's understanding of issues that matter in ordinary life. They are as valuable to read to seven and eight as nine and ten year olds, although one's choice will naturally be different. An eight-year-old boy told me recently that they were reading *Animal Farm* at school and it was 'jolly good', which does not mean that George Orwell is to be recommended for the junior school, but that an interesting fable, simply and vividly told, appeals immediately at all levels. For children one must find fables whose implications are also simple, relevant and able to be talked about. Ruskin's *King of the Golden River*, for instance, uses the machinery of fairy story immediately pleasurable to seven year olds to make them feel a moral that still matters.

Instead of Cinderella and the Ugly Sisters we have an attractive generous boy called Gluck, ill-treated by two mean and ugly brothers, Hans and Schwartz, who have 'over-hanging eyebrows and dull eyes, which were always half-shut, so that you couldn't see into *them*, and always fancied they saw very

far into *you*'. They farm a valley near the Golden River miraculously favoured by nature but are bad farmers, exploiting the
soil and man, and killing everything that does not pay for itself
in some way. Needless to say when other valleys are without
corn, they overcharge for their abundance. In the testing that
follows, the ugly brothers are destroyed by their greed while
Gluck's generosity wins riches, not the gold that seemed to be
offered but natural fertility, for the Golden River changes its
course and brings life back into the valley. This tale is quite
short, is beautifully written and beautifully balanced in its
action. But it lacks the creative power of Dickens or of Kipling.
For Ruskin is never, as they are, thinking, feeling, seeing as a
child while he writes. He remains a creative teacher finding
liberation while on holiday from his real work. His vision,
nevertheless, is simple and compelling.

Many teachers of seven and eight year olds, while recognising
the value of a story with an underlying simple moral, much
prefer one set in the real world and about real children. Paul
Gallico's *The Small Miracle* and Meindert DeJong's *Wheel on the
School* are such fables, evoking what at first may seem opposed
kinds of wonder and appealing to what are too easily accepted
as opposed kinds of imagination. *The Small Miracle* is concerned
with the power of a child's faith and as most people probably
know is about a ragged war orphan from Assisi, whose donkey,
Violetta, is not only his means of livelihood but a substitute for
home and parents, a creature to love and shelter with at night.
This is not sentimental if one remembers seeing small children
settle down to sleep in gutters and shop doorways in Italian
cities after the war. When Violetta falls sick, the boy is convinced
that St. Francis will cure her but is refused permission by clerical
officialdom to take her into the crypt. His refusal to take no for
an answer is not because of divinely implanted faith, but because
a G.I. who was a hero figure for him during the war told him
never to do this. He sets off for Rome, miraculously, it would
seem, obtains an audience of the Pope and is granted his wish.
The miracle is in the effect of his innocent expectation on the
imaginations and hearts of the officials he encounters. Their
own faith is stirred and renewed. Back in Assisi, when the old
entrance is unbricked to make way for Violetta, a small leaden
box is discovered, thought to contain the lost legacy of St.
Francis. They find only a piece of cord, a sprig of wheat, a
primrose and a bird's feather; but the saint's values are felt
afresh as a result of the find.

. *The Wheel on the School* is concerned rather with the power of childish endeavour and the energy it liberates. Meindert De Jong, an American writer of Dutch origin, grew up in a small village in Friesland until his family emigrated in 1918, and he draws much on his childhood experience. The story describes a primary school project in action, a project of an Outward Bound nature, demanding imagination as well as initiative. The children of Shora want storks to nest in their village as they do in many villages in Holland, for they are thought to bring good luck and anyway are fascinating birds to see at close quarters. Their schoolmaster makes them discover, first, why they don't come – because the roofs of the houses are too steep and also they have no wheels on them for the storks to nest in. Then he tells the children that by using their imaginations they may be able to alter this. As he puts it, 'sometimes when we wonder, we can make things begin to happen'. This leads to the children going off either alone or in pairs in search of an unwanted wheel and their separate adventures form the story.

This kind of form, of separate episodes linked by an interesting central idea, is particularly suited to reading aloud to children. Another book like this, although not a fable, is Elizabeth Enright's *The Saturdays*, which appeals strongly to first- and second-year juniors. This is the best of a series about a New York family of four children, who have no mother and a preoccupied father. Bored with their Saturdays, when they can never afford to do anything interesting with their small amount of pocket money, they form the Independent Saturday Afternoon Adventure Club, by the rules of which each of them gives up their pocket money so that one each week may have it all. The only condition is that it must not be spent on sweets or the cinema but on something unusual that they have been longing to do. Their four adventures form the main body of the story and take one out into the city, into an art gallery, to a matinée at the Metropolitan Opera, to a performance at the circus, to a down-town beauty parlour. For once, and this is rare in children's books, one sees the life of a great modern city not as background for a chase of some kind but as the source of interest and discovery in its own right. So although the characterisation and picture of the family is glossy and romanticised, what happens is illuminating and interesting, and can lead to talk and writing about individual experience.

When discussing traditional literature, I suggested a fundamental division between the heroic and outward looking, and that which charts some kind of inner journey. The latter was never introspective in an individual romantic sense and therefore is quite often enjoyed by children. Some important modern writers have chosen this approach in their work for children so that I think one can now find my original division occurring within fantasy itself. There is heroic public fantasy, drawing strongly on traditional mythologies but fresh in its creativeness and full of action. Children very much enjoy having this read to them. Other fantasy is private and individual, often having a rather introspective central character, and is more suited to private reading. J. R. Tolkien and C. S. Lewis seem to me very much in the heroic tradition, Philippa Pearce and Linda Boston to be more private writers, while Mary Norton has some qualities of both kinds.

Tolkien's books are steeped in Norse mythology, which is a vivid reality to him. Children love the precise topography of *The Hobbit* and feel at home with the ancient idea of rescuing a great treasure guarded by a fearsome firedragon in the bowels of the earth. The hero, while not a child, is nevertheless small, reluctant and appealing, and tends to be put upon. He only goes on the heroic quest in the first place because he is a burglar by trade and is thought indispensable. His favourite dream is of eggs and bacon. Yet he has some poetry in his soul and is drawn by the mystery of the journey. He shows himself capable of strategy on more than one occasion and, in the end, of a certain heroism, when he emerges small and vulnerable from the long tunnel under the mountain into the vast hall of the ancient dwarfs, where Smaug the Dragon lies, emitting smoke and a mysterious thrumming. Bilbo steals a great two-handled gold cup from the vast treasure. Smaug stirs a wing, opens a claw, the rumble of his snoring changes its note. Then Bilbo flees back up the long tunnel, his heart beating and a more fevered shaking in his legs than on the going down but still clutching the cup, his chief thought: 'I've done it! This will show them. "More like a grocer than a burglar" indeed! Well, we'll hear no more of that.'

This calls for an audience, not silent readers, to get the full flavour of its burlesque comic element. There is even more gusto and burlesque in C. S. Lewis's *Chronicles of Narnia*, where giants storm and jeer at each other in long meaningless words of about twenty syllables, foam, jibber and jump with rage, and lam each other with great stone hammers that bounce off their hard skulls and hurt their fingers. Yet children never question, for the space of the story, the seriousness of the Lion, Aslan, the God of Lewis's universe. This is Christian allegory, not Scandinavian, although Lewis drew on both traditions. He had a passion for the inventive, boisterous, mock-heroic Italian writer, Ariosto, and for Tasso, who was more serious in his blending of realism and fantasy; and once said that his ideal of happiness was always to be convalescent from some minor illness, sitting in a window overlooking the sea, reading their poems. One feels that writing the *Chronicles of Narnia* offered him something of this freedom and satisfaction.

In *The Silver Chair*, the second of the series, the children are very extrovert and ordinary yet are genuinely involved in the task set them and almost seduced by the Witch of the Underworld into accepting that there is no real world to go back to. The Underworld is another kind of Wasteland, sterile, windless, with no birds or sound of water, only sad cold creatures with smooth pumpkin faces and long soft noses like trunks. This world is finally challenged by the assertion that what the imagination conceives as real has its own reality. As one of the characters puts it: 'Suppose we *have* only dreamed, or made up, all those things – trees and grass and sun and moon and stars and Aslan himself. Suppose we have. Then all I can say is that, in that case, the made-up things seem a good deal more important than the real ones. . . . We're just babies making up a game if you're right. But four babies playing a game can make a play-world which licks your real world hollow.' This declamation of faith is enough to shrivel the witch back into her true serpent state and all is well. Children are gripped by the incidental excitements but also by the underlying sense of significance. The journey has a purpose and they are left with a sense of achievement.

Mary Norton's *The Borrowers*, and others in the series, seem at first to be doing much the same thing as Tolkien and C. S. Lewis, only in miniature: taking children on an heroic journey. Yet there is more irony in her comments on human beings than in either of the other two and her vision is altogether more individual and private. She is not reshaping traditional material for a new journey, with some kind of implicit moral satisfaction for children; but rather exploring, always ingeniously, often quite movingly, a fanciful private idea. There seems to me something slightly pathetic about the Borrowers, both in their having to exist on the scraps of human beings and, more centrally, in their being created out of the scraps of past mythologies. They never reflect human potentiality but can only be put on show in a miniature model village for humans to gape at. The author always respects her small creatures and her stories have inner consistency but one could not talk to children about what one had been reading without a kind of cheating, which is always bad, and I would therefore prefer to leave these books for private reading.

The other two women fantasists, Philippa Pearce and Linda Boston, are imaginative rather than fanciful. *Tom's Midnight Garden* and *The Children of Green Knowe* I would call poetic rather than private fantasy. If the allegories of Tolkien and C. S. Lewis are extended similes about extroverts setting off like Swallows and Amazons on a quest with a difference, the former are concerned with rather isolated introvert children who have some kind of visionary experience. This kind of fantasy, for adults or children, is more like metaphor than simile, in that it fuses diverse feelings, thoughts and sense perceptions into a new whole. Momentarily, at least, we share the vision.

The central characters in both books are very self-contained thoughtful small boys, spirited as well as imaginative. Both are believable but they are not very usual. Both move out of time back into the past and enter into the lives of the people who had once lived in the house where they are. Tom, particularly, in *Tom's Midnight Garden*, lives more intensely in his dream than in his waking life and in the end hates having to leave it for real life. Many robust, ordinary, modern boys will find it impossible to accept that he spends the daytime of his holiday not wanting to go out, not wanting *to do* anything his aunt suggests, longing only for everyone to go to sleep, so that midnight may come and the magic out-of-time existence can begin. Since as adults we know that this could not happen, that the journey into the past is essentially *imaginary* as well as imaginative, we are in difficulties if questioned on this point. And we are bound to be. Tom, too, questions himself and searches for rational conviction, which he finds when he comes upon the strange old woman who owns the house, and through whose memories of happiness the past lives. The appeal of both these books is very individual and subjective, and therefore teachers may prefer not to read them aloud but to see that they are in the library and that children are introduced to them. They are rather like the secret haunts of children, very important, but not always to be shared; and never to be desecrated, which casual or unfeeling comment might cause.

Significantly, both Philippa Pearce and Linda Boston have moved away from fantasy and recently found plots that allow their imaginative insight full play while at the same time deepening a child's sense of reality.

This is particularly so of Philippa Pearce, whose imagination is deeply rooted in the Cambridgeshire countryside. *A Dog So Small*, for instance, is a wonderful book to read aloud to younger juniors. They feel instantly and intensely for the small boy, Ben, who can't have a dog in London, although he longs for one. He is promised a puppy for his birthday by his grandfather but is sent instead a woolwork picture of a very small dog, brought home from sea long ago by an uncle since drowned. The desperate disappointment of this makes him withdraw into his imagination, create a dog there and live with it – and that is the only element of fantasy in the story, the kind of reality we are asked to allow this other life of Ben's and the dog in it. The plot, though, works credibly and movingly on the side of life, for his withdrawal leads to his daydreaming while crossing the road and the subsequent accident, happily not too serious, makes his parents see that he gets his dog. Plot summary is quite insufficient to convey Philippa Pearce's quality *as a writer*, her ability to create in words not only situations and characters, but the atmosphere of a place and above all the tactile quality of living things. When Ben first visits his grandparents he goes out to the sty where Tilly, his grandfather's dog, has her puppies and watches them sleeping, crowded together, while Tilly watches. 'Grandpa plunged his fingers into heaps of puppies and brought one out at random. He dropped it into Ben's cupped hands. Ben felt perfect happiness. He shifted the puppy into one hand – which it slightly overflowed – in order to be able to stroke it with the back of the forefinger of his other hand. Then he put it down and gently picked up another.' A little later on he is left alone with Tilly, who is now feeding her puppies. 'He liked being in the sty with the rain sounding on the iron roof just above his head, and the dim warm light from the lamp, and the smell of straw and puppies. He liked being alone with Tilly and her feeding puppies. Sometimes he could be of help. He brought home a puppy that had strayed or been pushed beyond Tilly's tail and was whimpering for lost food. He righted another puppy that – still sucking – had somehow got turned upside down. He unburied another – always sucking – that had been quite trampled under and out of sight by the others.' The natural active peacefulness of this has its effect on Ben, as it has on children listening to the story; many are made aware of a different tempo and to some extent of different values from those that seem important in their own homes.

The Minnow on the Say, also by Philippa Pearce, is not fantasy at all, but an unusually good story about a treasure hunt, that at the same time conveys the slow sureness of East Anglian life. Much of the description and action suggest what one finds in many successful children's stories, the lazy flow of a long summer holiday with afternoons made for dawdling. The plot itself, though, has not the same living quality as in *A Dog So Small*. It does not stir the author's imagination in the same way as the natural detail does. Linda Boston, while a slightly more pretentious writer than Philippa Pearce, also seems to me interesting and worth exploration. Her most recent book, *A Stranger at Green Knowe*, has both an imaginative plot and the vivid expression of it through natural detail. It is too difficult for the average nine year old to enjoy on his own but read aloud and talked about in class it makes an immediate appeal.

The first part describes a baby gorilla growing up in the 'immense privacy of the forest with his family'. The jungle assails our senses through those of the baby gorilla, with his bright eyes, gentle funny face and long thin puppy hair over the rest of his body. We see his father, the Old Man, 'superbly dressed in dense fur', his eyes 'deep set and far-seeing, but neither sly nor cruel'. Humans enter the animals' world and destroy this jungle life, putting the Old Man in one cage and the baby gorilla in another. He shakes the bars, strains at the door, bites the hard cold steel in despair, until he overturns the cage and brings a red-faced, hairy, human animal upon the scene to right it and comment upon the creature's strength.

Part Two introduces Ping, a human child, who also knew life in the jungle in Burma with a home and father until guerrilla fighting destroyed both. Ping is being taken round the Zoo with a school party when he first sees Hanno, now a full grown gorilla, but unreconciled to his captivity. Ping feels a sad horror as he watches this superb creature padding round and round his cage.

The development is credible as well as exciting. Ping is able to give Hanno three 'real' days outside a cage in the jungle-like garden of Green Knowe, before he is discovered and Hanno has to be shot. The boy is convinced that the gorilla preferred death to continued captivity.

H

Both these books strike me as fresh and individual in their language, true in feeling and direction of sympathy and, what is most rare, significant in action. What happens matters not only as something thrilling and delightful in the story but truly matters in the life of the central child character.

This is the kind of action that makes books like *Heidi* and Frances Hodgson Burnett's *Secret Garden* still immensely valuable for eight and nine year olds, although one would need to know the class before being sure that it was better to read them aloud than simply recommend them for private reading. *Heidi* absorbs young children from the moment they meet the heroine being taken up the mountain to her grandfather by an unsympathetic cousin. The child's vitality and honesty are invigorating and the fact that everything is new to her makes children aware of it with her. This happens later in the story also, when she has to go to Frankfurt. One's only criticism is that the author quite often makes Heidi bring out a Christian moral, not in itself sickly or sentimental, but with a faith well beyond her years. But a good teacher can cut or adapt this. What is valuable about the story is that it touches children's lives now at many points but with such differences in time and place that they are ready to talk about what is happening very openly. This applies particularly to Hans' jealousy. The way, too, that Heidi teaches him to read by brushing aside his and everyone else's estimate of his low ability is encouraging and enlightening.

The Secret Garden is a very Victorian tale, which makes some teachers hesitate to read it, especially to modern boys. This is to miss its robustness and the story's central criticism of everything mawkish, self-centred and self-pitying. The children in the story are changed and grow up through the action; while the self-absorbed Mr. Craven turns his face towards life again, like Scrooge but without the intervention of a ghost. Neither Mary, the heroine, nor her sickly, spoiled cousin, Colin, is held up to us for pity. Both are created in the round and understood. Both are capable of growth. One notices at once a remarkable astringency of tone. 'When Mary Lennox was sent to Misselthwaite Manor to live with her uncle, everybody said she was the most disagreeable-looking child ever seen. It was true, too. She had a little thin face, and a little thin body, thin light hair and a sour expression. Her hair was yellow, and her face was yellow because she had been born in India and had always been ill in one way or another.' Her father is always busy and ill himself, her mother, beautiful, selfish and pleasure-loving, wants to forget that she has a daughter. By the time Mary is six, she is 'as tyrannical and selfish a little pig as ever lived'. At nine, cholera carries off both parents and so she comes to Yorkshire.

Gradually her values are shaken and changed, first by Martha, the maid, and then by Martha's brother, Dickon, a convincing twelve-year-old Yorkshire boy, with a snub nose, large mouth and patched clothes. He knows all about birds' nests, otters, badgers; and brings seeds and bulbs and tools into the mysterious locked garden that she has discovered in her wandering about the grounds. Together they turn it into a living garden and in reporting on their progress to her sickly cousin, and generally ignoring or mastering his tantrums, she has the kind of effect on him that Martha and Dickon have had on her. Much in the action, and particularly the descriptions of the violent quarrels between Mary and Colin, is close to most children's experience but the difference in circumstance makes it natural and easy to talk about the children's behaviour. The effect of the book is both gripping and liberating. Above all it is full of hope.

For children at the top of the junior school, really good adventure stories give something of this sense of liberation and growth, and I talk about some of these in the chapter on 'Projects', for I think they are of most value read aloud in conjunction with other work. The same applies to good historical novels for children, which are essentially adventure stories that happen to be set far away in time, as most modern ones are in place. I discuss particular authors in the later chapter. More introspective books about growing up, like Richard Jefferies's *The Story of a Boy*, or ones without much action, like Alison Uttley's *The Country Child*, are best left to secondary level.

I should like to end this survey with a short comment on anthologies of story, which I suspect will become increasingly used in the next few years.

I am not thinking of books of short stories or tales for children, who in any case usually prefer a full-length book or linked incidents concerning the same characters, but books like the pioneer volumes of James Britton, *The Oxford Books of Stories for Juniors*, designed to help teachers make a more varied and interesting use of story in class and to realise how much this experience relates to writing and talking. In the *Oxford* series, the excerpts are long enough to be absorbing to a child and to encourage him to explore further both in reading and more practical ways. There are also teachers' books with creative suggestions for handling the excerpts. I hope that this series flourishes, as it deserves to, but one fears inferior imitations and their temptation to teachers anxious to save time. Publishers happily produce whatever looks like being profitable and the market is enormous. I would prefer books of stories to be used than that story should be entirely neglected, as it is in many top junior classes, but if we are to have books of excerpts I hope that teachers will not depend on them too much, but develop more individual choice. There is a danger also that excerpts may become automatically linked in teachers' and children's minds with writing to follow, which some children will not enjoy so much. Writing is sometimes a valuable extension of the experience of story but story is not primarily to be *used* at all. It is to be lived in and enjoyed.

Enjoyment of a wide range of story in class is the best incentive to private reading, which helps a child's technical progress in the first years and is in itself an important part of his experience. I discuss ways in which school and class libraries can play a creative part here, in the later chapter on 'Books and Libraries' while many of the writers just discussed and others mentioned in the chapter on 'Projects' will be enjoyed as much in private reading as in class. Where private reading is concerned teachers need to be aware of general expectations and satisfactions, but also of the individual point of growth. Any story that gives a child some genuine satisfaction and in some way refreshes him will be 'good' for him at this point. But children can undoubtedly be led to enlarge their range and capacity for satisfaction, and to grow dissatisfied with some familiar repetitive favourites, by teachers who know what they are ready for and what to recommend. One must be constantly exploring oneself. The best children's stories are genuinely absorbing to read and, compared with the average adult novel or non-fiction work, easy and short. One feels delightfully free reading them, as if playing truant from the best motive, and often one senses the same kind of liberation of imagination in their writers. The more one can give children the chance to experience this, the quicker will they tire of the spurious 'activity' of Biggles or The Secret Seven. One should never attack the latter but give every opportunity for informal exchange of views as well as books. Children may seem to share many needs and satisfactions in their private reading, mostly in the form of vicarious experience: to be one of a group of some kind, to have adventure, as frequently in pleasant holiday form as in situations of danger or suspense, to excel in some glamorous sphere like ballet or sailing, riding or flying, to serve the community as nurse or doctor. But they are also highly individualist, clear sighted and honest in their reactions to what they read. In many ways they are less easily taken in than some adults. They don't like cheating and more important usually recognise it when they discuss books. No matter how fantastic the setting, they mostly want a kind of truth in their reading – what could happen in life, or what might happen, with eyes open here to all the marvellous potential of modern science and also prepared in many instances to accept all the marvel of past magic. Above all I think they want that something significant should happen. In their eyes, *Dr. Who* is super – up to a point. Its genuine blend of realism and fantasy is far better than past magic carpets. They love being transported into past and future. But after a time most of them grow disappointed with what they are actually shown.

It is appropriate to end this chapter with a reference to television, for the latter is as important as books today as a medium for fiction and for many adults and children more important. Many teachers and parents deplore this as having an adverse effect on reading but often fail to ask what kind of reading it replaces. There is no evidence from children's librarians that television makes them less eager to read. After seeing an exciting programme children often want to find out more from books. After watching a good dramatisation many want to read the book and it is mere literary snobbishness to complain that some children will then think of it as 'the book of the television serial'. But a more justified complaint could be that television so rarely takes its opportunities to move children by the imaginative reality of a good story. In children's programmes fact is very often treated more imaginatively than fiction. Programmes about animals, travel, life in other countries, various aspects of science, are usually of a high standard, suggesting that the men presenting them believe in what they are doing. Fiction programmers too often seem to think that fiction must be comic in the Billy Bunter tradition or tough as in *Ripcord Inc.* There have been notable exceptions of course, especially in the BBC Sunday serialisations, but these are often of books that junior children are not ready to read to themselves. What I should like would be time and money to be found for midweek serialising of books like Frederick Grice's *Bonnie Pit Laddie*, Eilis Dillon's *Island of Horses*, Paul Berna's *Hundred Million Francs* and Howard Spring's *Tumbledown Dick*. If teachers themselves were more consistent and united in their belief in the value of good children's fiction, then something like this might happen.

A child's private reading is not something that can or should be programmed, though it will be much affected by his experience in school. Nor can its effects be measured, though one can see its influence in varying ways, especially on his writing. What is important is that junior teachers should feel it as a valid part of a child's experience. For some children it will become part of their way of life. Good story books stir their minds and feelings in ways that are valid in relation to a wide range of human life. They help children grow up, prepare them imaginatively for their own adolescent and adult life. Much of the pleasure of reading at this stage lies in the underlying excitement of anticipation. This is not happening to oneself — yet. Some of it will surely, for one is on the threshold of so much. Our emphasis today is very much on helping children to be social beings, to fit in and contribute to their community. But if they are to have something to contribute, they must also be able to withdraw sometimes, not simply into daydreaming but into a receptive thoughtfulness. Good stories foster this part of a child's being, and with it that openness to ideas and impressions and feelings beyond the immediate which is what one means by living in the imagination.

4

MIME AND PLAYMAKING

THERE is an amusing scene in *Tom Sawyer* when Mark Twain describes Ben Rogers 'personating a steamboat'. He 'was eating an apple, and giving a long, melodious whoop, at intervals, followed by a deep-toned ding-dong, dong, ding-dong-dong. . . . As he drew near, he slackened speed, took to the middle of the street, leaned far over to starboard and rounded to ponderously and with laborious pomp and circumstance – for he was personating the *Big Missouri*, and considered himself to be drawing nine feet of water. He was boat and captain and engine-bells combined, so he had to imagine himself standing on his own hurricane-deck giving the orders and executing them:
"Stop her, sir! Ting-a-ling-ling!"
The headway ran almost out, and he drew up slowly towards the sidewalk. (His right hand meantime describing stately circles for it represents a forty-foot wheel.)'

This kind of 'personation' comes naturally to children of junior school age. One sees them at play, showing the same combination of spontaneity and discipline as Ben, the same absorption and powers of observation. This essentially dramatic experience, extended and directed in a way their play rarely is, should be a natural part of their school life. It can certainly be a tremendously valuable one.

To consider for the moment mime only, it develops and concentrates a child's awareness of the outside world, as well as calling forth his power of feeling and expression from within. Children cannot mime any action in a play or impromptu dramatic situation – a priest carrying an urn to the altar, a woman made to drag coal in the mines, a smuggler rolling a wine keg up the beach – without transporting themselves into the situation and considering with some concentration what the action actually involves. This means discovering and taking hold of the relevant facts. An urn or a keg or a truck of coal cannot remain words, but must become things of shape and substance. Equally, a child cannot be the priest or the woman or the smuggler without some consciousness, translated in terms of his own experience, of the emotion belonging to the occasion: the fervour of the priest, the woman's deep fatigue, the alert concentration of the smuggler. With the right kind of talk and imaginative preparation beforehand children will produce dialogue naturally enough, and usually suitable in tone and mood. Once they taste the pleasure of making a play, they will want to create others from a wide variety of material which forms their experience in school: from stories, ballads, narrative poems, parables, the human substance of whatever history they are learning. And the impact of this experience is often sharpened by the anticipation of creating from it.

This kind of creative drama will not be a series of rehearsals for performance, although informal presentation to another class will sometimes result. Usually one will not want to use a stage but only the classroom for the first very personal evolving stages, then possibly the working area of the hall and some-times in the summer, if appropriate, somewhere outside. If one has movable blocks to give some change of level, so much the better. There will be no written script save possibly occasionally as a record. It will never be what the work was aimed at.

The value of this lies in the value of the experience for the players, which controlled and directed by an imaginative teacher can be considerable. Socially, it makes children co-operate and learn the need for self-discipline. It also helps them to express themselves through words and through their bodies in a way that increases their self-confidence enormously. Shy children especially, for whom direct participation in other forms or oral work is nightmare, are protected yet helped to find themselves in playing a part. In addition to its social value, dramatic work of this kind makes children think, and think creatively. At the same time it makes more concrete and real to them the substance of the play. The factual information of social history, for instance, makes a far deeper impression when it is lived through in their own drama, than when only read about and discussed with their teacher; although, of course, they cannot begin to make it into a meaningful play without this discussion.

Playmaking with children, one is above all aware how strongly their feelings are involved, with boys particularly, their aggres-sive ones. Sometimes one senses a boy, tense and quite with-drawn, awaiting his moment to grapple with the Minotaur or some other deadly marauder. Instead of the frustrations of real life, such children experience satisfaction in slaying the foe.

Their feelings find controlled release and this is important as art and therapy. More important than individual release is the rare sense this work sometimes affords to children of sharing emotionally in something significant.

In spite of this many teachers in junior schools are suspicious of dramatic work and not prepared to take it seriously. This is partly the puritan in them that believes no good can come of pleasure. More often it is the conscientious educator, that makes them try it out of a sense of duty and leaves them relieved when, because they do not believe in it, it does not go well. Then they have evidence of inferior work not rising above the level of a second-rate charade to support their argument that drama teaches nothing, wastes time and is disruptive of discipline. At bottom they may well be afraid, as many are with project work, of the overspill beyond the boundaries of lesson periods, and of the much greater demands drama makes in terms of their time and personal commitment than routine subject work.

As with children's writing, it is a mistake to press for quick results or to expect sudden and striking achievement. One must give time for natural growth. Students particularly, with a short period of teaching practice, perhaps finding themselves in a school where drama plays little or no part, need both conviction and patience, and to be levelheaded in their expectations. Best is a school where the headteacher and a majority of the staff consider mime and creative dramatic work an integral part of school routine, special enough not to be over-indulged in, but not so special that its rarity makes the children behave too excitedly. Then there is likely to be both relaxation and concentration. The children will take for granted that they sometimes go to the hall, and also on other occasions be adept and reasonably quiet at rearranging the classroom for acting. In old schools, with overcrowded classes, and awkward furniture, this is sometimes impossible although a combination of ingenuity and determination will often achieve the impossible.

One can use the word *Mime*, but there is no need to with children. I have seen students begin by asking a class if they know what it is. Acting without words, someone says, and for the rest of the lesson this abstraction hovers in many children's minds, preventing their complete absorption in whatever particular action they are being asked to 'personate'. Far better to get them to imagine themselves in a particular situation within their experience and likely to matter to them, and then ask them to do something within that situation. It is best to make this something they feel strongly about, either for or against. To make the action an indifferent one invites casualness and carelessness. Children accept quite naturally that they are not to say anything but to concentrate on the action. This could be opening a parcel on one's birthday, laying the table for a party, eating an ice-cream on a hot day; or for an action they will dislike, taking a dose of medicine, combing tangly hair, picking blackberries surrounded by prickles.

From the beginning it is valuable to develop children's awareness of different sense impressions, particularly of touch. They can imagine that they are walking first barefoot on pebbles, then on firm cool sand, then on a very hot day on dry sand where the sea never comes. They can be walking over rocks or daring to paddle on a particularly cold blustery day or walking along the cliffs against a strong wind. Girls can imagine they are chopping vegetables and cut themselves, so can boys as they are sawing wood. They can suddenly find themselves in a dark room or be using their eyes more than usually sharply – behind the barrier, for instance, waiting for their mother's train. Perhaps at first they cannot see her, think she has missed the train and then, suddenly, there she is.

It is important to involve everyone from the start of the lesson, either with all miming or with half, while the others watch. In very cramped conditions only eight or ten may be able to mime but the others should be concentrating on something specific in the action and know that their comment will be invited afterwards. Comment must always be encouraging, always in the spirit of 'How can we make this better?', not 'What is wrong with it?' Usually the brief talk beforehand is more important than the comment afterwards for it is through this that the action and the accompanying feeling take shape in children's minds, and make it possible for the mime to truly come from them. For instance, if they are going to be absorbed in imagining themselves in a dark room, they will need to think about why they are there, what size it is, how cluttered with furniture, and what kind of furniture, whether they need to be quiet or not, whether they are looking for anything or not. Any teachers who have seen Peter Schaefer's play, *Black Comedy*, will realise the exaggerated care that is needed. Children are stimulated, also, by the right kind of property, especially if one is concerned with the feel of something. The evocative power of objects is always greater for children than words.

The next stage is to involve them in a change of emotion.

This more complex response can quite naturally follow a simpler
original one. They are undoing a birthday present, for instance,
and instead of its being what they are longing for and expecting,
it is something they have already. They arrive home with some
exciting news to find that there is no one there to tell it to. They
have cut their hand and have to put iodine on it but then a
soothing ointment and bandage. One can also devise situations
involving a group of children in a similar change, caused always
by something that happens. For instance, they are getting ready
for a day by the sea, collecting bathing things, helping mother
cut sandwiches and fill the Thermos flasks when suddenly the
phone rings, and the trip is cancelled, for the time being anyway;
or some variation on this situation in reverse, with a sudden
invitation and hurried preparations. All the time in this work
one wants children to be actively imagining the situation, thinking and feeling within it and then going on to give spontaneous
and convincing development. One wants them to realise how
one's movement is affected by one's predominant feelings and
how character comes in when it is a question of behaviour in
face of disappointment.

Following mimes such as these, in which a child has explored
his sense reactions and his emotional ones, he will be ready to
be somebody else. At first it is best to be conventional and ask
for people known well from fairy stories: a princess getting
ready for the ball, a king receiving foreign ambassadors, a
wicked stepmother arriving uninvited at the feast. From a quite
early stage more than one child may be involved and after
practice with their own group, they enjoy watching others. The
important thing is that they should try out walking, standing, sitting as other people. This is only an extension of the
spontaneous trying on of a character that many children start
doing as one talks about him. Many children find it harder to
take on characters from nearer home, to be their mother coming
in from shopping, their elder sisters getting ready to go out or
father gardening. Or perhaps it is that they find it tempting to
play this near situation in an exaggerated way, from the outside,
and to some extent for laughs. Children can only create people
as they understand them and understanding of people matures
slowly. One needs talk and the placing of these people in
credible and interesting situations. They may need time for
first-hand observation where previously they have taken someone for granted. We are not asking children to act like someone
else but for the moment to *be* someone else, to think and feel

like him, again, of course, within the limits of their own experience and understanding. Their personal writing can often link in a helpful way with drama, in that it may be asking for some similarly observant understanding of people in the world around them.

One needs always to be vividly aware oneself of the children's environment, of the kind of people in it, its atmosphere and tempo. The seasons will affect the situations one devises, as will any special stimulus like fog or snow or storm, or important class outing. It helps focus difference of attitude and also physical movement if one gives a situation and then makes children imagine themselves very different people confronting it: in the fields on a hot day, for instance, as a lazy father, a butterfly collector, or an energetic child; being father or oneself cleaning the car; mother, father, or oneself at the launderette. One can ask different people to look at themselves in a mirror: a pretty elder sister, a schoolboy, the ugly sisters, a vain king. Similarly one can ask them to come in and sit down as a tired old man, a bossy woman, or a teenager.

Obviously how one develops this work, and how long one gives to the various stages, depends on the age of a class when one starts with them and what if anything they have done so far. The important thing is for a teacher to have a sense of direction which is conveyed to the children, and regularity, so that the work is looked forward to as a developing kind of fun. Any kind of Stop-Go policy is disastrous. There is much scope for individuality in devising and timing the stages, and in relating mime and other dramatic exercises to the beginnings of playmaking, especially exercises concerned with stimulating dialogue. But if one really cares about this kind of work, one will want some mime all the time. It is often essential as background preparation for all kinds of group work: being red coats marching in *The Highwayman*, smugglers hauling kegs ashore or up the cliff in Kipling's poem, children dancing after the Pied Piper, sailors confronting the storm in *Sir Patrick Spens*. Music will often be a vital part of this kind of miming. In any case, it is a tremendous spur to all mime and dramatic work to have related work in music and movement that sets children's imaginations free in a poetic and unconscious way. All kinds of life and growth have rhythms that they can explore. Children love expressing such forms of being or activity as corn growing, machines working, trains running. They love moving as animals, whether elephants or horses or cats or snakes.

Sometimes there can be a direct link between music and some kind of dramatic presentation. If children develop movements quite freely, for instance, to Saint-Saens's *Carnival of Animals*, they are peculiarly ready for and receptive to a poem like George MacBeth's *Noah's Voyage*, which I mentioned in the chapter on poetry. Here the poet works not through strong rhythm but the sharp appeal of language to the senses and the mind. He creates not only the animals but the natural life and forces that are part of the voyage: the oak and pine that have to be cut down to make the Ark, the thunder, rain and lightning that confront it on its way, and finally the 'salt-washed skin of the sand', the firmness of 'old hard land' and its green fur of soft grass, when it lands on Ararat. The intentness upon words and their closeness to things make us strongly aware of the inner being of whatever is presented as well as its outward appearance. The pine for the mast, for instance, first through the words of the narrator,

> Standing in place now,
> spun in a socket he sets like a
> maypole. An oiled bole of red wood,

then voicing his own being,

> *Screwed to the low deck, I*
> *rise to the cold stars. The sea waits,*
> *tossing a little. The black earth*
> *lingers to wave me a long farewell.*

Children of nine and ten respond to this and express it quite unself-consciously despite difficult words and absence of rhyme and they enjoy very much the expressive varied comic life of the animals: pig, for instance, glad to announce himself 'usefully fat', or rhinoceros coming aboard 'like a boulder'.

In this kind of work tape-recorders can help immensely in giving original sound effects but children are willing substitutes and gramophone records can supply the music, usually evocative 'programme' music, not concerned primarily with purely musical patterns, though the music of modern composers like Benjamin Britten or Richard Rodney Bennett, to whose rhythms junior school children are particularly responsive, are significant exceptions. Rhythm is always very important. Of other music, choice must be personal. For me it would include Beethoven's

Pastoral Symphony, Stravinsky's *Rites of Spring*, Wagner's Overture to *The Flying Dutchman*. Grieg's 'In the Hall of the Mountain King', from his *Peer Gynt Suite*, is wonderful for trolls and other grotesques, Bizet's *L'Arlésienne* for pure gaiety.

Once children have some experience of miming in character, and of the kinds of situation that cause a change of mood, they are creating drama. They will be ready and want to speak. And the words as well as the movements must come from them. However good in itself, and most of the available ones are not at all good, a script is an intrusion in this kind of work. It always inhibits children and, unless they are exceptionally fluent readers, demands an intellectual concentration that prevents their entering emotionally into the whole. I have seen children set to act with a text read out stage directions as well as their lines with no awareness that anything was wrong. It was as if they were telling a story to the class, not temporarily forgetting themselves and becoming the people in it. For children of this age this will only happen when they are freed of set words and can create their new person in their own speech.

However, sprung on children without the right kind of feeding of the imagination and sufficient conflict in the situation pressing for speech, a demand for words can misfire badly and destroy confidence. They must always have not only knowledge but some *feeling* of the character they are meant to be and also a clear idea of what the talk is to be about, what occasions it and what it is heading towards.

One can help by devising varied exercises to develop dialogue, beginning by expressing differences of attitude through simple greetings, and then with simple but interesting situations from which a few sentences would naturally come. One wants children to think a little about the ebb and flow of conversation in ordinary life. What prompts them to speak as they do? The actual situation, their thought in relation to what has just been said, their feelings towards the last speaker, probably all or some of these. Not that junior children will formulate this but they can be aware to some extent of the pattern and the give and take involved. In preparing individual or group scenes, one will get children to suggest the probable thoughts and feelings of the people in them, stressing what might be said but leaving the actual words to whoever plays the scene. Children soon gain confidence from this kind of stimulus and are ready to try dramatisation of a fuller kind. Then, provided that one plans the stages of the action with them in detail, and discusses the characters and how they would be likely to react to what is to happen, they will usually find words that are convincing, despite some incongruous idiom. One must guard, certainly, against ever letting playmaking become the occasion for showing off on the part of a few talkative children, but given the right relationship between class and teacher, the right choice of story to dramatise and the right timing in its presentation and early development, this won't happen.

Choice is all important and certain essentials need to be borne in mind. First, whatever form the material takes, there must be a simple strong action, with some conflict and development, and with no subplot. It should lead in a clear-cut way to a climax, after which there should be a satisfying rounding off. All the great traditional literature discussed earlier has strong action but it is not always simple and although the feeling may be quite well understood if the story is read to children, it may be too adult for them to portray themselves. They can dramatise Ulysses and the Cyclops, for instance, but not Ulysses and Calypso. On the whole it is better to choose an action set in the past than the present, for this calls for projection rather than the more secret identification which occurs with most private reading of modern stories, and which is difficult to convey unself-consciously to others. Stories with a modern setting tend to invite banality in dialogue, as all the stereotyped associations of comics and television flood in and prevent genuinely individual response. Also, modern stories rarely have the significant moral pattern of folk and fairy story.

From a more practical standpoint, the action must be manageable – that is, it must not have too many short incidents or impossible elements of magic that cannot be convincingly presented in a classroom. One can act *Sir Patrick Spens* or *The Wife of Usher's Well* but not *The Daemon Lover*. It should also be likely to produce clear-cut dialogue, without needing background conversation to establish atmosphere. In fact it is better on the whole if the action does not depend too much on what is said. If, as happens with some historical actions, well known words are associated with a character, it is often impossible for the intelligent child to disregard these. They stand out awkwardly, very much on their dignity, and impede the flow of his re-creation. This is only a problem with the very bright, who absorb and literally retain whatever they are told by way of preparation. So it is probably better not to give a good class too much, verbatim, from the sources but to recast as interestingly

as one can in one's own words. This would not apply to traditional
fairy stories, of course, or other well-known stories like *Alice in
Wonderland*, for there will be less discrepancy in these between
remembered dialogue and what children make up. One last
important need, the action should if possible have some creative
value, illuminate some aspect of experience and direct the
sympathies of the players in what one feels to be the right ways,
as well as genuinely gaining in effectiveness by being made into
a play.

As with mime in character the best starting point for dramatisation for younger children is probably the traditional story:
Sleeping Beauty, for instance, *Hansel and Gretel*, *Rumpelstiltskin*,
Snow White. The latter immediately shapes itself for playmaking.
'Presently in came the masters of the cottage, who were seven
little dwarfs that lived among the mountains and dug and
searched for gold. They lighted up their seven lamps, and saw
directly that all was not right. The first said, "Who has been
sitting on my stool?" The second, "Who has been eating from
my plate?"' and so on through the list. Three times the wicked
queen tries to entrap Snow White and the last seems successful,
with Snow White apparently dead and on her bier, when the
prince comes, dislodges the poisoned apple and she is restored
to life. Children enter in to this at once, especially in trying on
the characters of the dwarfs. The fascination they feel at the
power of wickedness, and their tension and sorrow, are resolved
in a creative way. The action has not been trivial or simply
amusing but literally one of life and death, which always
involves children.

Greek legends like those of Persephone, or Theseus and the
Minotaur, or Ulysses and the Cyclops, make marvellous short
plays, especially if this is part of other work on the Greeks, and
remain more vividly with children as a result. Other suggestions
for young children are fantasies like *The Sorcerer's Apprentice*, or
some of the incidents from Collodi's *Pinocchio*; folk tales like
The Wise Men of Gotham or Aesop's *Shepherd Boy* or Andersen's
The Emperor's New Clothes; ballads like *Robin Hood and the Bishop
of Hereford*. I have already suggested how well *Alice in Wonderland*
and *The Wind in the Willows* dramatise.

For older juniors, one can add to these much that is too
difficult in its original form for seven and eight year olds:
narrative poems like Kipling's *Smugglers*, Browning's *Pied Piper*,
Noyes's *Highwayman*, this last, stirring melodrama rather than
good poetry, which is why it works if dramatised. Chaucer's

Pardoner's Tale, of the three rioters who go off to slay Death, and are tricked by their greed into slaying each other, can be effective and stirring. His *Nun's Priest's Tale*, of the proud, complacent Cock and the fox who flatters him into showing off his fine voice and then carries him off, has the right dramatic qualities but to some extent lacks manageability, which is vital. For it is difficult to convey the carrying off convincingly while the climax, with the villagers giving chase armed with every imaginable farmyard weapon, needs sure control on the teacher's part and the right kind of involvement on the children's if it is to succeed.

Traditional ballads offer some wonderful material to teachers who are aware of the poetry in them and how it works: *Sir Patrick Spens*, for instance, and *The Wife of Usher's Well*, or the shorter humorous one, *Get Up and Bar the Door*, which has more development of character than is usual in ballads. The husband and wife in this, who quarrel over who shall lock up and vow not to say a word to each other until one of them gives in, are enduring types. Two passing strangers enter and insult both until the husband has had enough. 'Will ye kiss my wife before my een', he cries, 'And sca'd me with pudding broth?' But his chivalry is entirely wasted on his wife, who claims victory:

> Then up and started our goodwife,
> Gied three skips on the floor:
> Goodman, you've spoken the foremost word,
> Get up and bar the door.

Children recognise this situation quickly enough from their own experience or that of parents or other adults. People, especially married ones, still often make a stand upon some trivial issue and let stubbornness and pride keep them from going back on it. One can do nothing to alter a woman like the Goodwife. She continues to exasperate but at the same time arouses a certain admiring awe. All traditional ballads, especially the tragic ones, work powerfully through their words and rhythm so that they are often better mimed against the background of expressive reading than given speech. Timing is very important. To discover difficulties in the text, to summarise the plot and plan the action can kill the life of the ballad for children, who unconsciously absorb the experience and the emotional implications as they listen. With a good class alive to poetry of all kinds and always alert for the suggestion, 'Now, let's act it', mime can develop quite spontaneously after two or three intent hearings of the ballad. In the end the strong fatalistic or super-natural element may seem to take control.

Often with top juniors it gives more meaning and interest to make some kind of project out of playmaking or make play-making the climax of a project. In fact project work that does not lend itself to some kind of dramatic work may well be too impersonal for children. A possible approach for a dramatic project is to have a class divided into groups of eight or ten, with each group reading a different story with a view to play-making afterwards. They will read individually but talk as a group with the teacher about their story as they progress. Then each group can choose a scene or scenes and dramatise them for the others to watch at the end of term. I have seen this done by a class with such varied books as *The Kontiki Expedition*, *Black Beauty*, *Treasure Island* and *The Boyhood of David Copperfield*, with great enthusiasm and inventiveness, and such convincing miming on the raft that some people in the audience felt quite seasick. This method ensures more than enough parts for every-body and the helpful stimulus of wanting to produce something worth showing to the rest. Alternatively, scenes from a book like *A Christmas Carol* can be worked on in groups in the Christmas term.

Another sort of dramatic project can grow naturally out of the children's discovering something about the part the theatre played in people's lives in medieval and Tudor times. For instance, if children are engaged in a project about the medieval guilds and the coming together of church and guilds in the great cycles of mystery plays, it will mean much more to them if they are working at the same time at their own 'mystery' or simple nativity play. As with *Christmas Carol*, this will want to be in the Christmas term. I would recommend the *Second Shepherds' Play* from the Wakefield Cycle (sometimes rather confusingly referred to as the Towneley Cycle because for years the manuscript was in possession of the Towneley family). David Holbrook gives a good modern version in his collection of dramatic pieces, *Thieves and Angels*. One will not use a text with junior children but this version can help one tell the story to them vividly.

The shepherds grumble about the cold and hardness of the season, then about their particular ills, which are of their own age, not of Roman times. The characterisation is of enduring types, which gives children scope for individual touches. The first shepherd complains about the taxes and how poor men are oppressed by the rich and worst of all by the hired men of the rich, who – proud as crows – take their ploughs and wagons 'as if it belonged'. Yet, as he says bitterly, he were better hanged than dare complain. For the second shepherd a far worse oppression is the constant nagging of all wives yet as he admits men continue to marry. The third, the shepherd boy, is sure that the extraordinary storms and floods they are beset with portend disaster. The weather was never like this before. The other two think him lazy and only prepared to work for what he gets out of it. Moreover, he appears to have lost their sheep for he hasn't seen them or bothered about them since nine o'clock that morning. Having said all this, they settle down to sing to keep their spirits up.

They are joined by Mak, a sheep stealer, who shows off at first, adopting a 'posh' southern accent as if he were a nobleman. The others quickly laugh him out of this and then he complains bitterly about the size of his family and the constant additions to it. They all lie down to get some sleep but after a short while Mak steals off with one of the sheep. When the shepherds discover their loss they go to Mak's house where they hear a lullaby being sung as if to a new baby. They search the house but find no sheep for they don't think to look in the cradle. Just as they are about to leave they remember that they have not given anything to the child. They go back, look in the cradle and discover their lost sheep. As punishment they toss Mak in a blanket but one can easily suggest a more manageable alternative.

The shepherds lie down again to sleep and this time the Angel Gabriel appears to tell them of the birth of Christ. They follow the star to Bethlehem and offer their gifts with direct and simple reverence, the first bringing 'a bob of cherries', the second, a bird, while the third offers a tennis ball, saying:

> Hail! Put out your hand small
> I bring thee but a ball
> Have and play thee withal,
> And go to the tennis.

ITV recently showed a very interesting series of programmes, somewhat misleadingly called *Wonderworld*, in which a young drama teacher, Joan Haggerty, worked with London children dramatising stories from the Bible: *Noah's Ark*, *Joshua at Jericho*,

David and Goliath, an account of which she has since published, *Please, Miss, Can I Play God?* One immediately felt the spontaneity and involvement of the children. Modern urban civilisation often intruded but only as it presented itself to them, not as a show business gimmick, so that the underlying seriousness of what they were doing was preserved. For instance, an Israelite quartermaster stocked up with Fish Fingers, which was realism meaningful to the children and remarkably close to the naïve anachronism of the medieval shepherd's tennis ball. For children working on a project, there would not only be the simple power of the Bible story but strong interest in the Guildsmen playing the original parts and the practical considerations that determined the allotment of these: the Bakers, for instance, always presenting the Last Supper, the Shoemakers the long journey of the Flight into Egypt, the Shipwrights Noah's Ark. This, of course, is the miracle play that Britten uses as his text in *Noyes Fludde.*

The best short account I know to bring this to life for children is C. Walter Hodges in his attractively illustrated *Shakespeare's Theatre,* which is invaluable if one decides to do an Elizabethan Project. In this children can find out how the companies of strolling players grew up, like the one Rosemary Sutcliff describes in *Brother Dusty Feet,* from which evolved the later permanent companies associated with the new London theatres, and with Alleyn, the Burbages, Marlowe and Shakespeare. Most Elizabethan drama is not suitable for children yet such a project more than most should have a play at its centre. This could be a version of the traditional mummers' play, *St. George and the Dragon,* which Rosemary Sutcliff conveniently describes when her boy hero, and the travelling company he is with perform it in their travels, just as they perform *The Second Shepherds' Play* at Canterbury. It could well be scenes from *The Merchant of Venice,* not starting from the original but from a good retelling for children such as Ian Serraillier gives in his *The Enchanted Island,* or Charles and Mary Lamb's classic version. The basic fairy story element in the three caskets part of the plot make it particularly suitable. There is no difficulty in children's understanding the prejudice against Shylock nor the cruelty that this involves. Almost all Shakespeare's stories are interesting to children as stories, and many already know them in some detail, even though they have never seen him acted. This kind of creative approach before they come to the text is valuable, just as creative reading from Dickens is, in making them eager later for the real thing. How far the teaching that they get then does justice to it is another matter.

Instead of dramatising a story or earlier play or famous historical incident, children can work in groups bringing to life situations in the period they are studying: a villein brought before a manorial court, situations concerned with the plague in Elizabethan London, the press gang in the eighteenth century, child labour in Victorian times. There is more than enough material at all times, full of interest and dramatic potentiality. The important thing is to devise a sufficient action, probably quite slight in itself, but likely to provoke thought and feeling, and to give children a firm sense of direction for their dialogue. It is when nothing happens that they lapse into crude modern ad-libbing, without having entered the earlier period in spirit at all. Having given a group a situation and the outline of an action, one must get from them suggestions for the characters likely to be involved. They can be left to work out their scenes then, with help when they need it over feeling and atmosphere. Unlike the Israelites and their Fish Fingers, people must be eating more or less the right food and be preoccupied with probable issues. The greatest value often lies in the creative discussion by the class after seeing the scenes. 'He wouldn't have had to pay a £5 fine then, sir, would he?' (This referring to a manorial court.) 'They wouldn't have had Coca Cola in the eighteenth century. Would they have had pork pies?' This kind of point and the answer to it gets remembered more vividly than facts written about in their text-books, although of course they will go to these with added enthusiasm to find the facts for their play.

Having chosen what to dramatise, one has then to think actively about what this involves. One is not telling a story but presenting action. So one must consider what natural stages it divides into, where its climax comes, where the best starting point is. This may be just before the first event of importance or just after. The former gives time to establish atmosphere, the latter ensures immediate urgency. One will talk about this with the class and be ready for views very different from one's own. Then an action needs rounding off, there must be some equivalent for the secure 'lived happily ever after' element of children's story, and this is usually found in plays set in the past in simple ritual or ceremony. This kind of playmaking never stresses individual performance and does not aim to offer the kind of excitement and satisfaction that goes with this. Instead children should feel that they are taking part in something significant.

One must also think dramatically in working out individual scenes, deciding where the climax comes, seeing that everything else leads to it, and that there is no extraneous action. Each scene needs its own development, especially as the dialogue will never be very interesting for its own sake, as it may be in adult plays without strong action. I suggest this line of thought for a teacher but in effect he will make the class trace the events, decide upon the scenes and then on their development.

First, however, one must tell the story or legend, read the ballad, recreate in one's own words the historical situation. This demands knowledge as well as interest, and power of voice and understanding. For the historical situation particularly, one must be thoroughly master of the material, have thought about it concretely and anticipate questions. One quickly realises the value of incorporating playmaking in a project for then teacher and class are for the time being close in experience to the people and situation being enacted. The children will be absorbed in discovering varied details about the theme or its background. Pictures, music, a model of some kind, all or some of these are at work at the same time. Their imaginations need no artificial stimulus.

One's original presentation of the 'matter' of the play must be clear, alive and strongly visualised, with a pace steady enough to maintain interest but slow enough for the whole to sink in. The characters must be distinct and alive in one's own mind, so that one can bring out their individuality, wherever possible in direct speech. It is better to tell the story than to read it. Even if one is going to make a play from a story one has just finished reading, a condensed retelling helps to recreate and concentrate attention on the dramatic centre. As well as planning the action in detail with the class, one will want at the same time to talk about the characters, whether they were justified in behaving as they did and what such behaviour tells us about their natures. Then they begin to exist as people in children's minds and imaginations.

The third aspect of discussion will probably be the practical concerns of production, where the various parts of the action in any scene had best be staged, where one should have the wood in relation to the mill, the table to the throne, the witness-box to the bench, and so on. It is best to be acting with a surrounding audience or with something approaching the Elizabethan apron stage, with an audience on three sides, who are felt by the players more as participators than onlookers. If children have to come out to the front, one must get away from hampering ideas, linked with the proscenium arch, of never having one's back to the audience.

It is usually best to cast scene by scene, otherwise ome are disappointed from the start while others are so absorbed thinking about their own part to come that they pay no attention to the rest. One wants a good cast for the first scene but must be careful not to put all the best children in it so that there is a sad decline afterwards. If there are more children than parts, one can often suggest extra guards or citizens.

I have already suggested how helpful related mime is, both before one starts the play and, where feasible, while one is working on it. This is particularly necessary when children have to move as adults, as a body of soldiers, say, or have to handle weighty imaginary properties.

Often as valuable as mime in a play's development is brief talk after each scene. Did one always know what was happening? Was it what should have been happening? Were the characters convincing? Did the players stay in character throughout? Did they add anything from their imaginations that helped to bring their character to life? Could they be heard all right? Did they say enough? If not, what might they have said? Did anyone, or everyone, talk too fast? Or not fast enough? Did they play as a group, listening and reacting to each other as they should?

This is the sort of specific questioning that is briefly needed after a first playing. It need never be personal for one is always asking a class to consider a character, not a player. Above all it must only assist a live birth. Clumsily applied, it can lead to a still-born play.

Once all the scenes have been played, one has to decide how much time to give to making something more polished of the whole, to what extent in fact improvisation admits of polish. One's decision will depend on how much the class is involved and interested and one's own assessment of the value for them of going on. One must also take into account the progress as a whole of any project connected with the play. In general, I think a second playing is always worth while. If one class is going to entertain another, a good deal of spontaneous rehearsing will take place outside lesson times and children should certainly realise that concentration and effort lead to improvement.

On the other hand junior children's interest is quickly aroused but also quite quickly dissipated. Once a project has run its course, they usually prefer to turn to something new, rather than linger over any part that has got left behind.

This raises the question whether there is place in the junior school for anything approaching the secondary school play. There is not the same social need as with older children for some compelling activity going beyond the boundaries of separate lessons, and the less formal contact between staff and children that working together on a play produces. A good junior school has this integrated atmosphere all the time. The kind of playmaking I have described helps junior children to move with confidence and control, to speak more easily and adequately, themselves in turn to be objective and considerate as an audience, above all to feel they are taking part in some action that matters. Full scale performance, on the other hand, must be theatrical, concerned with footlights, make-up, personal triumph, none of which is in place in the world of eight and nine year olds. It tends to be exhibition rather than ritual and participation. For this kind of performance one must have a text, which as I have already said inhibits children from entering deeply into character, and in any case there are few good ones. There are exceptions in operas for children like Malcolm Williamson's *The Happy Prince*, and Britten's *Let's Make an Opera*, though this needs some adult principals. Gifted teachers create their own plays or operas. Valuable collaboration exists and is growing between schools and training colleges. I have seen junior children acting, singing and in large measure providing the accompaniment in an adaptation of Benjamin Britten's *Noyes Fludde*, and obviously the experience was significant and satisfying for them. Nativity plays, often best when created by individual teachers, have the same simple power. I would say the same of a musical play like the *Midnight Thief*, by Ian Serraillier and Richard Rodney Bennett, although I know that musically it is far from simple. Probably, though, the natural desire of staff and children to have a special incentive for high achievement and for parents to enjoy their work is best met by the informal open day, with different classes contributing their own parts to a varied programme. None of this, though, is important in comparison with what I think is the chief value of playmaking in the junior school – and that is the pleasure it gives all children, the sheer fun of it.

5

WRITING

LIKE everything else for junior school children, writing is an activity, not as easy and immediate as talking or listening nor such obvious fun as play but still a natural means of self-expression. But, first, children must have a reason for writing. They must have something that they are eager to write about, that is alive for them, actually, or in their minds, as they write, that touches their experience. Then writing offers very real and tangible satisfaction.

In these conditions what children write, even the least able of them, often puts the average adult to shame, it is so direct, spontaneous and alive. One envies them for they are closer to the roots of language than most adults, closer to things, and the feel of things, from which all language comes. They have no preconceptions about usages until adults create them. Their responses are not 'sicklied o'er with the pale cast of thought'. They are not ashamed of their feelings.

These qualities may not be sustained in their writing. Many teachers reading this have probably already recalled pedestrian monotonous offerings from classes they have taught: Then we got the train. Then we got to the beach. Then we did this, that or the other, or all three; or numerous flat statements strung together by *ands*. Are they certain, though, who is the culprit, who has been the more pedestrian and unimaginative, class or teacher? For it is not simply the subject that determines the quality of a child's writing but his feeling for it, his involvement in it, his excitement about it, and initially it is the teacher's *presentation* as well as choice that calls forth this feeling. Where there is some eagerness, it will flash out in an unexpected comparison, a vivid phrase, an unconsciously expressive piece of syntax that heightens meaning. Where there is none, a child will not care very much about his writing. It will be detached from his main concerns in school, its quality largely dependent on his dutifulness or otherwise as a pupil and his ability to assimilate and reproduce. It will also be very largely dependent on the expressiveness of the English he hears spoken all day, in school and at home. Where this has verve, it will come through despite dead teaching. But at the same time a false opposition may be created between negative 'correctness' and idiomatic life. This is often intensified at his secondary school with such effect that one finds various restrictive practices inhibiting and deadening the expressiveness of students who are preparing to go into junior schools and start the cycle all over again.

Children coming from a good infants school will unconsciously accept writing as natural and enjoyable. It is for junior school teachers to instil this attitude where it does not exist, and to strengthen and extend it where it does. Above all they must see that it informs their necessary task of developing a child's technical capacity. As children move up the school, demands on this increase, often of a utilitarian kind. Unlike their painting and modelling, their writing cannot always be purely self-expressive and creative. They have to develop a more or less neutral competence. Yet neutrality has no meaning for children. They will often walk sedately enough yet equally often break into a skip or a run if the spirit moves them, where an adult never would. They often have to walk in school and outside but wise adults will only constrain them from sensible needs of safety and orderliness that they are sure children understand. Not many nowadays will snuff out the spirit of life in their movement simply from repressive motives. And if children take pleasure in movement, they will walk as well as run with more vitality and grace. There is ample evidence that the same is true of their writing. If they take pleasure in expressing themselves in words, in discovering themselves through language, they will have a confidence and zest that shows in all their written work. None of this should or can be quite impersonal.

Yet more than once I have heard a teacher justify spending much time on corrections and remedial English exercises by saying 'They can't run before they can walk'. I don't agree. When the spirit moves them, they can. In any case walking and running are vitally related movements that flow into each other. Most exercises bear as much relation to true self-expression in writing as a lecture in anatomy does to running a four-minute mile. Teachers who give time to them may think that they encourage free creative expression at other times, without realising that this will be worth little if their attitude is inconsistent; if at bottom they are more concerned about what children mustn't do in writing, than eager to let them discover what they can; if they have never fully explored their own powers as writers. The conception of writing as a natural and deeply rewarding activity must be *felt* by the teacher before it can be so felt by the child. Even if he has not experienced it himself, the teacher must accept for the child the controlling stimulus of wanting to write, the pleasure in the thing made and the experience of making it. Once a child discovers that language work aimed to make him write better truly increases his pleasure in writing, he will be ready enough to concentrate; and this will only happen if such work is vitally related to his creative writing, springs from it and is felt to be connected with it. Then it will be an integral part of what has been so well called and so wonderfully demonstrated in the West Riding of Yorkshire Education Authority's book of that name, the *excitement* of writing.

No writing can spring from a vacuum, not for children anyway. Unlike the young man in the *Punch* joke, who scorned his aunt's inquiry, one always writes *about* something, one never just writes. Like speech, one is moved to write by some need, some experience and the pressure of a genuine personal response to this. For a child there will be no pressure to write, unless he is involved in and excited by the experience, whether actual or imaginative, unless it is of some concern to him. And he will not achieve much in writing unless he is honest about it, faithful to his own feelings, not substituting others that he thinks are expected of him.

Such tradition as we have in teaching children to write English has never bothered about this kind of honesty. It has concentrated much more on external rules of usage, which is not surprising since it derives from the long-dominant classical tradition in our education, in which learning to write automatically meant to write Latin and Greek. For a long time in junior schools, imitation did duty for experience, and the desire to please teacher in particular and authority in general did duty for personal response. The argument ran something like this (and many modern course books show that it still does): children learn to speak by imitation and to write, at first anyway, by copying. Give them exercises to increase vocabulary, encourage variety in sentence building, stimulate vividness in expression and give practice in paragraphing. As the external exam approaches (first, the old 'scholarship', now the eleven plus,) give an *idea* of a perfect composition, to hover like Plato's bed in the mind of child creators. Then all their practised skills can be put to work with 'successful' results. There will have been many exceptions, of course, but there was frequently an underlying dishonesty in such writing, which showed in uneasiness of tone, and stilted syntax and choice of words. Children were not expected to be themselves.

Increasing numbers of junior school teachers now repudiate this approach. But many still do not. Some adopt an uneasy compromise between 'free' and 'formal' in their methods, without conscious thought about their aims and apparently little awareness of their opportunities. Yet if English is central in its importance in a junior school, writing is central in its importance in a junior child's English. Unity between the free and formal elements is essential, not as a compromise but as a *condition* of fluency and true progress.

Yet the old imitative approach still flourishes. It is how most teachers were taught themselves and, in this sphere, we are all deeply conservative. To some extent a conscious approach to style does help an adult who wants to improve his writing, just as it helps foreigners learning English. But it does not follow from this that it helps children. Almost invariably it positively hinders them. This does not stop a new text-book published in 1965, having this under *Better Writing*:

'A school is a place where children go to be educated. A school has a hall and several classrooms. A school has a playground outside. A school has a headmaster or headmistress in charge of it. A school has other teachers as well. A school is either for infants and juniors, or for older children.'

This description of a school is very poor. Although it gives plenty of information, every sentence begins *in the same way* (black type, not italics, in the original) making it a very tedious piece of work. It would be much better like this:

'A school is a place where children go to be educated. It has a hall and several classrooms, and outside there is a playground. A headmaster or headmistress is in charge of the school, and there are other teachers as well. Some schools are for infants and juniors, others are for older children.'

Children are then told to notice that all the sentences now begin differently, and are asked to improve other 'tedious' descriptions of a hospital, a post office, a bank and a department store, *in the same way*.

Yet anyone who works with children knows instinctively that both the original and the improved versions are *equally tedious* to them (and, incidentally, to adults). School for a child is not a dead colourless generalisation. If a ten-year-old boy writes uninhibitedly about it, one gets something utterly different. This, for instance, quoted in *The Excitement of Writing*:

My First Day in Mr. W. . . .'s Class

That first day was awful. Everybody was doing a job, some washing paint-palletes, others tidying cupboards and I was helping to sort out books and put them in racks on the wall.

I did not think there was any point in it. I felt lost. Mr. W . . . told P . . . to get some test tubes out of a box and put them in some kind of holders. But P . . . was clumsy and slipped on a book that someone had dropped. Crash, two test-tubes splintered into little fragments.

The teacher flew into a terrible rage, his face went red with anger, he shouted and bawled at P . . . calling names like dolt, idiot, twerp, nit and twit. P . . . went white. I was quite nervous. Sometimes I fidgetted, I'm slightly below average height.

By play-time we had finished the jobs, and was I glad!

Is there any doubt which is the '*better* writing'? Everything here is particular, alive, very real and still frightening for the child as he relives the actual experience in his imagination. It is the pressure of this feeling that gives variety to his sentence structure, not recalling that writing is *better* that way. Any teacher who sets a subject as wide as *School* without seeing that some particular experience or aspect comes alive for children before they start deserves a dreary catalogue. But this does not seem to occur to the compiler nor presumably to many teachers who use the book. What genuine experience can come to life in a child's mind if he has to write about the Post Office or a bank? Does one ever see a child of junior school age inside a bank? Their writing would inevitably be derivative and conventional, full of masked men and bank raids.

Frequently the imitative approach is not even justifiable stylistically, not in the dogmatic terms of the text-books anyway. It is not 'always bad' to begin sentences in the same way. Sometimes repetition expresses powerful feeling. Dickens, for instance, often uses it in this way, as the second paragraph of *Bleak House* shows: 'Fog everywhere', then every other statement but one in the passage beginning with *Fog*, to make certain we get it in our nostrils. This is instinctive and emotional, and closer to the entwined roots of language and feeling than carefully organised 'variety'. A child may produce something like it and one will judge by how it works in the passage, not inhibit by an absolute rule. Sybil Marshall, in her exciting book, *An Experiment in Education*, has a chastening paragraph that is worth quoting:

When I was young, I once set a class of juniors to write about *The Milkman*. I knew no better then. One child handed me in a page full of neat writing. I read: 'The milkman brings the milk, milk, milk, milk, milk, milk, milk, milk . . .' a hundred and fifty three times. Since then I have often spent part of my summer holiday helping friends who run a large retail dairy to deliver milk. How right that child's perception was! After the two-hundredth bottle or so that is all there is to say about the milkman. The fault was not hers but mine.

Given the right kind of imaginative encouragement, almost all children will come to write fluently and expressively. It won't happen overnight but, if a teacher has insight and patience and faith in the value of creative experience, it will come. Children won't only express themselves in writing but in paint, in clay, in movement, in drama; and teachers will let their own creativity in one or other of these spheres react fruitfully with writing. They will encourage children in every way to use their senses, to be vividly aware of the natural world around them and of their environment. At the same time they themselves will be vividly aware of the true nature of children's lives, both actual and imaginative, so that they can suggest or help them choose subjects directly touching on this. Above all they will know how important their other work in English is. For this creates the imaginative climate children write in, this decides whether they bask in warm sunshine, enjoy writing, are responsive to words and rhythm in language, want to explore experience of all kinds *through* language; or whether they always go out armed with umbrellas and macintoshes, are afraid to run about or roam too far, and never really stretch themselves.

It remains to consider what experience, actual and imaginative, is of real concern to children and will move them to write well. This may spring direct from lessons and the school environment or may be much more individual and personal, concerned with the all-important world of home and family, of friends, pets, hobbies, holidays. Still more subjective and individual, it may be part of the world of their imaginations, of their fears and fantasies and longings. To this last belongs the creative spirit in each child, the unconscious desire often satisfied in writing to shape experience in an individual and significant way, and in some measure to come to terms with it in so doing.

Lessons take junior children into exciting worlds that they will naturally want to write about, the world of the past, of other countries and continents, of the physical universe, of nature, or of their own particular environment. Much will probably be in the form of project work, which I discuss more fully later on. With this a good teacher will always try to appeal to a child's imagination, and so to involve him. Then his writing, whether objective and factual, or more personal, will matter to him. There will be a positive desire to make it technically adequate. Much of this writing will be recording of one kind or another as a result of individual or group research. Selecting detail from reference books, recasting it for use in a scrap-book, writing accounts for one's individual book of the experience of a visit, writing and illustrating studies of pond life, birds, plants, sea creatures, all this gives many opportunities for creative shaping. It is the teacher, however, who makes the subject matter in every sphere as real for the child as he can, so real that he is eager to write about it.

At every point, but especially in writing about the natural world, teachers will give children the chance to touch, smell and observe detail for themselves. One cannot overestimate the importance of the child's feeling and of direct sensory experience as its source. Helped by a good teacher, he responds to the actual with wondering concentration. In these conditions he sees more acutely, touches more sensitively, is eager to talk about or paint or draw what he has experienced. Before he writes, there will be talk to help find the best words, the ones he knows he needs. This is the true sphere of most language work in the junior school — work with words under the pressure of a feeling need for them. This is the kind of atmosphere in which children will search for an individual simile, for instance, to bring out their own vision and response. This is the point at which sometimes a vivid poem may focus the recent experience and bring it specifically and helpfully into the realm of language. The strongest response is always to the actual. A hamster in the classroom is worth two in the pet shop and more than that in print. But a powerful written description of an animal, in prose or poetry, following the experience of seeing it for oneself, is often very stimulating for writing. There are many animals one cannot have in the classroom but photographs, especially good colour ones of the kind that abound in Sunday Colour Supplements and Geographical Magazines, are powerfully evocative for children. So are television programmes like *Look* or *The Rare Ones*, which one can sometimes arrange specially to watch the night before they talk and write. Good painting is equally if not more powerful and there are many sixpenny postcard reproductions that one can let children enjoy. George Stubbs's *Tiger* or Rousseau's *Storm in the Jungle*, for instance, which immediately arrests a child's attention and would make him particularly responsive to poems like Blake's *Tiger* or W. J. Turner's *India*, (which Edward Blishen gives at the end of his *Tribe of the Tiger* section in *The Oxford Book of Poetry for Children*, together with a wonderful prowling illustration by Brian Wild-Smith). The Stubbs is in the Tate Gallery as is also Hogarth's *The Graham Children*, which is a good accompaniment for any of the several cat poems discussed earlier. Children love to compile their own scrap-books of animals, with photographs and drawing and painting and writing. They 'see' animals with vivid objectivity. They often feel towards them, especially their pets, in a quite deeply emotional and private way. Some animals arouse strong instinctive fear, as they do in adults. The death of an animal will probably be their first contact with death. Cruelty towards an animal may give them their first taste of physical power, which they may both enjoy and feel guilty about. The same feelings may occur when they witness an animal's cruelty.

Writing from any class about animals – it may be about their pets, or an animal they have seen whose nature and mood they are trying to bring out, or some incident they remember concerned with an animal – at once shows this variety of response. The following examples from a third-year class bring this out:

The Rabbit

My rabbit is black and white and furry. He has two pink eyes and about eight little whiskers. His hind legs are very strong which enable him to jump very high. His two frount legs are not as big or as powerful as his hind legs. The main use for his frount legs are dig-

1(*a*). Beating the Drum: the dramatic power of rhythm liberates
and controls children's movement.

1(*b*). Pharoah confronts
Moses: projection through
dramatisation in a strongly
felt moral situation produces
natural dignity and
forceful speech.

2. Activities outside the classroom: good photographs recapture pleasurable moments and lead to intentness of concentration in writing.

3. Renoir's *La Première Sortie* offers a personal experience for the child to share. The detail from L. S. Lowry's *The Pond* appeals to the isolation of childhood, and its underlying sympathy with protest.

4(*a*). Cat from Hogarth's *The Graham Children*.

4(*b*). Henri Rousseau's *Storm in the Jungle*. Animals rouse strong instinctive reactions in children, of fascination and fear as well as tenderness.

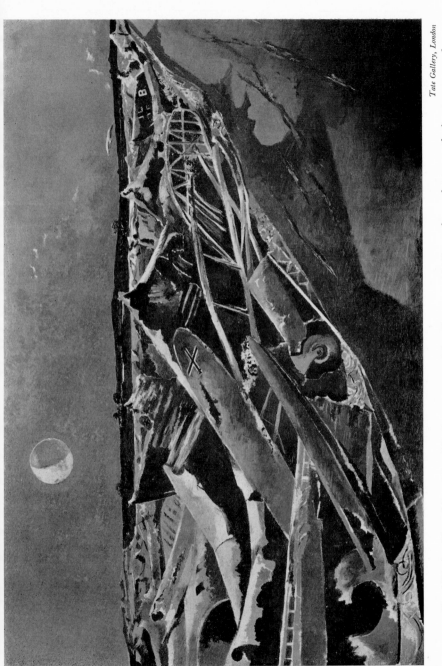

5. Paul Nash: *Totes Meer (Dead Sea) 1940–1941.* The German Air Force brought to earth, in strange and desolate contrast to the 'war thrills' of comics and films.

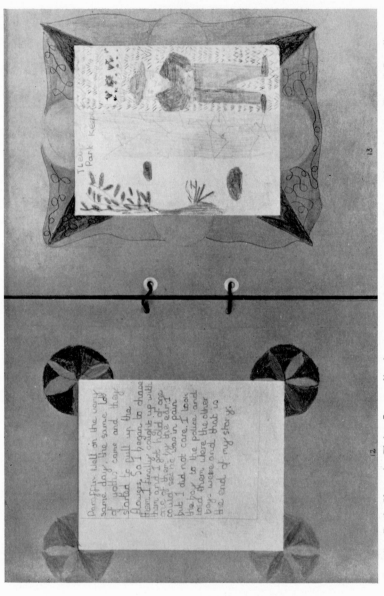

6. *The Park Keeper's Tale*: Jacqueline's story and illustration, from *Tales from a Forced Landing*, a third-year group's collection of modern 'Canterbury' tales.

7. Projects seen in human terms: a modern miner with his pit pony and a
lonely child trapper from the past.

Photograph Ashmolean Museum

8. The gold Mask of Agamemnon, dug up by Schliemann at Mycenae and the Gokstad Long Ship: the wonder of historical fact reinforces the realistic imagination of heroic story.

ging burrows. I have made him a hutch but he still likes to dig little holes in the garden. The rabbit likes to eat the flowers in the garden but I don't think father appriceates this very much. His main diet is carrots but he also likes lettice and pellets which you can obtain from the pet shop.

Bobby

In our avaiary at home I have a lovely bird called Bobby. Every time he eats he bobs his head up and down like a yo-yo. That is why we call him Bobby. His favourite place to molt is my head. Every time I come out of the aviary I am covered with his feathers. Also, he eats on my finger and sometimes takes bits of my finger as well. When a bird goes into Bobby's nest-box the bird rarely comes out without something wrong with him.

The Fox

One day in summer at four o'clock in the evening I saw a fox. It was brown and white with a tail that is black. My dad had his camera and he took a photograph of it. When it came it dashed off over the next door neighbour's garden and vanished. From then on I did not see it again. We don't know if it had escaped from a pet shop or not. He made a funny noise, it went like this: 'Ow, ow, oooow'. It had sharp teeth like a point of a spear that had been sharpened. It must have been fritend because it did'nt stay for very long.

The Vixen

Suddenly I saw a fox with a chicken in his mouth. It was a vixen. I followed it at a steady pace until she got to her den. I looked inside the den and saw eight cubs inside it. I stayed outside the den until 10–15pm. In the morning I saw the fox eat the chicken which was fat and juicy. The fox had first bite and the cubs ripped the chicken apart in about five minutes.

The Viper

Sliding along the grass no one knows it's there. Out in the woods suddenly the viper sees its prey it slides along as quietly as it can suddenly it strikes out in the dark. Its prey cries out with a loud squeak and falls on the grass then we know the poisonous venom

K

has been injected. The bird has fallen. It begins to be carried away by the snake no one knows after the snake has gone into its little burrow what it is going to do with the bird.

The Ferret

A greyish-whitish flash, a crunch and a crash – that was the seventh ferret my Uncle and I had caught that day on my Uncle's farm, *Ash*. Just then Uncle said to me, 'Would you like me to get you a ferret so that you can keep him when you come down here?' 'Oh yes please' I said very excited. So the next day Uncle said to me, Today we will go out and catch some rabbits and then you can choose which Ferret you want. 'Goody' I said and we went out. We got the ferrets and went out to the rabbit warrens. We put six of the ferrets down the hole. They took six minutes to clear out five rabbits but then the other one was put down. In three minutes he cleared out twelve rabbits. 'Can I have the seventh one, please?' I asked. 'O.K.' said Uncle. So I have Streaky as I called him because of the white streak down his back, every time I went to Ash Farm.

All children are delighted by the characteristics of some animals, others inspire strong dislike. This combination of strong feeling and objective observation usually moves children to write particularly well.

There is so much good writing about animals to read to children, from prose writers like Kipling, Henry Williamson, more recently Gavin Maxwell, to name only three, and many poets, that there may be a temptation to overstimulate a class. I have seen students read, and children thoroughly enjoy, several good poems about cats, followed by lively talk about reactions, yet the students have been disappointed when many children did not then seem eager to write about the animal themselves. Their feelings about them were exhausted. One always has to sense when children are ready and need to be left with their individual response. This may well be very early. Often it is better to make a different but related suggestion for their actual writing.

With older children, on the other hand, one must give time for them to explore some of the complexity of feeling in a poem or story and not rush them into writing. That can come a little later. William Saroyan's story, *Snake* (included in *The Daring Young Man on the Flying Trapeze*), for instance, stirs them deeply. It owes a good deal probably to Lawrence's poem but is easier for children to enter and understand. Many children have probably captured some animal, bird or insect and kept it for a time, probably with disturbing feeling. What they make of their own experience may emerge later. Saroyan, here, is in a New York park:

Walking through the park in May, he saw a small brown snake slipping away from him through grass and leaves, and he went after it with a long twig, feeling as he did so the instinctive fear of man for reptiles.

Ah, he thought, our symbol of evil, and he touched the snake with the twig, making it squirm. The snake lifted its head and struck at the twig, then shot away through the grass hurrying fearfully, and he went after it.

It was very beautiful and amazingly clever, but he intended to stay with it for a while and find out something about it.

The little brown snake led him deep into the park, so that he was hidden from view and alone with it. He had a guilty feeling that he was violating some rule of the park, and he prepared a remark for anyone who might discover this. I am a sculptor, he thought he would say, and I am studying the structure of reptiles. At any rate, he would make some sort of reasonable explanation. He would not say that he intended to kill the snake.

He moved beside the frightened reptile, leaping now and then to keep up with it, until the snake became exhausted and could not go on. Then he squatted on his heels to have a closer view of it, holding the snake before him by touching it with the twig. He admitted to himself that he was afraid to touch it with his hands.

He stood up and looked around. All was quiet. The silence was almost the biblical silence of the beginning. He could hear a bird hopping from twig to twig in a low bush nearby, but he was alone with the snake. He forgot that he was in a public park in a large city. At first he was afraid to speak aloud, but as time went on he became less timid, and began to speak in English to it. It was very pleasant to speak to the snake.

All right, he said, here I am, after all these years, a young man living on the same earth, under the same sun, and here you are before me. What do you intend to do? Escape? I will not let you escape. I intend to destroy you. As an obligation to man.

The snake twitched before him helplessly, unable to avoid the twig. It struck at the twig several times and then became too tired to bother with it. He drew away the twig and heard the snake say, Thank you.

He began to whistle to the snake to see if the music would have any effect on its movements, if it would make the snake dance. You are my only love, he whistled; but the snake would not dance. He tried a Brahms lullaby, but the music had no effect on the snake. It was tired. It was frightened. It wanted to get away.

He was amazed at himself suddenly; it had occurred to him to let the snake flee, to let it glide away and be lost in the lowly worlds of its kind.

He makes a last move to kill it with a stone, but cannot, for compassion for it as a living creature. But he wants to touch it.

Then, swiftly, he lifted the snake from the earth, learned the true feel of it, and dropped it. There, he said. Now I know the truth. A snake is cold but it is clean. It is not slimy as I thought.

He smiled upon the little brown snake. You may go now, he said. The inquisition is over. You are yet alive. You have been in the presence of man and you are yet alive. You may go now.

At first the snake is too terrified to move, which makes him ashamed, but then — Suddenly the snake turned from him and spilled itself forward and away from him. Thank you, he said. And it made him laugh with joy to see the little snake throwing itself into the grass and leaves, thrusting itself away from man.

English children may not have seen a snake but many will have felt towards some other wriggling creature in the mixed way Saroyan explores here. They will almost certainly have lain in grass themselves and sensed insect life about them. They enjoy writing from a snake's point of view, or a little later one can ask for a story with a title that may recall this. Learning its true feel — this reverent phrase of Saroyan's describes what one is after, not with one but all the senses and as far as possible with the emotions that accompany reactions to this kind of sense experience. This is what writing helps children to do.

The natural world affects us all through the seasons. Teachers will be aware of this, not only as the seasons transform the actual world, but also in the subtle ways that they affect the rhythm of our lives, our moods, the atmosphere at home, our thoughts and preoccupations. Snow can be exciting even in town, before it turns to slush and so can frost, while dense fog is always fascinating and frightening for children. If teachers encourage them to talk about their immediate experience and lead them through talk to particularity in writing, their own eyes will often be opened by children's wonder and exactness.

I heard a student give this kind of imaginative lead to a class
the day after a freak late snowfall. One boy wrote afterwards:

Walking Home

The path seemed strange, all you could see was sillouid of the
houses and the shadow reflected in the deep crisp snow. But most of
all the creepy unearthly silence. Now and again the silence was
brocken when the wind drove the snow around your legs and you
was reminded again of the cold cold winter. Suddenly the snow began to fall faster, faster thicker, blinding was the snow. I began to
run at an unsteady pace underneath my feet the snow crunched.
The tree in the feild i crossed every day seemed weid and casting
shadow of blue brown the snow was bitting bitting cold.

One would like to feel confident that this would everywhere
get more praise than blame for junior school teachers. Yet
would it? There is such discrepancy between spelling and punctuation, and vision and feeling for words, that many would be
instinctively prejudiced. They would possibly miss the natural
expressiveness of the syntax. They might even want to spoil the
second sentence with a verb. One must always remember,
though, how keenly and easily children are inhibited by
negative criticism.

Following these extremes of nature, where one senses that it
can add something and make children focus their own experience
more keenly, one can read some expressive description. Huckleberry Finn's, for instance, of the violent storm he watches with
Jim, the runaway Negro slave, from the comforting security of
their hide-out on the island in the Mississippi. Children may
not have known anything as lurid but all on some occasion have
probably felt glad to be safe in bed when it thundered and
poured with rain outside:

We spread the blankets inside for a carpet, and eat our dinner in
there. We put all the other things handy at the back of the cavern.
Pretty soon it darkened up and began to thunder and lighten so the
birds was right about it. Directly it began to rain, and it rained like
all fury, too, and I never see the winds blow so. It was one of those
regular summer storms. It would get so dark that it looked all blue-
black outside and lovely; and the rain would thrash along by so
thick that the trees off a little ways looked dim and spider-webby;
and here would come a blast of wind that would bend the trees

down and turn up the pale underside of the leaves; and then a perfect ripper of a gust would follow along and set the branches to tossing their arms as if they was just wild; and next, when it was just about the bluest and blackest—*fst*! it was as bright as glory and you'd have a little glimpse of tree-tops a plunging about, away off yonder in the storm, hundreds of yards further than you could see before; dark as sin again in a second, and now you'd hear the thunder let go with an awful crash and then go rumbling, grumbling, tumbling down the sky towards the underside of the world, like rolling empty barrels downstairs, where it's long stairs and they bounce a good deal, you know. 'Jim, this is nice,' I says. 'I wouldn't want to be nowhere else but here. Pass me along another hunk of fish and some hot corn-bread.'

Far more children live in towns and suburbs than in the country, and in drab surroundings than in beautiful ones. Yet if a teacher looks with fresh intentness at a particular environment, he will probably see some arresting quality in the everyday, whether in lorries rumbling by with gigantic loads, factory crowds emerging, a street market. If he is moved imaginatively by some aspect of the school's environment, he can make it of new concern to the children. One has to find what has meaning for different children in different environments. There may be a river and boats, or a dock and ships. There may be an airport near by, with jet planes coming in to land, or a main-line station, with express trains rushing through. Some children may live high up in a new block of flats and have their own view of the town beneath. Others may live in such respectable monotony that one would not expect them to be excited by it. *Our Street at Night* has meaning as a title for children in many industrial towns. One would not suggest it in Chislehurst or Surbiton. Where there is colour, where one would want to paint if one could, where there is life, that is where one will direct children's eyes. Often, since their environment means so much more to them when they experience it keenly through their senses, one may suggest titles that stress some physical activity. Where one can place it exactly and evocatively for them locally, so much the better. Cycling fast down hill, swimming in hot weather, tobogganing in cold, walking against a high wind, walking beside a rough sea, riding (if one happens to teach where girls can indulge their passion to do this), going on the big dipper, driving a dodgem car – there are many possibilities and scope for individual variation.

One would always seize any local chance to help children see the familiar in their environment with new eyes. Not long ago the *Observer Colour Supplement* had some good photographs of unusual aspects of the Thames. The third-year juniors I was teaching at Kidbrooke were engaged on a project on Shakespeare's London, and it seemed a good idea to ask them to look at their own city, the city of today, with fresh concentration. They wrote in any way they liked, simply describing the picture, writing a story suggested by it, writing a poem. Four of them wrote as follows:

1.   *A Misty Day*

It was a very sad day and the Thames was very calm – there were no boats on the water exept the barges that were chained to the shore and it was a very misty day.

The sun was shining down on the shore and the pebbles looked golden brown and some were green.

The barges were very faint in the mist.

In the distants you can see the chimneys and funnels of the oil tanckers.

(Paul)

2.   *The Last Long Look*

It was a sad day as I had just learned I was to move to a new house somewhere farther away from home. London was home to me and although I was to move to a different place in London I thought I would rather stay in the more central part. I wandered along until I came to Cherry Garden Pier which was dear to me. I looked down the grey river which was glistening silver in places to see Tower Bridge towering above the water which was lapping against it. It seemed just a grey figure in the distance. A few barges creaked and groaned and rocked gently with the tide. I saw a few birds flapping about and then gliding with the breeze and then with a last look I returned home.

(Brian)

3.   *The Cranes*

It was a dark night and very quiet as the big tall cranes swung to and fro on the harbour. The shining sun beat down on the black and grey dirty river and all the tubs were chained up to the harbour

with all the cargo packed on. I stood on the edge of the harbour
staring down at the river for it was a sad day for me because my
uncle had been killed. He was pushed out of his crane at the top
and fell in the river and could not swim and he went under and
drowned but the person that did it is not in captivity.

After standing on the edge of the harbour for about an hour I
walked away back to my house in Fleet Street. Then I went to bed.
I heard on the radio that the man that killed my uncle had been
captured and is now in prison. Then once again I went down to the
docks. The time was 9 o'clock. I reached the dock at 9-30am and
all the cranes were working fine.

(Geoffrey)

4.   *The Voyage*

It is a dark night. Abord the old Susyanna the night was as still
as a sleeping cat. Only the waves hitting the shore and the sparkling
moon. Daylight comes, all the sailiers on deck loading up the wine
and whisky. Down the river to the North Sea. Going up to Amster-
dam and Copenhagen to stay.

(Barry)

Brian's story shows, as do the pieces on animals, how impossible and wrong it would be to try to separate a child's home
environment from any more objective recording. Home is the
natural background for many accounts. Parents are there, as
they are in life, needed, taken for granted, sometimes grumbled
about, never consciously considered. Yet when one of them is
not there, this always shows in a child's writing. One may want
to concentrate for a time on *People*, at the same time, perhaps,
as some project like that described earlier on Chaucer's
characters, or when one was reading excerpts from Dickens.
Although not at all interested in them psychologically, children
see people objectively with remarkable exactness and write well
about them. Someone on the bus, a tramp, an engine driver, a
woman on a stall in the market-place, farmers in a market town,
men drilling the road, gypsies: one needs to look oneself, to
discover who potentially as well as actually is there, and to
allow children individual choice. Photographs here are often
the best starting point, those with a kind of documentary poetry
in them. The anthology, *Happenings*, that I mentioned earlier
has some black and white ones that are excellent; roadmen, a
young mother and an older housewife in a street market, a
very individual yet very typical study of a workman about the

age of many children's fathers. Colour photographs work even
better. Within this framework, children will frequently write
about people within their family, especially those they are,
vocally at least, most critical of. Big sisters or brothers getting
ready to go out, younger brothers or sisters having to be looked
after, a grandfather or mother to be visited: at nine and ten,
children are ready to explore such themes, as they also are to
consider the differences between themselves now, and two or
three years ago. Poems on people may be a good starting point,
such as those I referred to in *Here Today*, or a vivid short story,
like Dylan Thomas's *A Visit to Grandpa's*, especially if one can
let a class hear the record of the author reading it. This is
particularly so because the language with its exuberant extrava-
gant exactness, especially in his comparisons, is often remarkably
close to how children see things.

It was the first time I had stayed in Grandpa's house. The floor-
boards had squeaked like mice as I climbed into bed, and the mice
between the walls had squeaked like wood as though another visitor
was walking on them. It was a mild summer night, but curtains had
flapped and branches beaten against the window. I had pulled the
sheets over my head and soon was roaring and riding in a book.

'Whoa there, my beauties!' cried grandpa. His voice sounded
very young and loud, and his tongue had powerful hooves, and he
made his bedroom into a great meadow. I thought I would see if he
was ill, or had set his bedclothes on fire, for my mother had said
that he lit his pipe under the blankets, and had warned me to run
to his help if I smelt smoke in the night. I went on tiptoe through
the darkness to his bedroom door, brushing against the furniture and
upsetting a candlestick with a thump. When I saw there was a light
in the room I felt frightened, and as I opened the door I heard
grandpa shout, 'Gee-up!' as loudly as a bull with a megaphone.

He was sitting straight up in bed and rocking from side to side as
though the bed were on a rough road; the knotted edges of the
counterpane were his reins; his invisible horses stood in a shadow
beyond the bedside candle. Over a white flannel nightshirt he was
wearing a red waistcoat with walnut-sized brass buttons. The over-
filled bowl of his pipe smouldered among his whiskers like a little,
burning hayrick on a stick. At the sight of me, his hands dropped
from the reins and lay blue and quiet, the bed stopped still on a
level road, he muffled his tongue into silence and the horses drew
softly up.

'Is anything the matter, grandpa?' I asked, though the clothes were not on fire. His face in the candlelight looked like a ragged quilt pinned upright on the black air and patched all over with goat-beards.

He stared at me mildly. Then he blew from his pipe, scattering the sparks, and making a high, wet dog-whistle of the stem, and shouted: 'Ask no questions.'

After a pause, he said slyly: 'Do you ever have nightmares, boy?' I said: 'No.'

I said I was woken by a voice that was shouting to horses.

'What did I tell you?' he said. 'You eat too much. Whoever heard of horses in a bedroom?'

He fumbled under his pillow, brought out a small tinkling bag, and carefully untied its strings. He put a sovereign in my hand, and said: 'Buy a cake.' I thanked him and wished him goodnight.

As I closed my bedroom door, I heard his voice crying loudly and gaily, 'Gee-up! gee-up!' and the rocking of the travelling bed.

One needs always to distinguish between what is real for children in the actual world at a level that involves deep feeling, and what is everyday and often humdrum. In and through writing, one searches to release them from the latter into the former. One takes them away from the classroom and work. Home often means chores. One knows, through the overwhelming predominance of it in their story books, how they long to set out on holiday. They want to write about this in an individual way. It may arise quite naturally from a story one has been reading with them. Many adult writers write particularly well about this area of their own experience. Children are ready enough to imagine themselves in a holiday situation. It is for the teacher to help them, by related and more detailed work in language lessons, to recall and find words for what they saw and heard and smelt on the beach, in a rowing boat, on the moors. Can they get into words the *feel* of walking in the Highlands, or the stillness of a lake or mill pond on a hot day? One needs to be more than usually aware, though, of what their opportunities are, and especially to make tactful allowance for the children who never go away. Poetry is often a good starting point, so are evocative photographs. Only one, or copies of the same one, with the opportunity for every child really to look at it, and lose himself in it. It helps if one has a class with children at tables in groups rather than in lines of desks. Of the photographs reproduced in Plate 2 one of the boys fishing is likely to recall detail. The *Happenings* photograph, on the other hand, is close to most children's actual circumstance, but still makes them eager for the train to arrive and the day trip to start.

Evocative objects are powerful stimuli in this connection. For instance, a bucket and spade, a bright-coloured bathing cap, some unusual shells. This is so in other spheres, and is especially valuable if one is teaching older juniors who have not been used to much imaginative work. Opening sentences are also a way of releasing children from the immediate, provided that they are simple and sensuous. Brian Jackson, writing in *The Use of English* on work he did with seven and eight year olds, says that he found sentences evoking colours especially valuable: 'It was a very bright blue . . .' or green, or red, or gold. On the other hand, sentences that suggest some emergency situation taxing a child's ingenuity and ability to cope only engage him at a superficial level, and produce less feeling expression.

Many of the subjects I have talked of already will produce brief pieces from children that are essentially stories. The shaping spirit of their imaginations will have been at work, making something independent and real in its own right of the original experience. They will discover their powers here more fully if teachers are alive from the beginning to the need for integration within this world of actual and imagined. Then children will not make a false division of their experience, and tend to use artificial and unlikely fantasy material for what they make up, for 'imaginary' stories.

For young children of seven and eight, their world of fantasy is as real to them as what happens at school or at home. They will write naturally about it, usually making no division between it and the real world in their stories, except to halt proceedings at intervals for some necessary event like tea or bed. The world of fantasy is at once vivid and yet secure and domesticated. It is in writing about this that their real experience of their families often finds expression. Set them at this age to write directly about family activities and the result is usually pedestrian and apparently lacking in insight. The following, by a small boy of not quite seven, shows what I mean:

Once upon a time there was a little rabbit called Robert and he lived in a nice big burrow which had a table and three chairs and a wardrobe. The three rabbits lived happily on lettuce leaves and carrots and they liked them so much that Robert's daddy planted two nice even rows of each and he and Robert had lots of fun watering them and looking after them. One day when Robert and his daddy went to look at the carrots and lettuces they were big enough to eat so he pulled up two carrots and one lettuce for dinner.

After lunch Robert and all of them go off for a ride in a yacht but come home for tea, after which Robert puts on his pyjamas and has his daddy read him his favourite story, *Robert and the Fox*. Next morning he wakes up 'a happy little rabbit and when he smelt carrots for breakfast he hopped out of bed and tripped over the carpet'. Later on, after making his bed 'like I always did', Robert plays 'lots of games that I would play. The game that Robert liked best was cowboys and indians. When Robert played that game he was a cowboy and his daddy was an indian'.

Here identification is complete, but that does not prevent Robert the Rabbit being separate from his creator and very much alive. Very many children at this age, although less fluent and sharply observant of character and detail than this boy, show this unconscious power of projection and detachment, of involvement and placing. This quality is part of all good writing but it is easily lost when children have grown self-conscious about revealing how large a part fantasy plays in their thoughts and daydreams, and do not write about it freely. It is therefore very important in the first year or two of the junior school to encourage this kind of expression by one's awareness that it is natural and to be respected. Then there will be a continuity in their growth.

One should never encourage children at this stage by the suggestion of fanciful unreal subjects. It must be the child's own world that is explored, which as I suggested in writing of De la Mare's poem, *Myself*, is a secret one. Some teachers in their wish to get children away from the prosaic and everyday may be tempted to hold up seemingly 'imaginative' substitutes. The following example brings this out:

The Paint-Box

The colours of a paint-box held a meeting and the Brush was invited as well. Red said 'I am the President.'

'No, you're not,' squeaked Green loudly. 'I should be President.'

'Without me you would not go on the paper at all,' said the Brush.

'I think yellow should,' shouted Blue.

'No,' said Yellow, 'Blue, you be President.'   ·

'No, I think all of us are wong; all of us are equal, because with any of us missing, the picture would be spoiled.'

Just then Mary came up and shut the lid and the paints had to stop talking.

The seven-year-old girl who wrote this was not living in a genuinely felt world of fantasy. A fanciful idea has been neatly and quite attractively written about, probably because it was suggested to her as a subject, or because it was close·to something in the same vein that she had recently read. In a way the child has already grown out of it. Significantly, Mary in the story, (although this is not the name of the author) comes along and shuts the box. There is a natural inventiveness here that needs stretching, that is ready for more realistic reading and a different quality of imaginative suggestion before writing.

This must be an individual matter, so one can only suggest what it might be, and repeat that such suggestion must always be seen in relation to the stories and poems one is reading with children, to the environment of the school, to other living school experience, and as far as possible to the individual child's point of growth. In their first junior school years, not many children enjoy retelling in their own words stories they have particularly enjoyed. They enjoy writing their own stories, often carrying on for some time with the same central character, like Robert the Rabbit, who can then keep pace with his author's growth and they enjoy illustrating their stories and sometimes making puppets of outstanding characters. Conversely, stories may often spring from a drawing or painting they have already created. Sometimes a class in a quite spontaneous way will take possession of a character in a story, and want to make up more about him individually or as a group. He might be a clown, an animal of some kind, a foreign child from a country they are learning about. A teacher can provide suggestions for a new chapter or incident by way of an evocative title: *The Fancy Dress Ball, The Snowman, Lost*. The last mentioned, and other related ones could be a lead for something more personal, just as many of one's other ideas connected with the actual world of the children may well occasion a story. Children should always feel as free to produce this as a description. They need not feel that it has to have happened, but should come to realise that it must convince.

Children's fantasy changes markedly as they go up the junior school. The secure domesticity goes. Fears predominate, personal hopes and ambitions are explored or acted out. One senses that in writing directly out of such experience a child is contending with some aspect of his life in a way that talking does not allow for, although acting or mime may. To foster pretence about this world with growing children of eight or nine is more damaging to their imaginative being than with younger children. The six year old who wrote about his rabbit would undoubtedly have been convincing if told to write about the paints in his paint-box and none the worse for it. Two or three years later, to sense that an artificial framework had been imposed or literary 'fancy' held up as model would be more harmful. The following examples bring these distinctions out, I think:

1.   *The Dream*

All at once I fell asleep and went into a dream. It was such a hair-raising dream that I crept under the bedclothes. The rattling in my bedroom made my dream rather creepy. I dreamed about a fierce dragon who had Jack Frost riding on its back. Jack got off and came towards me. I was rather frightened in case he touched me, for everything he had touched so far turned to ice; but he said in a tinkling silvery voice. 'Please, don't be afraid, I have come to take you to see my snow castle. I will take you on my pet dragon, Jacko. Although he breathes fire, he is really quite friendly, he won't hurt you.'

We reached the snow castle and Jack showed me all his ice treasures, and his silver throne behind coral curtains. He even had an ice clock with silver and gold snowflakes decorating the edges. Suddenly he said it was time for me to go home. He put me on a magic carpet and off I went. Just at that moment I woke up, and in walked Daddy with the morning cup of tea.

2.   *A Strange Nightmare*

In the middle of the night I woke up with a start. I went down to Mummy, then I told her I had seen a ghost and he threatened to kill me if I did not go down into the cellar. Down there he told me to get some food. I did it for him. Then I went back to bed and called Mummy because I thought that there were snakes and worms in my bed. She stripped the covers off and showed me there wernt any and I went back to sleep.

3. (This was written by a boy who had fainted the day before.)

I was sitting near the dining room wall with my brother. He was standing by one of the optics that were situated behind a little counter that my father had had built so that we wouldn't have to go out to the public house for a drink. Suddenly I became hot and dizzy, I tried to get up, but I swayed and slumped back. My brother Will came over to me and loosened my collar, then everything went black. A storm broke out in my restless sleep, the ceiling cracked and came pouring in. I was trying to get out of the chair, then the storm died and a cool hand slid over my forehead. Then the sound of whiskey falling into a glass . . . every little thing echoed in my mind . . .

If one's own experience gives any means of judging, a 'creepy dream' was never like the first description. On the other hand, the girl wrestling with snakes and worms in her bed, the boy into whose restless sleep 'a storm broke, the ceiling cracked and came pouring in' while he tried to get out of his chair, these convince me at once of their fidelity to actual experience. Through their involvement in this and their writing about it, both probably became more aware of its nature and grew a little in understanding; whereas the first writer is being trained to think of the imagination as something decorative and fanciful and unrelated to her actual experience. She is obviously an able and inventive child, well taught formally, undoubtedly 'good at English', in the accepted sense of the phrase. To help such children write is not a major problem, although I think that they lose much as people if kept too long thinking of the imagination in these terms. More important are the majority, the average and less than average children, who unless there is some urgent pressure of their own experience never find themselves as writers at all, never have any of that essential confidence in themselves *as writers* that leads to technical progress. This only comes about when they are encouraged to be sincere in their writing, not by exhortation, of course, but through general attitude, atmosphere and suggestion of subject.

It is particularly important with older juniors, for whom the pressures of the actual world grow more insistent in their education generally, to keep alive their more purely imaginative writing and to make every natural warm provision for it that one can. At ten and eleven, only a minority perhaps wants consciously to make up stories. But an evocative appeal, always at a quite deep emotional level, releases most children into valid, often exciting expression. But the stimulus must always be individual, strong and clear, so that it can sweep aside the ready-made plot and character associations, and stock emotional reactions that their reading and television viewing provide, and set them searching for something more personal. If one asks for a ghost or mystery story from ten year olds, most will be stereotyped in their ideas. If one has just read a poem like *Flannan Isle*, or (by a poet usually too reflective and complex to be accessible to children, but also at times very simple and direct), Thomas Hardy's *Strange House*, the result may be different. The poem has in brackets under it the name of Hardy's beloved house in Dorset, Max Gate, and the date A.D. 2000. He actually died in 1928. The first verse reads:

> 'I hear the piano playing —
>   Just as a ghost might play.'
> 'O, but what are you saying?
>   There's no piano today;
>   Their old one was sold and broken;
>   Years past it went amiss.'
> 'I heard it or I shouldn't have spoken:
>   A strange house this!'

One can use a title only, again as evocative as possible, that leaves children free simply to describe something that they are likely to have seen or heard, or if so moved to shape and add creatively to their original experience. Titles of poems or pictures may help one's own inventiveness: *Sounds in the Night*, *The Quiet River*, *The Hunchback in the Park*, *Hunters in the Snow*. More moving for most than simply the title is a picture, especially if one chooses also what is suggestive of a story. The Tate Gallery has many sixpenny reproductions that do this. The National Gallery far less, for there is less contact in older painting with the child's world, and less often a point of identity in the picture that is meaningful to a child, both of which are essential. If one mounts the postcards on a cardboard stand, they can be placed on the tables many juniors work at. Otherwise this is not practicable. It is very important not to give children much choice here, for it only confuses them and arouses dissatisfaction that another group has the picture they think preferable. It is best to give a little time to working along these lines, so that a class may look forward to what their teacher will bring next week. Choice here would naturally be a very individual matter and would vary according to the nature of one's class, especially their imaginative nature. I make only a few suggestions. For the detail from L. S. Lowry's *The Pond* (see Plate 3) one would need to find other titles, although children should always be free to choose their own. Picasso's *Boy with Dog, Child with a Dove, Young Man and Horse,* work well with some children, as does Renoir's *Première Sortie.* Paul Nash's *Dead Sea,* dated 1940–41, the years when we defeated the *Luftwaffe,* has a quite different appeal and effect, especially with a top form. To write freely from a starting point like this does not mean in-discipline nor slovenly work, but rather concentration and some real attempt at ordering their response. More topical leads for a story usually produce something humdrum or, paradoxically, something wildly improbable. There is no tension to make children draw from genuinely observed experience, and every assistance to use the obvious cliché in language and situation.

Often the studies or short pieces of writing inspired in the ways I have been discussing will be close to poetry, far closer than if one suggests to children that they should write a poem. For at junior school age, conscious poetry writing almost always means concentration upon rhyme and simple verse form. Natural difficulties over this prevent the experience controlling the expression in any meaningful way, there is no tension, only a certain neat attractiveness. Often there is no real experience, only the desire to write a poem. On the other hand, if one suggests when one realises that a subject is of particular concern to a class that they write quite shortly, allowing a new line for each statement, the lines isolated on the page so that there can be concentration of meaning for the child writing, one often gets genuine free verse. The varying lengths of the lines, the omissions or short cuts in syntax, are themselves aspects of meaning. The experience would have less fulness, were the lines written as prose and logical sequences provided. The following, by a girl of ten, deserves to be called a poem.

The Tramp

Here he comes again
Slithering across dirty back streets
Talking to himself
A filthy face
Trousers too long for him

L

All shaky
He's digging in the dustbin
Shoes holes
Feet coming through
Hobbling with an old stick

Rubbing his hands together
Imagining a fire.
No money.

Home at last
Under a hedge.

The following, set out as poetry, could as well be prose. Yet the
writer may well have gained immensely in concentration
through setting it out in this way.

Big Sisters

Big sisters are very bossy,
　　They are always making up,
Sometimes make-up, sometimes lacquer,
Lipstick, powder, nail varnish all colours,
　　They start at six to do their hair
　　Don't finish until nearly midnight.
　　They go out at half past seven
　　Don't come home till half past eleven
　　　Next morning they are very grumpy.

Most children, given the opportunity and a stimulus that really
moves them, produce something in between these two, more
memorable for them than ordinary prose writing. This last
point is, I am sure, the important one for this gives children a
definite sense of achievement. The following, for instance,
inspired by the Colour Supplement pictures I spoke of earlier,
while not in itself remarkable had something of this effect.

The Thames

The River Thames goes drifting by.
In places barges bob up and down.
Cranes unload ships.
Water rushes in the shore.
Children play in the water.

Sailing boats sail by.
Everything is gay.
Ships toot in the night.
I wish I could live by the sea.
At night the silvery moon comes out.
To shine its brightness.
Everything is peaceful.
The noise from the cranes is still.
I wish I could live by the sea.

(Kenneth)

Given time for practice and growth in confidence, children
often develop surprisingly technically but I would not try in
the junior school to teach children anything about verse forms
and rhythms, nor set them models, although if one knows Old
English alliterative verse this is possibly an exception; and
given that one finds a situation with meaning for children and
having in it a genuine incentive towards action, so is the traditional ballad stanza. One way to start is through a group poem
with each child trying to say as exactly and expressively as he
can what the particular stimulus means or suggests to him,
what pictures or images it calls into his mind, what he actually
sees and feels, if it is something there for him to touch. This
will be largely objective description, but charged with immediate sensory feeling, helped towards words by talk with his
teacher and response to the suggestions of other children. A
poem can serve as a starting point provided that any literary
associations it possesses are felt by the teacher only. For instance,
Rupert Brooke's *These I have loved* was in a way the model for
the class poem of which this is an extract:

Our Likes by 3B Slade Green School
(a second-year class despite their name)

Train sets bright and new
Engines that shine in the sun
Signals gleaming with little red and green lights
Like buttercups.
The dew that sparkles on the grass.
The colour of flowers when you are standing on a high wall;
The sun that shines in the sky
Making the earth hot.
Beautiful shining horses
The twinkle in my hamster's eye.

An owl with big eyes, that lives
In a dark wood and flies at night.
Snow when the crystals sparkle.
The sun gleaming on the cool water;
Ships sailing on the shining sea;
The green grass, shining green,
The wing of a peacock butterfly;
The peacock with its tail so gay;
The peacock patterns of tropical fish
    All these things we like.

This was written for a gifted mature student during a five-week teaching practice, who had aroused remarkable interest in words and expression in her class. Rupert Brooke may lie behind it, but its life springs entirely from the children's vivid individual concentration, their focusing in their minds on what they most like, and searching for vivid and satisfying expression of this. Wherever there is this pressure to convey exactly some vivid actual sense experience or vivid recollection of it, or whenever vivid personal association is touched off in the child's imagination by a writer's focusing in poem or story, children will write a kind of poetry. For this is essentially what makes poetry different from straightforward prose statement. Older junior children and certainly adolescents, because of the growing complexity of their awareness of experience and their reactions to it, sometimes find unconsciously a form for their expression which makes their poems genuine poetry, and many teachers at both levels are discovering how the kind of release into truth encouraged by this appeal to the whole of a child's being is the controlling centre of their work. Much of what A. B. Rowe, for instance, says in his article, *Writing Prose and Verse*, in Brian Jackson's collection, *English versus Examinations*, brings this out, and although he speaks of work with children in the first years of the secondary school, much of what he says applies to juniors. If one uses poetry as a starting point, which he does not advocate, poems by other children are often more evocative than those by adults, because they have the same immediacy and intimate closeness to children's thought and feeling that modern poetry has for adults. One does need here, though, to guard against any false stimulus of emulation: any well intentioned suggestion that if a ten year old wrote this, why not see if you can do better? And as I have already suggested, it is usually best to leave children quite free to shape their own focusing. Some may well write a prose piece, while others write free verse and there should never be the implication that the one is superior to the other. On the other hand, the talk that arises naturally during work of this kind gives children a far truer insight into the nature of poetry and makes them far more likely truly to appreciate it later, than any attempts to discuss rhythms and verse forms for their own sake.

From the beginning of the junior school, children should be accustomed to write freely and regularly in the kind of personal way I have described for as long as their absorption lasts. A quarter of an hour will probably be the average time but if some want to go on they should be able to while the others turn to private reading. By the third and fourth year, a class whose English has come to mean much to them will want longer.

It is very important that, if possible, the writing should be in a special unlined book or on unlined sheets that can eventually be sewn together and given a paintable cover, with no crest to stamp it as part of the official world. Children like very much to keep books of this kind and usually give much care to illustrating them and finding a title. The loose leaf method has the advantage that the child need not include anything that he is not satisfied with.

It is equally important that children should be able to write in pencil. One has only to watch a seven or eight year old wrestling with a school pen to see how much of his effort and concentration goes into the process of writing. Even for an adult, surely, there is often a frustrating interference between conception and achievement, between knowing in one's mind exactly what one wants to say and losing that wholeness while getting it down on paper. One should do anything one can, therefore, to help children achieve a creative flow. There are other times when one can worry about handwriting. In any case, if the writing itself matters to them, and the book they are creating, there will be a strong unconscious desire to produce clean-looking attractive work.

At all stages children must know and *feel* that what they write is respected by their teacher. They are proud of their work and want and need the recognition of some form of marking. This should always be based on co-operation between teacher and child, and be measured by the teacher's knowledge of the child's capability and potential, not by a notional average. Marking should never be an end in itself for the teacher (just as mark seeking should never be a concern of the child), but only a means to liberate the child's full capacity as a writer. Where personal writing is concerned, marking can never honestly be numerical, but only by grades, if one feels that some means of relative assessment is essential, in which case these should surely be interpreted as generously as possible. For many teachers, though, marking of creative work can only take the form of individual practical comment, always basically appreciative. 'Tried', for instance, does not strike me as being this. Any full correction of the text is a waste of the teacher's time and, a far graver charge against it, destroys a child's confidence at a time when confidence is a condition of fluency. Where one can apply objective standards of correctness and usage, one should aim to show a child those mistakes he is capable of understanding and that he should be beginning to avoid, and although the size of classes makes this very difficult, this marking should wherever possible be done together with the child. For he can often then be helped to correct himself. Teachers sometimes like to concentrate on one aspect of the writing only for assessment, spelling, for instance, or punctuation, expression generally, or the flow and control of ideas, telling the class *after* they have written, not before, which aspect is to be marked. But whatever the objective method chosen, the subjective assessment of a good teacher will always be expressed in sincere personal comment, and be closely related to the developing individuality of the child's expression. This may be revealing itself in more adventurous sentence structures, more wide-ranging choice of words, new sensitiveness to feeling, new forcefulness of imagery.

Ways of helping with spelling and punctuation I talk about in the next chapter, though it is worth noting here that there is no value in the conventional writing out of corrections. Educational research as well as honest recognition of experience proves this to be a harmful chore. Nor is there anything to be said for writing a fair copy, save occasionally if for a special purpose. Other more valid occasions must generally be sought for practising handwriting. Three other aspects of writing strike me as relevant here. First, the atmosphere in the classroom when children are writing. For each child needs a certain withdrawal into self, a certain imaginative concentration. I know that most children of junior school age are impervious to noise, and that they often work sensibly in groups with the kind of quiet noise one knows is fruitful. But personal writing is essentially individual not group work. A slight tension of the right kind is more valuable than too relaxed an atmosphere. Tension of the right kind I take to be that springing from within and concerned with the personal grappling with story or subject. Tension of the wrong kind is any unnatural, externally imposed silence. If one wants quiet expectancy for poetry, one needs quiet concentration for writing.

Reading children's stories and other writing aloud from time to time gives pleasure and adds interest. I would only occasionally read the best, never read the worst; usually choose three or four that are interesting in different ways for general pleasure. I would not much encourage reading aloud by children of their own work. This tends to build up the wrong kind of pride in some children, and to fill others with a frightened tension that they recall long afterwards. (This does not apply when reading their own work aloud is the natural climax of some project work.) It also makes loyalty interfere with honest and constructive comment. A good teacher will sense when comment of any kind would be out of place, except very general expressions of satisfaction. Sometimes, on the other hand, especially where the internal consistency of some 'realistic' stories is concerned, comment can be valuable, as can discussion of particular words in the given context and the suggestion of others. Most children like to have their work displayed when it is good, and to have the chance to read what others have written, although here again I think that teachers should take care that it is not always the work of the same gifted children. One can let groups of children take over a display board for a week at a time, and see also that any piece of writing representing a genuine achievement for a particular child receives recognition. Where the work is alive, there will be constant interest and variety, probably with a wall news chart or magazine as well as other creative work. I have been in classes in early spring where there were still carefully composed set pieces about Guy Fawkes on the wall.

Reading work through is important and I think that help in this could play a larger part than it seems to, at all stages in the junior school. One can tell children a little about proof reading for magazines or anything printed and how necessary this is, and how the most practised sometimes let errors through in their own writing, especially if the experience of creating it is still vivid in their minds. It is best to separate the two activities by some quite different work. Children can set their writing books aside, then later in the day have them back so that they can read through what they have written, thinking more actively about spelling and punctuation, asking when in doubt, using dictionaries and rubbers. Sometimes older children, with a comparatively impersonal piece of writing, can be asked to correct each other's work and comment helpfully on it. This intrigues them and they take the responsibility very seriously. But of course the value lies in the conscious thinking about expression that is involved, not in the adequacy of the actual marking.

In conclusion, I would urge that as far as practicable children be asked to write about what is of genuine concern to them, not simply of interest. It is easy to interest children in many comparatively trivial but engaging topics and activities, but the interest soon flags, as mothers know during the holidays, unless there is deeper concern. For this to inform his writing, a child must feel quite free and want to draw on the whole of his experience. What T. S. Eliot had to say about the sources of poetic imagery in his essay, *The Use of Poetry and the Use of Criticism*, has bearing on what one wants a child's engagement in writing to be:

Only part of an author's imagery comes from his reading. It comes from the whole of his sensitive life since early childhood. Why, for all of us, out of all that we have heard, seen, felt, in a lifetime, do certain images recur, charged with emotion, rather than others? The song of one bird, the leap of one fish, at a particular place and time, the scent of one flower, an old woman on a German mountain path, six ruffians seen through an open window at night at a small French railway junction where there was a water-mill: such memories may have symbolic value, but of what we cannot tell, for they come to represent the depths of feeling into which we cannot peer.

By encouraging children to write from the whole of their 'sensitive life', to discover through an imaginative starting point what is charged with emotion for them, will mean that they take their writing seriously. There will be pressure to find adequate means to express their experience. We know as adults how vivid much of our childhood experience still is, which should make us realise what is there all around children to be drawn upon. We shall help best if we give them confidence, are interested, unfetter their imaginations, but do not over-press. It is no freedom for a child to sense all the time that his teacher is wanting him to write intensely, is always urging him to be as vivid, accurate, imaginative as possible. One must let him be. The experience he is writing about must shape his work, leading him to more or less forceful, more or less feeling and truthful expression, and as I have suggested teachers need most perception and understanding when they come to mark and comment on a child's work. Is the work truly personal? Is it the best the child is capable of? Is he perhaps trying something new and adventurous for him? Does he habitually write fluently and is he growing careless? Such questions may often be relevant. No piece of work can be judged in a vacuum, we must relate it to what we know of the child. Clumsiness is often better than glib adequacy. There can be no absolutes save in one's readiness to be sympathetic and encouraging. One should not hope for startling or quick results, only for signs of individual growth.

6

LANGUAGE

THERE should be no artificial division in teachers' or children's minds between language work and their personal writing. They should always be intimately related and should strengthen each other. Yet English Language in many schools is isolated, a patient 'etherised upon a table'. Often, as in the corny joke, the operation is successful but the patient limps for life, instead of running, leaping, diving, doing a handstand when he feels like it. A patient is a human being, however crippled. Some approaches to language work in schools, particularly secondary schools, do not conceive that there is anything organic and vital in language at all. It has become a machine to be tinkered with, its parts labelled, its functions analysed. All conceivable accidents are prepared for but, like a learner driver, its owner nevers gets near a motorway. Yet what essential connection is there between being a very good driver and knowing in detail what happens under the bonnet?

Unfortunately, many junior school teachers were taught English Language in this way and in no sphere of their work now do they need more vision and awareness of connections. Not many may argue openly, though some do, that constant emphasis on spelling and punctuation at this stage is essential, but unconsciously many believe that standards have fallen here and that to some extent free creative methods are to blame. Many parents support this view. They cannot believe that they ever wrote as carelessly as children do now. It is not easy to disprove this, though instances of children's work from twenty or thirty years ago are not inspiring. John Blackie, Chief Inspector for Primary Schools, discusses the point in his valuable book, *Good Enough for the Children*, quoting one composition written by a ten year old in 1935 that was picked out then as the best in a school well above average in its written work. Although clear and straightforward, the piece is entirely without punctuation and, more important, much less developed in its handling of language, in its range of sentence forms, unconscious awareness of rhythm, feeling for words, than good junior school writing today. Where children are not involved in their writing, it will be scrappy or neatly stereotyped. Where they are, it will often be careless, its punctuation possibly ceasing altogether and its spelling growing rich and strange. But at the same time there will often be unusual fluency and command of syntax. It is fluency at this stage that matters most, for this gives a child a genuine sense of achievement, on which in varying direct and indirect ways one can build. This will include steady underlying care for correctness, but always seen in perspective. If teachers are honest with themselves they know how little genuine development comes through drill and exercises. Publishers and schoolmasters churn out courses which, if the complacent optimism of their titles meant anything, would long ago have made successors quite unnecessary: *Clear English*, *Better English*, *Effective English*, *Complete English*, one meets them all at Foyles. Recently I came across *Mental English*, and a *First Aid Course in English*, complete with a St. John's Ambulance Cross on the cover. In junior schools that rely on these, what happens to the living body of the English language? The compilers of these books have no feeling for it. Children who have to work through them can have little either. There is far too much 'mental English' in junior school classrooms still, in both the accepted and colloquial sense of the word.

Happily many teachers utterly reject this approach, but some may use their freedom with a greater sense of purpose if they are more actively aware of the issues involved. Most teachers would say that they aimed in their language teaching to develop a child's power of expression in speech and writing. Not all realise or accept that this means, primarily, aiming to sharpen a child's awareness of experience through words, and helping him come as close as he can to conveying this when he talks and writes. Talk is all important, in its own right and as essential preparation for writing, and in language work as well as every other kind of English there should always be a core or substance felt as experience by the child. Whatever passage or group of sentences one may be talking about it must add up to something, offer some experience in its own right, whatever one may be 'using' it to demonstrate. Language work should also gradually come to be regarded by children as experience of a peculiar kind, not that they could write about, but that begins to give them a sense of the power of words and the possibilities of sentences, and that begins to make the experience of writing more satisfying. A classroom in language lessons should not be full of children 'occupied' in filling in gaps or distinguishing between *their* and *there*, *who's* and *whose*, *it's* and *its*. (This is catching. I watched a student not long ago add *rite* to *write* and *right* upon the board, then have to give some time to telling children what a rite was.) It should be much more like a workshop, a junior Renaissance studio, with sometimes group activity, sometimes individual, with lively interest in and constant opportunity for hearing work in progress, and genuine concern for good craftsmanship. And there must, of course, be a master and a master vision.

Teaching of this kind will recognise the nature of a child's learning processes and work with, not against, their natural growth. It will always remember that language begins with speech, and that spoken English remains more important than written English for most people throughout their lives. Children learn to talk by hearing adults and by imitating them. In situations where they need to communicate they try out language while they are in the process of discovering it. A child beginning to talk often makes up words or uses his special form of existing words possibly only recognised and understood by his parents. These are perfectly serviceable for communication between them but like dialect are limited in range. All the time the adults he is with share the situation with him, divining his needs and interpreting his meaning, helping him to understand theirs by gesture, by pointing at the object spoken of, by doing the action named, by constantly providing new words for new experiences. Gradually he assimilates the forms and vocabulary of the speech he hears around him. *He never learns words or sentence forms isolated from usage.* All the time talk with his parents, with other adults, soon with other children, and then with his teacher, is the prime means of learning. At school his range of activities is greatly extended but it is the constant interaction of doing, and talking about the doing, which gives the experience meaning for him, and which makes him learn from it. All this language is rooted in and remains very close to first-hand experience.

Teachers of junior children sometimes concern themselves quite early with nouns, and even make children start distinguishing between common nouns and proper ones. Some text-books go so far as to give exercises on collective and abstract nouns. One doubts if teachers or compilers have stopped to think of nouns from the child's point of view. For him, at first, every thing or person he can name has the unique status of a proper

noun, beginning with Mamma and Dadda, or whatever
appoximation fond parents recognise as his first utterance. He
rarely names objects without first touching or holding them. It
will be some time before he realises that other children have
their Mummies and Daddies, still longer before all but his own
are de-personalised to the extent of losing their capital letter
and becoming mothers and fathers. That mothers and fathers
belong to a larger class, parents, will come still later. That
mothers belong to a larger class, women, and fathers to the
class, men, while all belong to the embracing class, human
being, is something he may never know intellectually in the
sense of being able to formulate it like this. But he will know
it fairly early in experience. In his own life people will early
belong together for him, distinct from inanimate objects, just
as he very quickly distinguishes children from adults. A toy
train will be his special Chuff Chuff or whatever name he gives
it, a girl's doll will have her name, before either owner knows
that the word, *toy*, includes both of them. Yet both children
know soon enough what mother means when she tells them to
put all their toys away. One tendency, then, of the perceiving
cognitive faculty of the human mind is to classify, but far more
power to evoke actual experience of the thing or person named
remains in the special, the proper name. Mum and Dad,
Mummy and Daddy, spelt with a capital letter, have a special
significance for most people all their lives. This division of
abstract and concrete greatly affects the impact of adult prose.
The more comprehensive the noun, the further from actual
experience what it names. *Sleet* or *fog* mean more than *bad
weather*, in that they bring us closer to the particular form it
took, although they are also, of course, more limited. Our
mouths water more at *raspberries and cream* than *dessert*. When
children learn to write, it is first-hand experience of one kind
or another that they write about, and concrete and particular
words that they need. It is the living language experience of
talk, particularly talk in the classroom, led by a good teacher,
that helps them find these, not work based on various, often
false principles of classification in a text-book, that mean nothing to them.

At the risk of repetition it is worth stressing this, that language
in the infant and junior school should never be taught for its
own sake, but encouraged in every way to grow out of the
needs and pressures of experience. To be creative in a valuable
way, talk will not foster 'excitement' for its own sake, but allow

this to be the natural by-product of the child's realising for himself through words the actuality of what is being looked at, touched, listened to and thought about in the classroom. For language is his prime means of laying hold of all the varied knowledge of experience.

Good work in language presupposes and depends on a real knowledge of things . . . *I never taught language for the PURPOSE of teaching it*; but invariably used language as a medium for the communication of *thought*; thus the learning of language was *coincident* with the acquisition of knowledge. In order to use language intelligently, one must have something to talk *about*, and having something to talk about is the result of having had experiences; no amount of language training will enable our little children to use language with ease and fluency unless they have something clearly in their minds which they wish to communicate, or unless we succeed in awakening in them a desire to know what is in the minds of others. . . . Teach them to think and read and talk without self-repression, and they will write because they cannot help it.

This was not written recently, close though its conclusions are to much modern thinking, but comes from an account written in 1894 by Anne Sullivan of her experience in teaching Helen Keller. (It appears as an appendix to the latter's *Story of My Life*, and the italics are Miss Sullivan's.) For her pupil, blind and deaf from the age of nineteen months, language was not a special subject, like arithmetic or geography, but her 'way to outward things'. Our pupils are not so handicapped. Sight and hearing make their impact more immediately and earlier than speech. But until they can talk about what they see and hear its meaning for them is incomplete, and unless language work for them in school continues and reinforces what happens for them in life outside school, it will be isolated and largely barren.

When a child learns to read, the same process of assimilation of meanings is at work as in learning to talk, as is also the reinforcement of them in varied contexts. He has first to master a new technique that will turn printed signs into words for him, so far only recognised by their sound. He no longer has an adult to share the situation with, but only the author, although while he is acquiring the technique, he is helped orally all the time by his teacher. Once he can read to himself, talk about what he has read often helps to bring it alive for him. The more a child reads, the greater will be the range of situations which he encounters in language and much greater, also, the range of language. His own command of English will be immensely strengthened by reading but a teacher's awareness of this should not make him treat a child's reading experience as more grown-up and valuable than his speech experience. The two are complementary and in the junior school should all the time strengthen each other. Both introduce children to new words in a context of meaning directly or closely related to their experience, and make it possible for them to learn in varying ways from this.

All this would apply just as much to a French or Russian or German child, yet there are certain essential ways in which English as a language is freer and more flexible than most European languages, with far less formal grammar, yet presenting more pitfalls to foreigners because of that. Teachers, I think, should be more actively aware of this than many are. As far as English words are concerned, very few have any fixed inherent meaning without a context. They all have a range of possible meanings, some of which differ greatly. The word *red*, for instance, probably suggests a more or less similar colour to most people, but given a slightly contemptuous tone, and a capital letter, has a quite different meaning, although the one derives from the other through the colour of the Communist flag. To children, whatever the tone, it would suggest the colour, unless there was a context to make it clear that Communists were being referred to. *Mary disliked her aunt's red china* has a quite different meaning from *Most Americans dislike Red China*. Most English words can be used to illustrate differences between such extremes.

In addition, unlike Latin, few English words indicate by their form that they are nouns, or any other part of speech. This means that we are free to use them in different ways in different statements. 'But me no buts', wrote Shakespeare, and 'Uncle me no uncles', which one would not like to have to turn into French. The word *cut* can be a noun in *The cut was a deep one*, a verb in *She cut herself*, an adjective in *cut prices*. Metaphorical meanings extend in various ways in *cutting someone socially, cutting a corner, cutting a lecture*, while there are many compound verbs: *cut out, cut off, cut through, cut up*, as well as slang examples like *cut it out* and *cut along*. English works very actively and concretely through its prepositions, which is what makes it so difficult for foreigners to speak idiomatically. This also gives it a different kind of exactness from more analytic languages like French or Latin, involving a closeness to actual experience not perhaps always possible in them. One could argue that this is related to differences in national character, and is proof of the living quality of language.

Children are always aware of primary meanings first, the ones that they need to express first-hand experience. They cut themselves early enough, they are warned not to try to cut things with mother's scissors. Soon they are old enough to cut out models from magazines, or help cut up vegetables in the kitchen. Those who live in Lambeth, or any other town where the railway age has left a street called *The Cut*, will make no connection between this name and hurting themselves with a cut. Metaphorical meanings always come late, and many adults always have a rather limited perception of these. The other extensions of meaning I suggested belong to later experience, but will probably still be learned in family contexts. The child whose father drives is more likely to hear abuse hurled at the 'other fellow' who 'cut in', than the child who rarely goes out in a car. With cars, though, most boys because of *intense interest* know all the words anyway, from talk among themselves, specialist articles in their comics, car spotting on long journeys, etc. This shows teachers the way round to work. Where there is great interest, children eagerly amass an exact and specialised vocabulary, and know what they are talking about when they use it. Few of them at junior level have any but a latent interest in words for their own sake.

Few modern children would know the meaning of my last example, *cut along*, since it is dated public school slang only met with in a certain kind of school story, never very vital in its language. On the other hand some modern slang may be forceful in fifty or a hundred years time, if the idea expressed through it still has some application, and its phraseology some creative force. The living idiom of a language, its current metaphor, cannot be kept alive solely by books, but it always gives life to books. This is what makes Elizabethan English so alive. The language itself was developing with the rapidity of an eager child's, a child with exceptional opportunities for first-hand experience. To find a modern parallel in concreteness and extravagance, I think one has to turn to African writers in English. One is constantly aware of this exuberance in children's writing where they are really free and confident in their approach. With young children all language work should aim to kindle these qualities, not damp them down.

A child has to meet a new word several times in varied contexts, before he will use it himself, especially if he first met it in a book. We all recognise far more words in reading than we ever use in speech or writing. It is not simply laziness in speech and our tendency to understate. It is much harder to define a word in isolation than in a context. Psychological research bears this out. Recognition is stronger than recall. If asked who was at a party some weeks ago, there would be gaps in one's memory. Given a list of names of all the guests, the task would be much simpler. Even now, when we learn a new word, we are often surprised that it then seems to recur so frequently. All that has happened, of course, is that it now registers, it has an active meaning for us independent of context. Before, when we met it in print, we had an idea of its meaning that was good enough *in the context*.

One cannot overestimate the importance of this contextual nature of meaning in a child's learning of language. Yet most of the many English course books for juniors totally ignore it and some seem openly to flout it. Instead of recognising the need to reinforce existing half-formulated meanings, instead of showing relationships between groups of words and how meaning may be extended in varying ways, most text-books erect a series of more or less impossible meanings so that the child may select the one 'right' one.

'Our baby has just learned to .... on the floor,' naïvely announces one exercise. Most children with a baby at home will promptly supply their own answer, and it won't be *crawl*, which they are supposed to select from an accompanying list.

A person who plays the piano is called a (genius, pianoforte pianist, spendthrift).

The only likely confusion for a child here is between *pianoforte* and *pianist*. If the teacher supplies or allows the bright children to supply the meanings of *genius* and *spendthrift*, the random unrelated nature of the whole approach is only emphasised. There is no context to fix these meanings in children's memories. I have seen no exercises that suggest we draw children's attention to how English has grown rich in vocabulary and expressiveness, and to how words are sometimes related. Often people who play an instrument, or make a special study of a subject, or drive a vehicle, are described by words formed *like* pianist. Suggest *violin, cello, chemistry, botany, cycle, motor*, to a class of ten or eleven year olds, and they will quickly see the connection

M

and suggest other examples themselves. There are many variations on this kind of approach that could valuably come into
the periods of *Work Study* appearing on many junior school
timetables. For instance, one common type of exercise gives a
phrase in definition of a single noun in a sentence as a means
of helping children to find the right word.

> *The man in charge of the books* helped me to choose an exciting
> detective story.
>
> Mr. Ryder has *a place for housing his car* attached to his house.
>
> Graham and Janet walk to *the place where a lot of birds are kept.*

There is a right word here and one wants children to know it,
as one wants them also to realise that it is only when grown-ups
are, as we put it, 'at a loss for words' that they are reduced to
substitutes like 'what d'you call it' and 'thingumajig'. But I
would not work in an artificial way like this, which can only
be random in its effect, but in a context that suggests to children
that we often have a word of a general kind which includes
many exact, more particular examples. Obviously one would
not say this to children. However, most of them probably live
in a *house*. If one asks who lives in anything else, one will get
flat, or *maisonette, bungalow* or *cottage,* if one is in the country,
and conceivably rarities like *houseboat* and *caravan.* A small
amount of questioning will draw from children a number of
words for places where human beings live. One can then suggest
that there is usually a special word for the 'house' of an animal:
what does a dog have? a rabbit? a bird? bees? What about a
cat? Why is there no special word here? One could follow this
up by asking what we call the home of a large number of
animals all brought together. They will almost certainly know
zoo. Words like *aviary* and *aquarium* can follow quite naturally
from this.

Intelligence tests, however, work in a quite opposite way.
'My pet is a .... (tap, dig, cat, net)' is a typical example from
a Kent test for eight year olds. These are now set by some
authorities to such young children so that the process of testing
a child's abilities shall be spread out, and not depend entirely
on performance in the one test at eleven. Any extension of this
practice will be disastrous, if teachers allow themselves to relate
English language work to preparation for this type of test.
Happily many don't. But the temptation remains, since although

one can do no more by way of preparation than make a child
focus his attention on the alternatives offered, and think carefully before answering, practice does undoubtedly improve
performance. However intelligently handled, such work is
bound to suggest that there is a right and wrong in language
far more often than is the case. The same is true of work on
opposites and other crossword puzzle elements of language that
abound in text-books. These exercises may well reveal a child's
power to see connections and differences, but they extend only
his purely intellectual knowledge of words, and with a majority
of children, not even that. For a child either knows the answer
or he does not, although when he is asked to select the right
word as opposite from a list there is some help, compared with
having to supply an opposite unaided. But there is nothing of
much interest to fix the meaning for him once a brighter child
has supplied the answer. If the work is written, he is driven to
guessing, which is profitless. In addition there is the same
continued unconscious suggestion that there is an inherently
right answer.

A *quiet* child is the opposite of a . . . . child.

Seven year olds obediently write in *noisy*, and certainly in this
particular respect two entirely hypothetical children may be
said to be opposite. Two actual children may be very alike in
other ways, in the degree of their intelligence, in generosity, in
physical daring, in spite of being quiet and noisy respectively.
Isolated instances are not important. It is the cumulative effect
of various related tendencies, particularly the *generalising*
tendency, of all this work with words which is harmful.

Most work on synonyms in text-books illustrates the same
tendency. It could be argued that no two words ever mean
exactly the same, although for practical purposes they frequently
do, especially the more colourless and abstract the word in
question. But everything depends on the context. Feelings are
frequently involved, of approval or disapproval. *Slim, slender,
scrawny, scraggy, thin*: are these interchangeable, for instance,
without some change in one's attitude towards the subject
described? If one were concerned with secondary children, one
would want them to become aware of this, not so that they
strive for neutrality, but for expression of honest feeling. It is
enough for juniors to search for the most expressive word in a
context of some interest and concern to all of them. This will

mean considering more than one possibility and will certainly mean being very much alive to the many onomatopoeic words in English (although one won't use the term). The approach of most of the exercises is to ask children to work out by an artificial and abstract process of elimination which word fits. This is then labelled *right*, and is easily marked. The following instance illustrates what I mean:

> Horses build
> Authors gallop
> Soldiers leap
> Bricklayers write
> Kangaroos fight.

'Put the *right* verb with each noun' says the book. When the child has done this, is he likely to care in any way? The substance of the exercise, as with so many, is random and pointless, and quite detached from any experience that has interest or value for the child. This is quite apart from the fact that bricklayers sometimes write, that soldiers might upon occasion leap across some obstacle and authors gallop along the sands with their children if they feel like it.

This is part of an exercise about nouns and verbs for seven and eight year olds, which wants them to realise that both are so important that we can make whole sentences with just one verb and noun. It is quite wrong, in my view, and a complete waste of time, to try to teach junior children abstract categories like this. They are not ready for them, they mean nothing to children, they offer no experience. In addition, this instance illustrates the false emphasis that abounds in adult conceptions about grammar. Human beings do not make whole sentences using only nouns and verbs because these parts of speech are, in the abstract, more important than all the rest. They cannot communicate in speech without using the words which they came to call nouns and verbs long after they had been first spoken and understood. Nouns and verbs are structural to all our utterances. Something has to be named, out loud or in our minds, before we can say anything about it. We cannot make any statement about it except by using a verb, again out loud, or understood. Adjectives and adverbs are usually decorative of this structure, while prepositions and conjunctions connect its parts. *But the categories come after the human experience.* They reflect it, they in no way determine it. I would never want to do any work with children on nouns and verbs as such, although plenty

of work to draw from them exact words to name things and
describe actions, in relevant and interesting contexts. I would
never leave them to sort out the 'right' answer, but try to find
a context in which they need the particular words one has in
mind. For instance, to start with statements as simple as the
book's, how do horses move? They *gallop*. Fine, but how else?
Trot, walk. With a little help, one can get *canter*, probably, and
help fix it in their minds, after they have envisaged the nature
of the movement and how it differs from a gallop, by mentioning
its connection with pilgrims travelling to Canterbury, and the
easy pace at which they rode. Is one kind of horse more likely to
gallop than another? A *racehorse*. What do we call a horse that
goes very steadily and slowly along, but has great strength? A
cart-horse. This would take children away from the classroom
back to the farm, if they are country children, and to recollections of the country if they live in towns. Words called to mind
from this context or new words learnt *for* it will become part of a
child's language in a way the language of an exercise will not.
It is all important, though, that the original questioning about
horses and their movement should not simply be illustrative, but
because the children are genuinely concerned about horses *at that
point*, are reading a story in which they play an important part,
are perhaps going to write a story about horses themselves or have
been talking about some pictures and photographs of horses.

The wheel *turned round and round* slowly — Write *one word* which has
a similar meaning to the words in italics.

This is a typical vocabulary building question from a text-book
for top juniors. What happens? The children learn the word
rotate. The original sentence happens to be more expressive,
suggesting what is happening by the way it moves and by the
repetition in the traditional phrase, *round and round*. 'The teacher
said Geraldine's work *was getting better and better*' is another
example from the same exercise. The 'right' answer, presumably
improving, does not give me the same sense of emerging achievement as *better and better*, the same sense of the child's effort. A
certain analytical precision is gained at the expense of syntactical
life and movement. For English naturally expresses itself through
phrases in a way that Latin, for instance, does not. I am not
advocating any kind of primitivism here, such as happened
with German under Hitler, when a Greek derived term like
Telefon, for example, was ousted by the native *Fernsprecher*: but
simply that our language teaching should not buttress false

attitudes about what is right, or better. Practice at this kind of exercise must give children unconsciously the idea that the single, rather difficult (very frequently Latin-derived) word is better than the everyday natural phrase. These exercises are always this way round. *Children are never asked to find a good phrase to replace a long word.* This, I think, reflects assumptions of the compilers about English which are for the most part untenable.

Many of these assumptions concern style, about which one can never be dogmatic. To be so at once suggests insensitiveness to its essentially individual nature. Yet one often reads this kind of thing: 'Now you have learned already that sentences are dull and not very interesting unless we use adjectives.' This groundless belief still lingers. If a passage is peppered with adjectives, it must be *descriptive*, though of what is usually not specified and their use may well be as revealingly repetitive as this rubric's *dull* and *not very interesting.* An adjective may simply identify a vague or neutral noun, where an exact one would have dispensed with the need for more description: a *tall* building, for instance, where *skyscraper* might be what was meant; just as an adverb may modify a general verb like *walk*, where choice of *dawdle*, say, or *stroll* or *stride* would give the kind of walk much more exactly. In most books there is no spur whatever to individual choice. Usually a group of adjectives to be 'used' is supplied in a context provided by the book. The child is not given two or three that approximate in meaning, so that he has to weigh them up and decide which he prefers, which makes him consider their relative descriptive power; but as with so much text-book work has to allot by intellectual process of trial and error. For instance, one book for second years has six pictures, of an elephant, a very-smudged looking house, a crooked walking-stick, a toddler on all fours, a kite and an open window. Underneath are written the nouns only, with *boy* instead of toddler.

Here are six adjectives:

crooked, dirty, huge, young, open, square.

Then the child is told:

Match each adjective with the *right* thing in the pictures. (My italics.)

The instructions continue:

Then write a sentence saying what there is in each picture.

Begin like this:

There is a huge elephant in the first picture.

An elephant is huge compared with most other animals, but some elephants are more huge than others and the one in the picture looks quite a youngster. *Young*, however, is needed for the boy, who might otherwise be dirty, and so it goes on. The house looks smudged – one can imagine the illustrator being given rather vague instructions to make it fit. Yet if one made a child picture the houses in his own town or, still more specifically, his own house – he would find more exact words than *dirty*. 'Old shaggy buildings', for instance, was the phrase a girl used for me recently, catching instantly the kind of decay apparent in the coloured photograph she was describing of a mouldering London back-street.

All these exercises positively encourage conventionality in expression. Yet it is not difficult to involve children imaginatively or actually in situations that make them want to specify, to find the necessary noun, the best adjective. One can start in any classroom. What colour is Jane's jersey? Red. Has anyone else a red jersey? Is *red* the best word for all these? Crimson, pink, scarlet, may well be suggested. This could lead to associations that can be tested on the spot. What does the wool of a jersey *feel* like? Would one use the same word for a quick-knit as for Jane's three ply? Again, though, it is important to have some purpose behind this, such as the interest of a project on wool.

More often one will want to leave the classroom with the aid of colour photographs or evocative objects like shells or fruit, ferns or seaweed. If the classroom has tables rather than desks, children can work in groups on a description, which can then be read out and commented on. Or children can journey in the mind. If they were by the sea, for instance, instead of in school, who and what would they see on the beach or along the front? What words might they use to describe the rocks? the seaweed? What about its smell as well as its feel? They have found a very fine round pebble – what words would convey best its feel? It is a hot day, and they scoop up a handful of sand. What is the feel of this? Supposing they were farther out, walking on sand only, just uncovered by an ebbing tide, what would be the difference?

This work is very close to what one might be wanting them to explore individually in their creative writing, and suggests the kind of constant interaction that should exist between writing and language lessons. The class will have been 'using' nouns and adjectives, although there is no need for the term to be used and no value in children's knowing the abstract category. For them all writing must explore experience. Any kind of categorising, any kind of instructions about style, kill life and individuality and actively prevent fluency. Yet the text-books abound in instructions, especially for seven and eight year olds, often going beyond work with words and providing a pattern for their developing thought and feeling as well. If young children are to write at greater length than usual, to attempt a whole paragraph, they are told how to begin, what to put in and in what order. For instance, after a picture of a girl looking in at her pet mice in their cage, one book gives two short paragraphs of information about them and then tells the children to write their 'own' paragraph. In case they should show any dangerous signs of individuality, though, they are given plenty of 'help'. The instructions go on:

Start like this — *Margaret keeps two mice as pets.*
1. Say what *Margaret keeps* as pets
2. Write down where *they live*
3. Tell where *they sleep*
4. Now say *where they have their meals*
5. Write down *what they like to eat*
6. Say what *the mice are called.*

One can easily imagine the stereotyped little paragraphs that will result; for how could anything personal and individual come from such an approach? Yet even the intellectual structure is not self-evidently 'right'. One could as justifiably follow 1 with 6, and just as convincingly say what the mice liked to eat before saying where they had their meals. One wants children to order their material but this must be mainly an inner order, coming from their own feeling and sense, from their own grappling with what they have to say. The sad thing is that a vicious circle tends to be set up. The teachers who fall back on this kind of approach do so, or so some have told me, because their classes have so little to say, because their written work is so pathetically scrappy. And so it is. But one knows at once who lacks imagination here, who it is who needs to see the connection. The children may limp, but these teachers are only providing heavy crutches instead of unimpeded exercise such as doctors now usually advocate. The cure, surely, is go direct to experience: some mice in the classroom, a hamster that the children can feed and clean and feel and watch, talk about their own pets. Then they will write about them freely.

Imagery is a particularly individual and important element in any personal writing, often springing for adults, as T. S. Eliot suggested, from unrecognised sources in their past. Children naturally see the world around them with immediacy and sharpness. This is a time when vivid comparisons easily suggest themselves. Yet most text-books fail to recognise this. Most work on comparisons fosters cliché, children being asked to complete traditional phrases like bold as brass, proud as a peacock, once fresh enough but now no more than conventional counters. Sometimes they are given some very hackneyed phrase like *letting the cat out of the bag* or *getting into hot water* (in the book in front of me this is accompanied by a gay little picture of a boy stepping gingerly into his bath) and told to allot them to the appropriate meaning from a list that follows. These are all dead metaphors used only by adults quite insensitive to the life and possibilities of language. Very rarely does one meet any invitation to create an individual comparison. But children if made to focus imaginatively are full of fresh and striking images. A form of ten year olds asked to describe themselves produced the following:

A bunch of mice squeaking in class and giving teacher a headache
Fishes with our mouths opening and shutting
A herd of bulls (boys anyway) charging across the playground.

Their parallel form were variously and vigorously denounced as:

Stoneage Beatniks
Ruffians
Zulus
A herd of warthogs wallowing in the mud.

Crude no doubt, as group feelings often are, but they felt and enjoyed the power of language in expressing them. More individual images came from more individual focusing, valuable often if they are later going to write at greater length on some connected theme. An old man's hand to a class of third years felt:

cold like ice
like the inside of a fridge
like a large slimy slug
like the North Pole.

In imagination, water slid over their bodies:

> like butter over a hot frying-pan
> like an eel slipping over rocks
> like a snake slipping through grass.

Among other examples: The fog rolled in from the sea like a tidal wave in slow motion. The fish on the bottom of the boat jerked like a Mexican jumping bean. One usually needs to give a lead by some evocative opening. For instance:

> The moss round the edge of the pool was soft like . . . .
> The noise as the express plunged into the tunnel reminded Peter of . . . .

Children are even more likely to produce good images if they have objects to feel and look at closely: a piece of marble, an unusual shell, a glass duck. If teachers look at their own possessions with fresh eyes, they will probably find something highly suitable. Bubbles blown in the classroom always fascinate them. Brian Jackson has an interesting exercise in the second volume of his *Good English Prose* called *Examining a Tulip*. Three boys and a girl were given a red and yellow tulip to examine. They were told to look at it closely and make notes together of what they saw, heard, touched or could smell. This is what they wrote:

Sliding my hand up the stalk I found to my surprise that it was quite firm. It felt and looked like a green snake. I noticed another boy holding it upside-down and it immediately reminded me of the little coloured bells that are painted on Christmas cards. The petal that had come off I squeezed and smelled. It smelled sappy and stuck to my fingers when I opened my hand. The tulip smelled like celery, and the centre piece called the pistil looked like a propeller on a boat. The tulip was yellow with brown stamens.

(David)

The pistil was like a torpedo and the stamens were like splashes of mud after the torpedo had plunged into the mud. The bottom of the stem was like a quill's point. If you crack the stalk it sounds like a gun's report.

(Martin)

Rubbing my fingers along the leaves I thought I was rubbing a very smooth piece of wood, the grain being very straight.

(Robert)

It had a smell like a smoky coal factory. The stem and the leaf had a lovely, cool, glossy feeling. It looked like a deep red cradle within a yellow stand. When it got caught on Linda's chair a dark green streak went across it.

(Susan)

Children are immediately interested in this. It is a real situation for them, they are eager to comment. They notice differences between the comparisons, suggest certain differences in character that they may denote. Asked why it was the girl who likened the tulip to a cradle, they discover something about the homely natural sources of our imagery. This leads to talk about why writers use them, not for their own sake, although they may incidentally be beautiful or stay in our minds, but to bring readers closer to sharing the writer's experience. Given something quite different to handle and describe in this way, they set to with zest and with no sense of an artificial activity such as 'finding comparisons' easily become.

The kind of perception being awakened here is essentially part of any true comprehension, or understanding, of what one reads and it involves reading with the whole person alert and sensitive to what is there, with feeling and intelligence working together. Yet to growing children nowadays, and to most students and sixth formers, comprehension means simply 'reading a passage and answering questions on it'. They approach the passage forearmed with intellectual instructions, as if they were taking part in a treasure hunt or car rally in beautiful countryside instead of exploring it for pleasure and with something of a naturalist's eye as well as a painter's. 'Comprehension' as almost universally practised in junior and secondary schools is possibly the most harmful and powerful of the many false categories teachers have erected over the last thirty years or more.

One would not mind so much if the average offering showed reasonably intelligent understanding on the part of the compiler. But passages for juniors frequently do not. Too often there is no inherent interest for children in the passage chosen, there is nothing to involve them in any way. Many passages are obviously made up by the compilers so that questions may be set on them. They are usually innocuous, sometimes mildly interesting, but they have not been created through any genuine imaginative pressure and so there is little in them that calls for insight from the child, little to call forth the beginnings of sensitive understanding.

For top juniors, and in many schools for lower classes too, there is considerable written practice at this kind of thing, which is treated in a detached way as a necessary chore connected with some kind of exam or grading. I have been in schools where the children are graded within the class and set to work on 'A' or 'B' comprehension books. The latter, needless to say, tend to be older, more dog-eared and generally less intelligent in choice, as befits the lower orders. In any case most books are preoccupied with superficial testable elements. Some concentrate on the simply factual, which some children find much more interesting than others, and this often makes the lesson more relevant to geography or social studies than English. There is no harm in this, of course, provided that children are also sometimes led to consider passages of genuine merit in their use of words and power of feeling. One of the few text-books I know which does approach these matters with feeling and intelligence, and which all the time aims to make children actively consider the merits of language in a living context, is the one I quoted just now, Brian Jackson's *Good English Prose*. In his second volume he gives an excerpt from *Adventurer's Fen* by E. A. R. Ennion:

The sun climbed out of the morning haze. Its low beams lit the fringes of the pool and warmed the air. It had risen high enough to dry the reeds before we stopped for breakfast. We sat there on the long grey nose of the duck punt, legs dangling in the water — one if not both soaked through in spite of thigh-long waterboots — content as only men knew how to be who are happiest in their oldest clothes, munching bread and cheese and drinking beer.

There were admittedly some minor troubles of the fen — biting midges and mosquitoes; horse flies with their chequered wings and transparent green-gold eyes; dull grey clegs who settled unbeknown and got their blow in first; capsized punts and sprawlings in the mud; slinkings-home in sodden, reeking clothes and squelching gumboots. Such trivialities only came to redouble the joy of all the rest.

The excerpt is followed by these questions:

1. What is the difference between a fen and a swamp?
2. What is the difference between a punt and a rowing boat?
3. What does Mr. Ennion consider the best things about breakfast among the reeds?

4. What are the drawbacks and difficulties? Would they be more important than the pleasures for you? Are they for him?
5. Why does he write:
   'The sun *climbed* out of the morning haze'
   instead of:
   'The sun *came* out of the morning haze'?
6. What does —
   'horseflies with their chequered wings and transparent green-gold eyes'
   — mean? Is it well written or not?
7. What does Mr. Ennion mean by:
   'slinking-home in sodden, reeking clothes and squelching gumboots'?
8. From your reference books discover what *clegs* are.

This is far too difficult to be tackled alone, but most ten or eleven year olds, having the passage read aloud to them with interest and feeling on the part of the teacher, would wish they were there having breakfast in the open air on a punt and so, one imagines, would most junior school teachers. They are taken away from the classroom, and all the questions are designed to make the particular experience of the author more exact and alive for them, which means, eventually, touching on how he does it. The questions concerned with fact at the beginning are not there merely to test a child's general knowledge in an unrelated way, as so frequently happens, but to make him place the particular kind of countryside and boat involved. This is quite opposite to the trick purpose behind giving pointless alternatives, as in these questions on a passage from *David Copperfield*. The passage describes an inn where David finds Mr. Micawber staying, and the word *dumb-waiter* occurs in it. The set questions are all followed by four suggested answers. For instance: *What is a dumb-waiter?*

1. A waiter who cannot speak
2. A stupid waiter
3. A lift or trolley for conveying food
4. A waiter who is pretending to be stupid.

Without the hyphen and in *other contexts*, both the first two meanings are possible, but it would be profitless and distracting to bring this out here. The questioning should be directed towards helping children distinguish between dumb-waiters and other things of the *same kind*: trolleys, dinner-wagons, trays, serving tables. Most children will only have experience of trays, anyway. If one wants to test a child's ability to sort out facts, and with seven and eight year olds close reading is largely concerned with this, one should ask a simple question that makes him refer to the passage, not refer to a host of confusing possibilities. *Why did David think that Mr. Micawber's room was over the kitchen?* as a question on the passage given is reasonable. But this compiler must give four possibilities, only one of which, the third, is supported by evidence in the passage. These four are:

1. David could hear the pots and pans
2. He could smell a roast dinner
3. There was a warm greasy smell
4. He could hear a man speaking in French and though he was the chef.

What kind of comprehension is such questioning after and what kind of comprehension does one feel the compiler has himself? An additional point worth making here is that in text-books for juniors one frequently finds Dickens cut without acknowledgement. It is usually his luxuriant and alive imagery which is hacked out, presumably because it offends the compiler's sense of what is fit for children and possibly their own stomachs. For instance, this passage has the following as part of the description of Mr. Micawber's room: 'I think it was over the kitchen, because a warm greasy smell appeared to come up through the chinks in the floor, and *there was a flabby perspiration on the walls.*' In the text-book excerpt the last statement has gone, yet far more children know what perspiration is than have ever heard of a dumb-waiter, and they can vividly be made to see the force of the comparison. They may well have been scolded more than once for leaving a kettle boiling soon after their mothers have cleaned the kitchen or for having too much steam in the bathroom.

For much younger children 'comprehension' in simpler form is often attached to pictures, usually of unrelieved gayness in colour, and the same addiction to pointless alternatives in the questions. For instance, a child looking at a picture of a woman in a grocer's shop is asked, among other things, if she is at the circus. Or following a picture of a girl walking: Elizabeth cannot go by bus

because she has no money
because there are seven days in the week.

'Choose the *better* ending' says the rubric. One answer is a convincing probability, the other a ridiculous *non sequitur*, so that degrees of comparison don't arise. But it is typical of the strange ingenuity of compilers, quite unconcerned with ordinary life and experience, that here they should say *better*, whereas so often when there is a real choice in the matter they are dogmatic and say *right* or *correct*. There are of course many exceptions to this kind of stupidity, there may even be a majority of text-books that show more sense than otherwise, but the stupid ones still sell. Where 'comprehension' is concerned, I know that teachers must consider what children have to do in their eleven plus, or whatever equivalent method of grading exists in their area. Younger children need to be trained in reading in different ways, but their pleasure in it should remain paramount in one's mind. At seven or eight they should only be questioned about simple objective writing, although this need not mean, as it does not with direct objective presentation in poetry, that they feel nothing. There should be interest and enough of the extract to give a taste of the book it comes from. Excerpts from books about children in other countries, about railways, birds, animals, etc., meant for children of this age are usually quite sensibly dealt with. But teachers should wonder more than many appear to how much this kind of work should be pre-packed, and whether there won't be an infinitely fresher taste and flavour in what they discover for themselves in children's books or in what springs naturally from books they are reading to their class, which gain sometimes by close study. I know this often means the additional work of making master sheets but these always increase children's interest and can be used subsequently with other classes. However, one should be careful not to let reading become automatically associated with questioning, especially not of a written kind. The approach at first should always be oral, aiming to increase interest through increased awareness. One wants primarily, as with poetry, to share the experience of the passage with the children. If one builds up the expectation through one's oral work of this kind of shared interest, it will then be possible sometimes to withdraw and leave a class to share a passage with its author, and write their answers on it with some involvement. As with any questioning on poetry, one will try to see that it is concerned only with what matters in the passage from the child's point of view, that it is directed to where his senses need alerting, his understanding exercising, if the whole is to come alive. Most important of all, one will only choose passages with life in them. Any written work that asks children to find out certain facts from a passage should be part of some kind of project, where there is a need for this information and the spur of interest in the subject matter.

A number of teachers have worked individually on principles close to these for some time and a few text-books are informed by them. Clearly more will be as more teachers grow independent, confident and discerning in their choice, and there is encouraging evidence that this is already happening. For instance, Rupert Hart-Davis's new series, *Enjoying English*, by Ronald Deadman, offers varied and interesting material based on unusual insight and understanding of children's concerns and reactions. There is an imaginative use of photographs throughout while the illustrations by Gloria Timbs are sensitive and individual, which is very rare in course books. The poetry is mostly modern, good in itself and immediately relevant for children, while children's own poetry and prose writing contributes valuably. Children are encouraged to talk as much as to write and the comprehension questioning is genuinely concerned to increase their understanding without this being limited to passages in isolation in a text-book. For example, following an interesting opening paragraph from a children's book about astronomy, children are asked what questions they would put to its author if they had the chance and also, if they had written the book themselves, what three questions they would ask a reader to make sure he had followed their meaning adequately. They are also asked what they feel when they look up at the sky at night. Such questioning demands close reading but not for the sake of the exercise. Rather it makes the passage open out like the sky itself and through the child's imagination seeks to arouse his curiosity and wonder.

The main deep objection remains to any approach to language, not through meaning and experience, but through categories for which language simply serves as illustration. It is not that one is against categories as such. Human reason has advanced at every stage through perceiving order of one kind or another in the material it has been concerned with. But all the significant advances have come from its working with imagination, with the faculty that sees beyond existing categories to the discovery of new ones. Emphasis on analysis and intellectual organising for its own sake has always been arid. It is

worth recalling Wordsworth's lines in *the Prelude*, where he
speaks of our analytic faculty as

> that false secondary power
> By which we multiply distinctions, then
> Deem that our puny boundaries are things
> That we perceive, and not that we have made.

Grammar consists entirely of mental categories erected by man
to *describe* his speech processes, not to fix them for eternity. They
are not there, like the properties of matter, to be discovered
and demonstrated, nor are they unchanging like much of the
reasoning of mathematics. Earlier grammarians have differed
in the number of parts of speech they discerned or thought
existed, while many modern ones reject this traditional mode
of classification altogether. Grammar is descriptive, not pre-
scriptive, although such is the weight of the conservative
educational establishment in this field that this is rarely
recognised. Grammar can tell us what is accepted usage now,
historical grammar can tell us what used to be accepted,
although not in a living context as literature does. It has no
power as a science to tell us what must be, only a very strong
social sanction to tell us what ought to be. But what rules it out
completely for children, in my view until thirteen or fourteen,
certainly for junior school children, is that *it offers no experience*. Ingenuity may make it quite entertaining and even colourful,
but children can in no way enter into it. The clever ones will
remember quite well some things they have been taught and
if they like their teacher and want to please him they will
certainly do their best. But it has no meaning for them outside
the dead world of the particular sentences they have been
dealing with. I watched a student recently, after she had carefully explained and given the children examples on the difference
between singular and plural forms of possession, point to
ladies' handbags in her example on the board, and ask how we
know that more than one lady is meant. A small boy called out
scornfully, 'One lady never carries two handbags.' One could
easily multiply such instances. Grammar at any level must
always be closely related to logic and meaning but for juniors
only meaning matters. And for juniors *language must represent
experience before it can have meaning*. Once it has meaning, there
is often point in making them consider the validity of that
meaning and if it is a question of intellectual validity, simple

N

logic will come in. More likely for juniors, action and emotion will be the main elements, which one aims that they should enter into and enjoy, not criticise in any way except by their own spontaneous comment.

Most junior school teachers will protest that they do not attempt to teach grammar, that they know better than to do that. Yet it appears depressingly often on timetables, students are frequently asked to 'take' seven and eight year olds for nouns and adjectives, and most text-books assume that there is some value, presumably for its own sake, in knowing the main parts of speech. Some have quite extensive exercises on these and, if the new course books continually coming out are any guide, the habit is growing rather than dying out. One published in 1965 has the following on *Past Participles*:

> Jean was *singing* a carol
> Peter was *painting* a picture

These sentences are in the *past continuous* tense, and the main verbs (in *italics*) are in the form of the *present participle*. The present participle of all verbs ends in *ing*.

Then it gives further examples of sentences with past participles telling children (since it is not content to start with the simple perfect tense) that the verbs in these sentences are in the past perfect tense – i.e. Vera *had* fallen – and follows this up with examples of verbs forming their past participles in different ways.

Have such compilers any idea how children's minds work? One can only quote Mrs. Marshall's classic instance of the zealous child running up to announce that 'Johnnie's putten "putten" when he should have putten "put"'. I sat at the back of a second-year class recently while a student dutifully took the children through some work on *was* and *were*, because their writing was so full of errors on this point, and then settled them down to further written answers. The boy next to me had finished and I asked him if he had been to the circus which had been talked about earlier. His dad had taken them, he said, but 'we wasn't able to get in'.

When children make errors of this kind because of what they hear around them all day and every day, the only way to help is to make English alive in the classroom in every conceivable way, spoken English even more than written. They should be encouraged towards fluency in expression, and particularly towards discovering pleasure in reading. Teachers could well encourage older juniors to be more aware of the idioms and slang they use, to debate their merits with them, to confront them, if possible, with relevant tape-recordings. Children always respond when they find that one takes an interest in their slang and knows at least some of their terms. Ten year olds gain from discussing how forceful these are or how long-winded, how changeable and to some extent how limiting. There is need for something more perceptive and positive in teachers' attitudes than a more or less even level of disapproval. We may have got rid to some extent of the two nations but the two languages, one for home, one for school, remains a deep-rooted source of uneasiness in expression. Many teachers and training college students would probably admit that their own attitudes towards what is good or bad English have been affected by this. To take the excerpt from *Huckleberry Finn* quoted earlier, I remember a parent who was herself a teacher telling me that she was surprised this should have been set for examination purposes in English Literature, since one could hardly say, could one, that it was written in good English. This is true, in that it is in good *American* English, but people like this would obviously be as insensitive to natural idiomatic ease in a Yorkshire or Somerset Huck. If awareness of local forms, interest in regional metaphors, discussion of them with children, were part of the natural background of English work for juniors, they would be far better equipped than many are to face the uprooting that going on to secondary school often is. Often there should be more cause for pride than uneasiness. A regional form like *anyroad*, for instance, is an exact metaphorical parallel to *anyway*; historical accident only led to one's becoming standard rather than the other. One should look closely at one's prejudices about slang terms and colloquial usages and realise how predominantly social they are, although one may rationalise them to oneself as disapproval of inexactness or some other objective defect of the particular form. This is especially true if one has climbed a social rung or two through education.

Paradoxically, while I am convinced that children need far less grammar (or pseudo-grammar) than they get, I think most teachers could do with more, with some active post 'O' level consideration of it but in a full context of language, meaning and style. Our schools offer nothing on this nor do many training colleges, although I am certain all should. Then many teachers would feel more at ease in their own language than they do, free to take liberties with it, free to follow their sensible instincts in expression, instead of hearkening always to the negative voice of 'O' level days. Ending sentences with prepositions, for instance. This is a genuine English idiom of long standing, found frequently in all writers of natural prose, but it is not a possible construction in Latin, which works through case endings and not, as English does, through word order. The long classical domination of our education system was a very mixed blessing, for two languages could not be more different than English and Latin. Yet for many years educated people have tried to make Latin a touchstone for English (often succeeding best with those who know little or no Latin) and there are still teachers and students and training college lecturers who think it is better to write *the age in which I live*, for instance, than *the age I live in*. I am not concerned with what one would 'correct' in junior children's writing, but with one's own prejudices about language. I am sure no junior teacher would try to make children write unnaturally here, but I suspect that many hold their hands simply through concession to their tender age and think that later on things will have to be different. This suspicion of the naturally idiomatic in writing is strangely deep-rooted. I am not saying it is better the other way about, better to write *the age I live in*, rather than *the age in which I live*. Both are equally acceptable English constructions, both, if one accepts the particular as instance of a general habit, indicate something about the nature of the writer. For it usually depends on circumstances and one's natural instincts which is better, because more natural, for oneself. But over a long period of time an educational establishment, by its nature more at home with the more formal constructions, has inculcated a belief that these are 'right', the others acceptable only in speech and 'wrong' in writing. Teachers' attitudes to language are very important, because in using language and developing their capacities whether in speech or writing children need from their teacher what a good home offers: security and ease and some love. Any divorce or separation between one's deeper instincts and one's surface code, any insincerity or lack of integration in one's own attitudes to language, affect those brought up in these surroundings.

Basically confident especially over priorities teachers can decide for themselves and their particular class what few grammatical concepts are necessary, which means *what they cannot do without* if they are to be able to talk sensibly about their writing. These concepts together with our usual terms for signifying them can be naturally introduced in the course of looking at some writing – a group description, for example, of a picture or an object, or an individual one in a context of practical concern to help the child to make his expression adequate to his intention. The writer will be aiming, in whatever situation he is describing, to make readers feel as if they were actually there. In discussing how well this has been done, one will need to talk about certain *sentences*, whether this one does not go on too long, whether the fact that several begin in the same way is not a hindrance, whether the *verbs* John chose to describe what the rocks felt like to his feet were the best ones, whether one could not find a more interesting or exact *noun* for something he has named. Proper nouns they are always interested in because these name something special. Third- and fourth-year children can see how *pronouns* help us to avoid clumsy repetition but only simple personal ones are ever in question by name. Awareness of relative pronouns will be entirely practical and should arise only when children are considering ways of combining statements and eliminating repetitive *ands*. The only syntactical concept besides that of a sentence that one needs to speak of to children is the *subject*: what John was talking about. But there is no question of demonstration or illustration. It is simply that if one chooses to use these terms, and not all teachers will think it necessary, children will become accustomed to hear them accurately used in discussing writing, the main aim always being *to help them write better*. Those who are more able to grasp concepts of this kind than the average will be able to relate this work to punctuation, where they will also be concerned with sentences. They will not be able to tell you what a *sentence* is or a *verb*; but let any teacher who thinks this an easy task try definition for himself. Nor will children be able to pick out the nouns, verbs and adjectives in sentences, which is the exciting reward of formal grammar teaching at this stage. But a certain realisation of the concepts will nevertheless have been implanted in the *same few children*, ten per cent at most, I would say, who actually grasp anything adequate from formal instruction. In correcting children's work one will never cross out anything unless one can make them understand what is wrong or what one objects to and why. This is almost always possible and better done in terms of style and usage. 'We usually say ....' or 'Wouldn't it be better if .... or neater if .... or be more forceful ....'

Once they feel really at home in their own language, teachers can concentrate on giving children the best up-bringing that they can. They will allow for and respect individuality, give freedom but ensure that there is an underlying sense of order and direction. The best qualities in junior school children's writing, its springing alive quality, its vivid directness and simplicity, its closeness to speech and to experience, they will recognise not as childish qualities only, but of the essence of good English writing from Chaucer onwards. The prime business of all language work should be to draw forth these qualities where they are still only latent, and develop and strengthen them in every way.

Having jettisoned the categories of grammar as abstract and irrelevant, and the paraphernalia of most text-books: opposites, synonyms, 'comprehension', etc., as false and contrary to children's natural development, teachers can find order unobtrusively enough in categories of experience. I mean the senses and the natural order of things in the world outside our own minds. Thus based, language work is a natural part of all other work, in that it is vitally concerned with extending children's experience and with awakening them to it, and also with all their varied learning from it. However, since like any approach in teaching it can be misused, it is worth making clear that this is no kind of sensationalist doctrine. Language work should be concerned with the senses not because any and every experience is valuable, nor because stimulation is valuable for its own sake, but because only if children's senses are alert will they come close to that 'real knowledge of things' which alone can make the language of the average child keen and exact.

In devising language work related to the senses, there is no need for children to be actively conscious of the different sources of their impressions. After all, these usually come to us simultaneously and it is artificial to separate. One must give them opportunities to look, to listen, to touch, to smell, and then, after talk, to record the experience in words in an atmosphere of fidelity to what is there, not of any forced excitement. Language is only one of the ways of responding to and completing our experience, and specialist teachers of English need constantly to guard against their inner conviction that it is the most important. Photographs, film, pictures, tape-recordings of sounds, objects with strong associations for children, these are all means of creating the kind of concentration that one wants, as are imagining oneself in a place or mood or situation, or

engaged in some kind of sharply defined physical activity. As
the last chapter sought to make clear, this work will often be
closely related to their more extended personal writing, especially in the area of experience being explored. Quite often,
though, it will be independent, expressive and enjoyable in itself, or spring from work in art or nature study or music. BBC
Series like the recent *Living Language* and *Listening and Writing*
often have good ideas for close work connected with the poems
and stories to be broadcast, and so has James Britton in the
teachers' books of his series, *Oxford Books of Stories for Juniors*.
As long as one keeps alive all the time the sense of exploration
and the possibility of discovery, a particular plan of work does
not matter, or, rather, is for individual teachers to decide.

Young children in their first year in the junior school need
plenty of practice in the valid objective categories of the outside
world that adults take for granted: the seasons, the months of
the year, awareness of left and right, the idea of past, present
and future *in experience*. The latter does not stretch with much
accuracy for young children beyond today, yesterday and to-
morrow. One knows how tremendously old children think most
of us are and how complicated things become if we try too early
to teach them how the Western world dates time backwards
from the time of Christ. Time shows itself in language, of course,
through tense but it is a waste of time to attempt formal teaching, as many books do, with practice in changing tense in
sentences made up for the occasion and added information on
the differences between strong and weak verbs. One can only
help children individually through their own written work,
pointing out or trying to draw from them what we usually say,
to help them see where they have gone wrong. Older children
can sometimes consider a passage that they have written, or
one with relevance and interest that one has made up, to see
how continuous tenses alter the effect. There is no point in
trying to make them know these *by name*. But they can be
aware in experience of the difference in effect between them
in use: between *I went*, for instance, and *I was going*; or 'Last
week, John *read* another exciting adventure story' and 'John
was reading an exciting story when suddenly . . .' Illustration,
though, should always spring from the need for it in their own
writing and as far as possible this should be the basis of the
illustration, so that one can draw from them the best tense for
the situation. It is well worth the work involved sometimes to
present excerpts, or any other illustration from children's

writing, not on the board but for individual consideration on sheets run off a Banda. For as with passages for comprehension a class is always more interested and becomes much more involved.

There are certain fundamental aspects of language valid in society as a whole outside the pages of an English course book, and young junior children need help and simple practice with these. For instance, alphabetical order itself, and its application when they need to look things up; how we show that we are asking questions, making a statement negative or plural; the simple fundamentals of punctuation. Many text-books for first and second years do produce good simple material here, but I still think that it is better for a teacher to use these only for ideas and suggestions, rather than have class copies, for children will take any text-book as equally valid throughout, and once a class has a set there is always the temptation to rely on it far more than one had intended.

Far and away the most important aspects of English in the eyes of most adults, aspects which tend to count most in any assessment of quality in writing, are punctuation and spelling. Many teachers realise, however, that too much stress on these prevents many children from writing fluently and that the quality of a child's spelling in particular is a poor indication of the essential quality of his writing. If children enjoy writing and take some pride in their work they will want to reach an acceptable standard. It remains to consider how best and most practically to help them here.

Punctuation for adults is partly an expression of style and so to some extent individual rather than rigidly fixed. Someone who tends to use semicolons and colons will write quite differently from someone who never does. People who are fond of exclamation marks or make a liberal use of dashes reveal something of themselves. Some people carefully punctuate all adjectives in a series, while others do not. But fundamentally punctuation is concerned with syntax, with the shape of our thought as expressed in sentences, and in clauses and phrases within these. It speeds up communication by revealing this quickly to the reader. For junior children, as with grammatical concepts, punctuation is best approached functionally, according to what they need, which means what they cannot do without. Occasion must be found for conscious application, thought and understanding and, unlike grammar, for practice in interesting contexts. Full stops and capital letters are all they need at the start of the first year, with commas and question marks fairly quickly following these. The first stages in learning should always be reinforced visually in the classroom, just as new stages in number are. Interest in handwriting can reinforce awareness of the various different forms involved in capitals, which can then head lists of words beginning with the difficult ones that are relevant in some other context. A few new sentences can be added every day to a class story or one can give children interesting openings to sentences and ask them to complete these. They can be given two sentences without punctuation and asked to divide them, or sentences with proper names unmarked by capitals and asked to supply these. One can do some work on *necessary* abbreviations. Some text-books give interesting simple material here from which one can get ideas, but there is no need for the children to have a book. Short but regular practice is valuable, with opportunities for children to supply what is wanted on the board, as well as write for themselves.

Commas are much more difficult than full stops for adults to handle logically and consistently, and few do so. Like adults most children tend to use commas where they need full stops, however well they are grounded in these, and one has to accept this, while at the same time giving them help and practice over using commas to separate nouns or phrases in a series, which is where they mostly need them. As well as asking them to supply the commas in such sentences as: 'Mary asked Jean Paul and Jennifer to her party' or 'John bought apples pears bananas and a pineapple at the greengrocer's', one needs from time to time to make children think objectively about what they are doing. Where would they put a comma in certain sentences and why? What effect do commas have on meaning? What difference does it make to have a comma here instead of there? The kind of exercise Brian Jackson gives in the second volume of his *Good English Prose* is what I have in mind:

> If we put a comma in the sentence:
>   'The sun slanted on the still brown water' and change it to —
>   'The sun slanted on the still, brown water' — would that change the meaning at all?

The idea of a question is not difficult to convey especially if one gives children some answers and asks them to decide what questions led to them. They enjoy coming out and asking the class a question of a general knowledge kind, the only stipulation being that whoever asks the question must know the answer. These questions can be written on the board so that children have practice in forming the question mark. They will still often fail in their own writing to mark the fact that they have asked a question but some will begin to take a pride in punctuating well. Apostrophes and inverted commas (or speech marks, if one prefers that term for children) should not be taught until one is sure a class is ready for them, which means their being reasonably competent for their level in handling commas, full-stops and question marks. There will always be unevenness in readiness, some children being much ahead of others, but generally one would expect to need these new punctuation marks during the third year. It is helpful to separate the use of apostrophes to show omission as in *can't*, or *mustn't*, from their use to mark possession, and to allow some time to pass before one introduces the second usage. Children can be asked to collect instances of omissions to add to lists on display in class but without any suggestion that the full form is the right one, the other to be avoided. The apostrophe to show possession can be very simply introduced and illustrated for singular nouns, but plurals are difficult and not worth much time being spent on them at this stage. Children will continue in practice to be careless in their use of apostrophes generally, and there is little point in worrying about this. They need practice in recognising which words are actually spoken in conversation as a basis for using inverted commas and, although this is difficult, I think it is probably wise to make clear from the outset that these are always used in conjunction with some other punctuation mark. We often ask questions in converstation and so need a question mark before we are ready to close our speech marks. If we haven't asked a question, we usually have a comma before closing them and completing our sentence with *said Mary* or *replied John*. Comparatively few children will remember to use these additional punctuation marks when writing but some are helped by the initial link and begin to think of both together.

Some kind of punctuation corner works well, provided that the children are genuinely interested in writing and eager for their presentation to be of a high standard. With top juniors a simple project on printing can help to reinforce awareness of certain aspects of punctuation. The main need, though, is for regular short periods of objective practice throughout a child's time in the junior school but no formal stress when he is writing creatively. Here one can help children when going through their writing with them individually and one's tone and attitude can bring out that punctuation is a helpful part of our expression. Children can be asked to look at their own work sometimes, from the point of view of an interested reader who needs help, which will probably mean supplying additional punctuation or amending what is there.

There is no need to say much about the peculiar difficulties of English spelling, except that there is a quite good historical reason for many of them, usually connected with preserving an existing pronunciation, and that standardisation in any full sense did not take place until the time of Dr. Johnson. The important thing with children is not to set too great store by correctness, not even *unconsciously*, and also to realise that because one teaches one is more aware of spelling mistakes than most adults. One tends to look for them. Yet proficiency in spelling is not a criterion of quality in writing. Yeats and Scott Fitzgerald, to name only two acknowledged writers in this connection, were both weak spellers. Generally, though, the child who is weak tends to be less good all round simply because weakness in spelling is one sign of a weak or careless visual memory and sometimes, although far from always, of a lack of interest in reading. Many intelligent children continue to produce highly bizarre spellings right through the junior school and little is gained by worrying over this. Others with more even, more dispersed, more fundamental weaknesses will never find any kind of fluency in writing if one hammers away at spelling. It is also educationally of little value to bring together, as so many remedial exercises do, words that tend to be confused, like *their* and *there*, etc. Brief steady practice in an atmosphere of interest in and concern about words is what one must offer, with every opportunity particularly in the first and second years to *look* at words, in lists of connected ones compiled in the classroom, in labelling of every kind, in spelling bees or other forms of simple entertaining competition. Children enjoy having a nature table or corner. A word corner is well worth developing with groups taking turns to run it. Apart from lists of words relevant to other work of all kinds, *Words We Shall Need*, for a project, for instance, or *Words We Have Learnt*, this is the place for lists of spelling oddities: the words beginning with *kn* or *gn* for instance, simple ones like *knock*, *knee*, *know*, rarer ones like *gnat*, *gnaw*, *gnome*, words beginning with *wh*, or a group like *dough*, *cough, rough, bough,* with parallel spellings but quite different pronunciations.

Other words with silent letters like *psalm* and *pneumonia* can be collected and children encouraged to find new ones for the class or group list. They can also work in groups to compile lists of ordinary words that they often misspell and then can give these as a test to the rest of the class. A few endings that show form can be concentrated on and lists compiled. For junior children the most useful here, because the most often misspelled, are probably *ful,* in adjectives like *beautiful,* (not *full*), *ly* (not *ley*) for adverbs and *ed* for the ordinary past tense of weak verbs: *opened, happened* (not opend, happend). Children enjoy demonstrating adverbs as in the game 'In the manner of the word' and this can help fix the *ly* formation. If a class is keen and one is sure that they are sufficiently advanced to be helped, not confused, one can extend this approach to groups of words with variant forms of a similar ending. For instance, we have large numbers of agent nouns, names for people who do things of one kind or another, which end sometimes in *or* as in *sailor, author,* sometimes in *er* as in *teacher, grocer.* Historically this is because the borrowings that came to us through Norman French adapted the French *eur* ending as *er,* whereas later borrowings direct from Latin came in with *or.* There is a small group in *ar* like *beggar* or *pedlar,* but these are mostly coinages from existing English words. Naturally one would not tell children this, unless a particularly good top form, but one can collect groups of these words, give children the stem only and let them complete them, using dictionaries if necessary. The same can apply to nouns ending in *tion* or *sion,* as in *attention* say, and *extension,* and adjectives in *ious* and *eous: glorious,* for instance, but *gorgeous.* Children frequently write *os* so it is quite helpful to establish that this is never used for an anglicised word. Handling the words as a group helps give an underlying sense of unity, but makes able children alert to the surface variations. And of course much of the difficulty of English spelling comes from the fact that there are far more of these than in other European languages. It is important to realise, though, that this kind of approach only confuses some children.

Some top classes are helped by and interested in simple work on prefixes, which if reinforced visually through word lists can help spelling as well as understanding of language. *Dis/appeared* for instance, but *dis/satisfied, mis/spell,* but *mis/call* or *mis/aim:* examples of this kind make it easy to decide whether it is one *s* or two, not simply a matter of guesswork. If children know that *tele* means *far* in Greek, it becomes interesting discovering how that meaning comes in to words like *television, telephone, telegraph.* Simple examples of prefixes for number, such as *triangle, triplets, tricycle,* for three, *bicycle* or *bifocal* or *bigamy,* for two, and *uniform, universe, unity,* for one, can be explored but teachers must be ready to do some homework here, for children will quickly produce what seem like instances and one may be unable to show why they are not. But one can make clear from the beginning that one is not infallible, that one is working with them finding out and that dictionaries are fascinating books to browse in sometimes. Another group of prefixes one may like to look at, particularly since many tests ask children for words of opposite meaning, are the different ones used to show this: *un* in *unkind,* say, or *unpleasant, in* in *inadequate* or *inaccurate* and then perhaps a few examples like *impossible* and *impolite* to show that the *in* has in usage often been adapted to the word following it, usually with a view to helping pronunciation. Variants such as *illegible* and *irreparable* can well be left unless one has a class that is obviously interested. *Dis* and *mis* have already been mentioned and one can add *anti* if one likes. If a teacher is interested himself, he can do much to help children at an impressionable age to make sense of difficulties where otherwise they might give up, especially when they hear adults talk of spelling as if it were something mysterious and arbitrary which one is born either good or bad at. English spelling is certainly exasperating but many of its vagaries can be accounted for, even to ten and eleven year olds, who often have an appetite for minor detail. But there must always be some practical effort from the child. Individual spelling books are an excellent idea provided that they are spurs not props. Children using these sometimes come and ask how to spell words that they are making no effort at all to spell for themselves. There needs to be some sort of questing spirit here as much as elsewhere. However, all this practical work on spelling should only be incidental to the more creative purpose of letting children constantly 'practise' their spelling in writing. Miracles won't happen but, in the kind of atmosphere I have been describing, some progress probably will.

Most teachers give some time at different stages in the junior school to letter writing. Adults expect correct 'instruction' here and teachers feel that for once they have a valid framework, since letters of a kind are probably the only personal writing ninety-nine per cent of children will continue to practise when they grow up. This is not an abstract category nor one that teachers have made up. Yet it is often handled as if it were.

Children need to be taught how to set out a letter and address an envelope. This last is easily enough done practically. Children enjoy addressing an actual envelope – they can be asked to bring one from home – and then putting an ingeniously forged stamp upon it. Better still, provided one can find a genuine occasion, they can post a real letter.

First, though, a child needs a simple model on the board and practice in some context that calls for a letter. It might seem unnecessary to say anything about the model, if some text-books did not produce such questionable ones and students show such uncertainty in their own practice, the result presumably of the wrong sort of 'instruction' at school. Some text-books are straightforward and sensible. Some must bring in here, as everywhere else, the pointless 'unravel-the-mystery' approach. A recent widely used book gives a good model of a likely letter by a boy to his parents from his uncle's farm. Then in case simple imitation should be too easy the child must be made to work something out. So the parts of the letter are numbered and set out on a blank sheet, and the possible answers all jumbled up for him to puzzle over (see opposite page). If a child who could write, but who had never seen a letter of any kind, were told to give his parents news of himself on holiday, he would never produce this travesty of simple common sense. He would not sign his name until he had written his message. An adult is left with a dancing picture of the letter, because the eye has to run back and forth among the sentences and then up and down the numbers. At eight years old, reading is a tentative but cumulative process, the eye moving from one sentence to the next, not hopping about grasshopper fashion. Children learn by doing, certainly, but the doing must be relevant and meaningful. For instance, if you want a child to look up Canadian lumberjacks in the encyclopedia, you don't suggest it would be fun to try the Z's first, instead of the C's or L's. This seems so obvious as to be insulting teachers to say it, yet much text-book work in English is shored up by such extra-ordinary anti-educational thinking.

What letters do children write at eight? And at later stages in the junior school? If one is honest, the answer is not many and those they do write are invariably thrust upon them by adults. It is worth talking about why people write letters, why

He signed his name here.

He wrote his ending here.

John wrote his address here.

He greeted his parents here.

He put the date here.

Here he wrote all that he wanted to tell his parents.

their mothers and fathers like to hear from them in any kind of separation and what kind of things they are interested in hearing. Some books suggest a letter to a friend or cousin asking him or her to stay and again it helps to talk about the essentials of such a letter and the kind of news that might interest. For instance, what would they talk about if they could meet the friend or cousin, instead of having to write?

Thank you letters are inflicted on most children, especially after Christmas, or a birthday. They are not easy for grown-ups so one should try to help children by making them imagine that they really have received something they particularly long for. Perhaps it is their birthday, they have had presents from the family and lots of cards; then mid-morning the postman comes again in a van, with a large and bulky parcel. It can follow quite naturally from their response to this that they write a letter to thank whoever has sent the present. Visits in connection with a project provide the occasion for writing to thank whoever is involved. Children should not be helped too much in this sort of situation. One sees sets of letters with obviously dictated sentences common to all standing out rather awkwardly among their individual revelations. This underlines the need for talk first, so that children recall what happened, what they enjoyed and the trouble that other people probably took on their behalf.

Projects often provide the best incentive for children to write letters. Teachers sometimes also make a kind of project out of letter writing. If one can arrange for a local postman to come and talk, this arouses much interest. If they have contacts with a school in a different part of the country, they can put their class in touch with one there. Group letters at first are best, I think, because then one can discuss with the groups what someone who does not know their area would be most interested in learning about it, and how most accurately to describe it. Objective information is a better starting point, usually, than the rather artificial situation of an individual letter to an unknown recipient. Then, after one or two group letters between classes in schools far apart or very different in environment, those children who want to start a personal correspondence can be put in touch. Students are often keen to try something like this between each other's classes on teaching practice, but there must be a significant difference in environment between the schools so that each side has a genuine curiosity about the other, and this is unlikely in adjacent suburbs. I had a student who had spent some years in Southern Rhodesia, who put the children of her English class in touch with a class there, linking the work with a project about the country. The children were most enthusiastic about this, the only irritation being the time-lag between letters. Some geography departments in training colleges are now arranging for students to be put in touch with schools in other countries, which leads naturally to letter writing as a means of discovering about each other's way of life. Some classes have written letters to children's hospitals or children's wards in hospitals, and the same kind of approach seems best here: initial group letters following the children's discussing what would be of most interest to someone forced to spend a long time in bed. Individual correspondence can follow where there is a genuine wish for it.

Much of one's work in language lessons is directed to helping children constructively with technique. This may well mean trying to eliminate certain weaknesses but one can still approach this in a positive way. How can we make this clearer, neater, more interesting? Children who are already enthusiastic about writing are very ready to discuss passages from this point of view, provided that the examples are convincing and *worth improving*. It helps first for a teacher to think a little about a class's writing as a whole, to see what the main weaknesses seem to be: poor vocabulary, overworking unexpressive words like *get* and *did*, stringing statements monotonously together with *and*, writing very brief sentences that are dull in their effect. I would not use particular instances here unless I was sure that the writer as well as the class would profit. This probably only happens if the essential quality of the writing is worth much praise yet there is some comparatively minor clumsiness in technique. It is usually better to make up an interesting passage, as interesting anyway as one can make it, allowing for its having to illustrate some weakness. One must always be careful not to impose one's own stylistic dogmas but draw from the children what they think is wrong or inadequate in the passage and discuss the effect of this with them. There is little value in simply making *get* a forbidden word if this leads to the more intelligent and literary starting to produce rather pompous alternatives, people 'alighting' from their trains, for instance, or 'boarding' them, instead of getting on and off.

In encouraging children to enjoy language work, everything in the end comes back to the teacher and his convictions about language, as well as his feeling for it. According to the author of the text-book whose model letter I quoted, the great advantage of using such a book is that 'this self-help method . . .' makes 'pupils work far more correctly than ever before', and a teacher's time 'is not swallowed up by masses of unprofitable corrections: *he is freed to concentrate on more creative matters*'. (My italics.) Unhappily this book and many like it show a complete unawareness of what creativity is in children or teachers. Certainly let teachers be given every help to free them for 'their true creative function', but let them consider deeply what this is and whether the average text-book can give access to it. Correct grammar, spelling and punctuation, neat and varied sentences, no muddling up of *their* and *there*, *who's* and *whose*, *were* and *where*, do teachers in their hearts consider these are the controlling forces behind good writing at this level? Rather is one not aware in every aspect of language work of the child's

o

growing individuality, his growing knowledge of the world, of people, of himself, and of the varying pressure of his desire to express this in words? To help creatively here, teachers need imagination, knowledge and understanding, and above all a genuine personal feeling for language as a medium. They need to sense not only its power but also its limitations. It is something to be wrestled with, shaped, enjoyed, and if they take pleasure in this process their class will also. It is in giving children this pleasure and opportunity for growth as actively in language work as in story, poetry or playmaking that teachers seem to me to exercise their 'true creative function'.

7

PROJECTS

PROJECTS of one kind or another lie at the heart of junior
school work and are the source of its vitality. In the hands of
really good teachers, the best ones fuse the practical and the
imaginative and create a new whole for children from diverse
aspects of experience and knowledge. This has its own reality
for them while the project lasts and its memory usually remains
when surrounding routine lessons have faded. The knowledge
they gain from it derives from their experience. One knows
that children who have enjoyed work of this kind will, at the
moment, be lucky to meet anything very like it again in their
secondary education. For its approach is quite different from
the separate subject disciplines of grammar schools and the
diluted version of this favoured for status purposes by many
secondary modern ones. One hopes that the present change-
over to a comprehensive system will alter this and there is some
evidence to suggest that it may. The Newsom Report urged
the need for a much greater sense of relatedness in secondary
schools, particularly between the substance of the curriculum
and the true nature of pupils' interests and probable future
lives. The comprehensive system is rooted in a belief in wholeness, which at the moment means primarily social wholeness.
However, there is an underlying awareness that this is only
part of the issue and that other kinds of integration are equally
vital, between different parts of the curriculum, and between
intellect and feeling in response to the experience that these
offer. In training colleges there is increasing concern that
students should be motivated at a much deeper and more
individual level than the immediate vocational one of getting
a certificate, and some recognition that an answer may lie in
learning from the approach of the best junior schools. Different
kinds of knowledge need to be felt as parts of a significant whole
by students as much as by children. This is no argument against
intellect but one for a much more creative and imaginative
application of it. Given some intellectual excitement, intellectual
discipline will follow. But of course the excitement must be felt
by the teacher before it can be conveyed to the taught.

It is up to junior school teachers to produce increasing and valid evidence that project work is valuable, which means a readiness to assess the average project, to see how far it provides this integrating of genuine experience. There is not much point in undertaking a project solely because one feels one should, as happens sometimes with students on teaching practice. On the other hand, the habit of thinking actively in terms of possible explorations of an idea or theme probably increases the teacher's own creativity. It is worth considering what makes for fruitfulness here, what will produce an eager response. One sees work on such subjects as the *Post Office* or *Local Government* that is quite sound but is certainly engendering no excitement. And this is hardly surprising, for although the children working on these subjects will have discovered some useful facts, their imaginations are not stirred, though of course visits from a local policeman or to a local post-office help enormously. Usually, though, it is not easy for children to *live* in the subject, for it offers little imaginative experience to bring the facts to life. There are no good stories that I know with the world of the Post Office or Local Government as a background and the BBC's *Swizzlewick* should be warning enough to anyone who thought, however fleetingly, of playmaking. One cannot conceive children writing in a personal way about such subjects as these although the former provides a valid situation for practising the external techniques of letter writing. There is, too, W. H. Auden's fine poem, *Night Mail*, already quoted.

I still have a vivid recollection from my school days of seeing the original documentary film made before the war and before projects were thought of, with Auden's words and Benjamin Britten's music. This immediately brings a sense of adventure into what ordinarily seems humdrum and gives children some awareness of how necessary processes affect people's lives. If teachers genuinely feel something of this adventure themselves and can find ways to bring it out, then subjects like *Transport* or *Communications* or, of course, *The Post Office* can have considerable interest and variety for children. One can see, although to a rather lesser extent, the potentialities of *Oil*. On the whole, though, subjects of this kind deal with predominantly social fact in an increasingly complex and in many ways increasingly impersonal society. Children need a fullness of emotional content before such subjects come alive for them and it is only through the insight and imagination of teachers in themselves conceiving a subject in human as well as factual terms that this can happen.

Good documentary film as well as charts and diagrams, stories as well as facts, poetry, a sense of the subject's history, its existence in time as well as place, these are the ways in which it can be enriched.

A project on *Coal*, for instance, could easily be dealt with in a predominantly impersonal and factual way, and the National Coal Board's P R O department is well able to provide charts, statistics, and other helpful data, including photographs of modern housing for miners. They also have photographs of miners working underground and these make a more immediate and deeper impact on children than the charts and surface photographs. They respond with much feeling, also, to the pictures of pit ponies and to the factual and human details about their underground life: that there are still about 4,000, for instance, while in 1917 there were eleven times as many; that in deep mines their health would not stand the change of temperature if they were brought to the surface when not working; that miners have great affection for their ponies and rarely ill-treat them. One story is told in the Midlands of a young driver on a stretcher after an accident remembering to ask that his pony should have a driver he liked; another of two Northumberland miners who died in a gallant but unsuccessful effort to save their pony from being killed by poisonous mine gas. In addition to photographs and illustrated booklets, the Coal Board will also supply film and the head of their Public Relations Department himself visits junior schools to talk to children.

Whatever form the children's individual and group work may take, given this kind of detail, they will begin to be able to enter into it, the facts will be rooted in some awareness of a way of life. Then one can let literature reinforce and extend this awareness. There is no need to restrict oneself here to books otherwise suitable for children. No one would suggest reading extensively from George Orwell to children but he had a powerfully documentary imagination that holds children's interest provided that they are already concerned with his subject. For instance, in the second chapter of *The Road to Wigan Pier*, reprinted as *Down the Mine* in the Penguin edition of his *Selected Essays*, he describes the descent:

You get into the cage, which is a steel box about as wide as a telephone box and two or three times as long. It holds ten men, but they pack like pilchards in a tin, and a tall man (which Orwell was) cannot stand upright. The steel door shuts upon you, and somebody working the winding gear above you drops you into the void. You have the usual momentary qualm in your belly and a bursting sensation in your ears, but not much sensation of movement till you get near the bottom, when the cage comes down so abruptly that you could swear it is going up again. In the middle of the run the cage probably touches sixty miles an hour; in some of the deeper mines it touches even more. When you crawl out at the bottom you are perhaps four hundred yards under ground. That is to say you have a tolerable-sized mountain on top of you; hundreds of yards of solid rock, bones of extinct beasts, subsoil, flints, roots of growing things, green grass, and cows grazing on it – all this suspended over your head and held back only by wooden props as thick as the calf of your leg. But because of the speed at which the cage has brought you down, and the complete blackness through which you have travelled, you hardly feel yourself deeper down than you would at the bottom of the Piccadilly Tube.

Apart from the exceptional vividness of this, Orwell is showing in the latter half just that power encouraged by good project work, exact awareness of physical detail and the same exactness of imaginative awareness of what he cannot see but knows to be above him. It is well worth reading the rest of his description, when he discovers that to reach the coal face he has to walk as far as from London Bridge to Oxford Circus without being able, save very rarely, to stand upright.

Orwell wrote this in the thirties but if one wants more modern testimony one can read an excerpt from a book called *Weekend in Dinlock*, also available in Penguin, by the American writer, Clancy Sigal, and discover no really fundamental change. Sigal's walk to the pit face was deliberately made even more painful than it would have been because he was given boots that were too small for him by a surface official who, as he acknowledges, resented his brief reporter's intrusion into their permanent underground world.

One may want children to know something of earlier mining conditions and here Jonathan Cape's excellent *Jackdaw* series of collections of contemporary documents are very helpful. Number 7 on *Shaftesbury and the Working Children* provides moving evidence in facts and pictures from that time of what children had to endure, particularly the utter loneliness of some of the jobs they had to spend twelve or fourteen hours a day doing. Its being such distance from their own world makes it hard for modern children to feel the reality of this and that children like themselves actually experienced it. They would come closer to doing so if, instead of the other excerpts I have suggested, one chose to link with the project regular reading aloud of Frederick Grice's *Bonnie Pit Laddie*, which is published by Oxford University Press and attractively illustrated by Brian Wildsmith. This evokes strikingly the life of a Durham mining village sixty years ago, tells a good story and is unusually perceptive in its treatment of relationships within the family. One quickly realises how a passage like the following would add to children's emotional experience of the miners' way of life. It would bring them nearer to understanding how the child trappers of the Victorian period felt, as well as conscious in a fuller way of miners' affection for their ponies: (The hero, aged fourteen, is setting off for his first day underground.)

It was a bright cold morning when he left for his first shift. The starlings were whistling on the roofs of the colliery houses when he set out, and he never forgot the clear penetrating sound of their calls as he walked down the street. He felt awkward in his first pit clothes, in the jacket that was far too big for him, and the heavy new-studded boots that clattered on the uneven pavements. His white bait-poke was slung around his left shoulder, and his jacket pocket bulged with his pit bottle. He felt that everyone was looking at him as he trudged with Kit past the depots, along the line, across the pit yard, and into the lamp-cabin.

. . . All the men who were to go down the pit on this shift were gathered together at the pithead. As they waited for the cage they seemed to Dick to grow quiet. There was plenty of noise all round them — the turning of the pulley wheels, the knocking and bumping of machinery, the upward and downward thrusting of the pumps, and the far-away sound of the rapper stopping or releasing the unseen cages; but the men seemed to be composing themselves for the quietness of the mine. At last it was their turn to ride, and Dick watched the rope slipping upward, the cage chains appear, and then the cage itself. As the men entered the cage they sat down on their 'unkers'; they believed they could better take the shock of any unexpected bump or jolt if they were crouching. When they were all in, the gates closed with a clang, and the cage was rapped away. The pulleys began to spin, the cage fell at first gently then rapidly until the sides of the shaft down which it slid were all one blur, and Dick's stomach rose. He had the strange sensation of going not down, but up; but before he had time to realise fully what was happening to him, the cage had stopped, the doors were flung open, and he was at the bottom of the shaft. He had entered his new world.

He had to work first as a trapper, and all he had to do was to stay by a wooden door that closed one of the galleries, to open it for any traffic that might want to pass, and close it after it had gone through. It was not an exciting task, but someone had to do it, for on the correct opening and shutting of the trap-door depended the primitive ventilation system of the pit.

But it was a lonely job. He had to sit by himself, with no light except the faint gleam of his pit-lamp, for long silent hours when the traffic was slack; and sitting there, he had strange fancies. Sometimes he thought he saw figures coming towards him out of the darkness, and he had to take up his lamp and shine it into the shadows to reassure himself that there was nothing. All the features of this new strange world impressed themselves upon him – the uneven slope of the wagon-way, the pools of muddy water between the short sleepers, the black and brilliant sides of the seam.

His first day seemed endless. When he felt that half of the shift was over, he ate his bait and drank some of the cold tea his mother had put in his pit bottle; but when he asked the time he found that only a quarter of the shift had passed. By the time he came to the end of his first day he was aching with hunger, and as he stepped out of the cage the upper world seemed something he had not seen for a year.

Dick worked as a trapper for a month. Then another boy came to take his place, and Dick, to his great joy, was sent to help Mr. Turnbull who was in charge of the pit-ponies. Alec Turnbull was as fine a master as the boy could have wished for, a proud conscientious man who took great pains with his work, and kept his stables as clean as his own house.

'Because my ponies are underground,' he would say, 'that's no reason why they shouldn't be looked after properly. This is how I look at it, Dick – when ponies never see the light of day they deserve the best and nothing but the best, and that's what I try to give them.'

As a climax in this story there is a vivid description of a pit disaster which, although it ends with a rescue largely due to the hero's courage and level-headedness, nevertheless brings home to children something of the constant sense of danger present in a mine. This brings children quite close to understanding the state of mind of a ten-year-old miner's daughter, quoted in a recent report on mining accidents, whose recurrent dream is of her father's being trapped and killed. They will be able to appreciate and understand, in these circumstances of unusual interest and awareness, a poem like George Barker's *Miners Above Ground* ordinarily beyond them.

> Dead men and miners go underground.
> Deeper than vegetables or the rock,
> Than the Cro-Magnon arrowhead or sounding
> Whale, deeper and darker than a black
> Burial, they both go down into dirt.
> But the dead stay down. We forget them.
> The sometimes smiling miner of Glynneath
> He comes up as murky as his shirt
> Out of the belly of South Wales. Let them
> Elated this Saturday be happy beneath
> An unfailing bright sky. Their work is done,
> Rigging a drift, riding a spake,
> Hacking the seam. A week's work done
> And — fine and unlikely as a birthday cake —
> These men enter the Saturday of the sun.

(Cro-Magnon is in the Dordogne, where remains of Early Stone Age Man were first found.
A *drift* in mining is an inclined tunnel underground.
Rigging means making safe.
A *spake* is the South Wales term for the carriages men ride to and from the coal face.)

The difference in significance for the child when a sociological subject like this is made vivid in his own imagination shows most powerfully in the quality of his writing about it. Reactions to *Milk*, for instance, may be straightforwardly recorded in a useful way, as when a child writes:

At the dairy we saw huge tankers which carry 3,000 gallons of milk. We were taken into the bottling plant where the bottles were being washed, filled, capped and crated. All this was done by machinery, without once being touched by hand. Before we returned to school we were given a lovely tea, which was a grand surprise to us all.

On the other hand, in a project on *Our Food* carried out with nine year olds living in the Old Kent Road area, during which the children had seen a vivid filmstrip of wheat production and breadmaking, and had listened to the old folk-song, *John Barley-Corn*, they were asked to write personally. One wrote:

I was born in my father's ear with my brothers and sisters with several more around. I was born on a lovely summer's morning, the sun shone bright and the rain came out to give a drink. After several days had passed I heard the sound of a machine. Then the next thing I knew was that the stalk was pulled away from me by some sort of machine . . .

I was thrown backwards and forwards. I was in the threshing machine being ground up into pieces and put into the big bag. I had a lovely ride on a lorry. I was taken to the baker's and baked in the oven and made into bread and ended up in some one's belly. And that is the end of my story.

In this same project, milk, too, became something to get one's teeth into:

When Sir made some cheese, we had a bite of it. I thought it was very nice, but I expect some boy or girl didn't. I will tell you how Sir made it. First of all he cut some bread to put the cheese on, then Sir let three pints of milk go sour then poured it into some butter muslin and hung it up to dry and about three days after he put some salt in it, then the next day we had a bite.

In most projects children have to write accounts of some visit or process or other activity in connection with the subject, and this relevant focusing of their powers of observation helps them to write economically and well. For a project to be more deeply fruitful, teachers must conceive means in their presentation which will cause the same focusing but of the inner eye; and, still more important, in their original choice have vividly in mind the need to find such means. In general the subject that does not provide it had best be left alone. The true imaginative sphere of projects is not literary. It lies in fact so presented, the natural world so looked at, some way of life in past or present, far or near, so re-created that the mind is kindled to new insight and awareness. The possibilities are inexhaustible as many teachers have discovered, but for those starting out I would most warmly recommend the School Library Association's book, *Using Books in the Primary School*, brought out in 1962 by their Primary Schools' Sub-Committee. This shows the essential part played by factual books in project work and also how good teachers supplement these with film, maps, models, wall charts, visits of every kind. Most important of all, as one senses in all the first-hand accounts of projects, whether of *Seashore Shells, Our Neighbourhood, Homes through the Ages* or *The Queen Elizabeth Story,* is the teacher's imagination, developing, directing, discovering. This sees that the pursuit of fact and information is always illuminated by insight, and also realises that this often needs the complement of art and modelling, collage work, playmaking, story and poetry, and the children's own imaginative writing, if the children are going to be fully involved.

In view of the many elements that contribute in a good project, it is perhaps misleading to speak of a sociological, an historical, a geographical one. Yet one knows that in practice most are usually centred in one sphere, at least their main emphasis lying there, with other elements contributing. It may be helpful, therefore to make some suggestions of what particular 'English' elements, what story, poetry and possibilities for drama and imaginative writing seem to me to offer most in these different spheres.

HISTORY

Children do not focus different periods in the past in relation to each other at all accurately. The Victorians will be as remote as the Greeks, unless they are set on the track of the right kind of social detail, the kind that will involve them in vivid comparisons of then and now, and also helped to relate the significant events and achievements of the age to something comparable within their experience. In any case, much history teaching will cut across chronology by making children aware of various processes at work that have affected people's lives, developments in their houses, for instance, or their transport, in their means of communication, their means of killing each other, and also of controlling disease. Teachers will often want to reinforce this with study in depth of a period, while at the same time bringing home to children that history is something that is happening to us now as much as it happened to other people over the centuries.

In view of this it does not seem very imaginative to march chronologically through history, as some syllabuses do, simply from habit and general orderliness, rather than regard for what access a child has at a particular age to the feeling and ideas as well as the events of the time. For instance, the peculiar *gravitas* of the Romans and their administrative and governmental powers are beyond the grasp of second-year juniors, among whom they nevertheless seem very often to turn up. Greater flexibility of approach would seem possible if teachers could develop a livelier sense, when they are choosing a particular period of history for study, of what there is in story, ballad or dramatic potential to bring it within the emotional range of the children they are teaching. If I discuss some possibilities chronologically now, it is purely for convenience.

Story in this context will often be traditional literature such as I discussed earlier, which one wants children to experience and enjoy for its own sake, but which is always made more alive and real for them if at the same time they are finding out about the way of life of the people in the story and other relevant historical details. The work on the *Iliad*, *Beowulf* and *Chaucer* that I discussed earlier are instances. Sometimes, though, one's emphasis will be on the period, one's main aim will be to bring to life for children the world of the Saracens or Elizabethan England or Roman Britain. Yet in these periods there will be no epic poetry or story telling of the age suitable for them. In such circumstances modern historical story for children can often be of great value.

Four writers in this field seem to me outstanding: Cynthia Harnett, Rosemary Sutcliff, Henry Treece and Ronald Welch. One finds oneself gripped by the exciting quality of the actual story as well as absorbed by the genuine feeling for the period, by the detail and atmosphere. Most of their books are too difficult for the average ten year old to read to himself, but read and adapted where necessary by their teacher, many can be understood and enjoyed, particularly as they coincide with other related work. This incentive of related interest is strong and cumulative provided, of course, that its centre is something that stirs the imagination from the start. It would be misleading, though, for teachers to think that it is enough to get hold of a book that sounds 'useful', treat it primarily as a tool themselves and then automatically expect children to be excited by the age it is concerned with. Their own imaginations must be fired first so that they are to some extent at least drawn into the period and are living in it imaginatively. They must also be prepared for all the work involved in implementing this in exciting ways for children, and one knows that this asks much.

The Greeks

I have already suggested what Greek literature has to offer junior children and that its intrinsic experience is so valuable that one would probably not want to make it the centre of a full-scale project. This would be much more likely to centre in social history and there is much helpful material in history text-books. The simplicity and graciousness of the Greek way of life appeals to quite young children, who love to create their own Athenian family and to make up a story about them. Roger Lancelyn Green has written several novels on Greek themes for children which one can draw upon, while many teachers let history and geography combine actively here and set children to discover about life in Greece now as well as in the past. Colour photographs and film of modern Greece are a great help, as is correspondence with Greek children. There are many fine books of photographs of ancient Greece and wherever the emphasis of one's project lies it can be enriched by play-making based on Greek stories and legends.

The Romans

Although Roman literature has nothing for children, which is reason enough for thinking that Roman history is not a wise choice for the younger forms, historical stories can help greatly. These are more often concerned with the Romans in Britain than in their own country, which suggests that this aspect of their history is the most profitable to concentrate on. For instance there is a chapter of *Puck of Pook's Hill* that takes the young hero and his sister north in imagination with a Roman centurion, on a twenty-day march to a command on Hadrian's Wall. They become aware of change and disintegration taking place in the past, as modern children listening may for the first time begin to apprehend underlying historical and geographical reasons for the greater hardness of northern life, still felt today. One also becomes aware of the stability and duration of Roman rule.

Of course, the farther North you go the emptier are the roads. At last you fetch clear of the forests and climb bare hills, where wolves howl in the ruins of our cities that have been. No more pretty girls; no more jolly magistrates who knew your father when he was young, and invite you to stay with him; no news at the temples and way-stations except bad news of wild beasts. There's where you meet hunters and trappers for the Circuses, prodding along chained bears and muzzled wolves. Your pony shies at them and your men laugh.

The houses change from gardened villas to shut forts with watch-towers of grey stone, and great stone-walled sheepfolds, guarded by armed Britons of the North Shore. In the naked hills beyond the naked houses, where the shadows of the clouds play like cavalry charging, you see puffs of black smoke from the mines. The hard road goes on and on — and the wind sings through your helmet-plume — past altars to Legions and Generals forgotten, and broken statues of Gods and Heroes, and thousands of graves where the mountain foxes and hares peep at you. Red-hot in summer, freezing in winter, is that big, purple heather country of broken stone.

Just when you think you are at the world's end, you see a smoke from East to West as far as the eye can turn, and then, under it, also, as far as the eye can stretch, houses and temples, shops and theatres, barracks and granaries, trickling along like dice behind — always behind — one long, low, rising and falling, and hiding and showing line of towers. And that is the Wall.

There are usually two or three children in a class, in London schools anyway, who have driven to Scotland, possibly one whose parents stopped so that they could explore the remains of the Wall, which they probably found disappointing. If not one can provide the contrast oneself. Either way the conception behind the Wall, as well as the form it took, comes alive for children still and is exciting. Awareness of it marks a significant point half-way through Rosemary Sutcliff's fine book, *The Eagle of the Ninth*, which one may prefer to Kipling, as offering a much more interesting and fully developed story that can be made the centre of much exploration by the children of the Roman way of life in Britain. Her description runs:

From Luguvallium in the west to Segedunum in the East (that is, from Carlisle to Wallsend) the Wall ran, leaping along with the jagged contours of the land; a great gash of stone-work, still raw with newness. Eighty miles of fortresses, mile-castles, watch-towers, strung on one great curtain wall, and backed by the vallum ditch and the coast-to-coast Legionary road; and huddled along its southern side, the low sprawl of wine shops, temples, married quarters, and markets that always gathered in the wake of the Legions. A great and never-ceasing smother of noise: voices, march-ing feet, turning wheels, the ring of hammer on the armourer's anvil, the clear calling of trumpets over all. This was the great Wall of Hadrian, shutting out the menace of the north.

Once he has crossed this, there is no going back for the young Roman hero, who is dedicated to discovering the truth about his father's lost legion, which he is idealistically convinced was loyal to the end. The first part of the book establishes, with varied and interesting detail, the way of life of this young legionary, posted to Exeter soon after the erection of the Wall in A.D. 123. A severe leg wound from fighting off a tribal attack on his fort destroys his romantic plans for a distinguished military career and during his long convalescence with his uncle, who has retired in Silchester, we discover the kind of contact that existed between the Romans and the British 'upper-class'. But his aim in life is to find out what happened to the lost legion. The familiar quest element never fails to work with children. Here it serves also to bring out, through vivid descriptions that are part of the action, the deep difference in culture between the Roman and Celt. The action has value for ten and eleven year olds also in that the hero grows up through it. There is no easy and glorious vindication. The Legion was not loyal to a man although a small core remained so, among them naturally – for children's stories must never be ugly or tragic – the hero's father.

Rosemary Sutcliff has written other books on Roman Britain: *The Silver Branch*, *The Lantern Bearers*, and most recently *The Mark of the Horse Lord*. Henry Treece is worth exploring also, for in his book *The Eagles Have Flown*, concerned with a considerably later period than *The Eagle of the Ninth*, fifth-century Britain, he gives a picture of King Arthur, who though doubtless legendary will be met frequently by children in various contexts at school.

The Vikings

There is an account in *Using Books in the Primary School* of work in an Oxfordshire rural school that was inspired by reading the description of Grendel's meeting with Beowulf, not in a prose translation but in Ian Serraillier's verse one. The children visited the British Museum and saw the Sutton Hoo treasures as well as Norse manuscripts and other exhibits. The strong appeal of the poem's language was reinforced by hearing a BBC Sound Broadcast and this had a marked effect on the vividness of their own vocabulary when they came to write about the encounter. They consulted many books about life in the time of the Vikings and the account of their work is followed by a helpful book list. In addition to *Beowulf*, I have already mentioned the novels of Henry Treece about the Vikings, which greatly humanise their world for children. I would also recommend Rosemary Sutcliff's *The Shield Ring*, concerned with the Vikings in this country, which, if one is ready to give some time and thought to adapting it, could make children realise something of their impact.

If one has read *Grettir the Strong* and there is already an interest in Iceland, children would enjoy listening to Naomi Mitchison's *Land the Ravens Found*, while there are also two very good stories about Iceland by Alan Boucher: *Path of the Raven* and its sequel, *The Greenland Farers*. But on the whole the way of life here, as I have already suggested, is probably too grim for one to want to stay with it for very long.

The Crusades

It is not easy to give children a balanced meaningful picture of the Crusades, since any intellectual and emotional understanding of their causes must be beyond them. For most adults this period of history tends to remain over-simplified, for on the misguided principle of chronology most of us 'learnt' about them at a tender age, as we did of the Normans and their strip system. Modern teachers may be very practical, getting children to make models of castles and concentrating on military details of weapons, armour and siege tactics, and also genuinely concerned to be fair to the Saracens. But the weight of folk tradition is against anything but simple opposition: Saracens, ferocious and treacherous to a man, Christians, all noble *cœurs de lion*. For a class to have read to them Ronald Welch's *Knight Crusader* while they are discovering about Saracens and Crusaders heightens their interest and deepens their grasp. For one thing the hero has always lived in Palestine, in Outremer, his father being lord of one of the Christian castles permanently maintained along the coast line. The silken hangings of this, its floors covered with rugs, its painted ceilings and wide windows letting in sea breezes create a feeling contrast with the discomfort of an English castle, to which he goes home at the end. There the stone floors are sparsely strewn with smelly rushes, rough stone walls drip with damp, slit windows allow little light while acrid fumes are billowed by strong draughts from the wide fireplace. The civilised qualities of the Turks are well brought out, as well as their ferocity, while one also realises the quarrelsome nature of the Christians. Most vivid are the battle scenes, which have tremendous excitement in them but no glorification of war. Rather the reality of its cruelty often shocks. Jousts and the art of jousting play a part in the story and, as well as the richness and brilliance of the settings and elaborate exactness of the ritual, children gain some insight into the subtle but necessary relationship, then, between playing at war and the real thing. For children the primary interest is in the story, and the hero, though soon a grown man hardened by experience, remains convincingly boyish at heart. Ronald Welch gives a brief exposition at the end of the facts on which his story is based and how he has used these, which appeals very much to the literal-mindedness of top juniors.

One can now get Henry Treece's *The Children's Crusade* in Puffin Books. This is based on the strange Joan-of-Arc-like vision of a shepherd boy in 1212. In many ways this book is more moving for young readers than Ronald Welch because the main characters are young also, but this closeness makes their eventual disillusion more painful than the grim horror of adult battles. The child crusaders face drought and starvation by the roadside, the sea does not dry up at their arrival to give a miraculous passage to the Holy Land and many are eventually sold into slavery in North Africa. Those who stayed in Egypt probably led a relatively comfortable life, some acting as interpreters and secretaries to a civilised ruler who made no attempt to convert his slaves. Those taken to Baghdad were less fortunate and we hear of eighteen put to death for refusing to become Moslems.

The Middle Ages

This period is rich in possibilities, some of which I have already spoken of. There are many good stories for children set in this time, but I would like to draw attention particularly to those of Cynthia Harnett. Her book, *The Woolpack*, for instance, available in Puffin Books, has a genuinely exciting story concerned with an attempt by some unscrupulous Lombard merchants to smuggle large quantities of wool from the Cotswolds to Italy by a secret route, thus avoiding the dues payable to the Staple at Calais. The hero's father appears to be implicated but his son's part in vindicating him is entirely credible, with no Biggles-like, supra-human qualities. The Burford setting and the daily life of a boy of the prosperous sheep-rearing *bourgeoisie*

P

is first established and then, the seeds of mystery already planted, the hero has to journey with his father to Newbury, for his formal betrothal to a clothier's daughter. This forms a perfectly natural occasion for description of roads and wayfarers, and for visiting his prospective father-in-law's varied centres of work, so that we get a vivid factual account of the processes of the cloth trade as seen through the eyes of an alert and partial scrutiniser. First we see the cottage industry where the wool is taken weekly by the master clothier's packers and then collected the next week as yarn; next the weaving on the most modern of existing looms, in the large attic of the master-weaver's house; followed by the dyeing, in troughs like bricked in washhouse coppers. Then comes fulling at the fulling mill, 'where the cloth was steeped in water and pounded with a sort of smooth clay called fuller's earth, which left it clean and soft and pliable, with all its wool felted together. After fulling it was hooked on to the tenters to be stretched and dried. Then the nap was raised with teazles, the thistly head of the common blue teazle plants which he had often seen growing without really knowing why people grew them.' There is an equally alive and detailed description of the great Newbury Cloth Fair conveniently occurring during the visit on the eve of Corpus Christi day, when throughout the late Middle Ages the guilds used to present their versions of the Mystery Cycle. All this detail woven for children in the course of an enthralling story gives them the chance to handle the stuff of history, the social and economic fabric of early Tudor England. In addition the book has delightful inset illustrations of things and places and activities being described: weekly practice at the targets; jesses and lures from the hawking mews, jesses with bells, to strap to the hawk's legs, lures shaped like birds' wings which concealed pieces of raw meat to coax birds back to their masters; Nicholas tying his points; shepherds' tools; a brass rubbing of Nicholas's grandparents, and many others. One may like me have only reached the actual through the literary, knowing from Shakespeare's Feste that points kept breeches up and what jesses were because Othello callously threatens, if Desdemona prove unfaithful, to toss her off even though her jesses are his dear heart strings. Yet one knows that the other way round is healthier and should make for a more immediate recognition of Shakespeare's realism later on.

There is a fascinating account in *Using Books in the Primary School* of the *Woolpack Project* of an Oxfordshire school. The children visited Burford, photographed and drew the houses, made sketches and brass rubbings in Northleach Church and accompanied all this by a study of the modern wool trade. They were able to visit a blanket factory at Witney and compare modern processes with the medieval ones. These were discussed thoroughly, the children collecting samples for a book about wool. Their final activity was to visit a sheep farm just at the end of the lambing season and see where wool came from. Clearly being near the Cotswolds was a great incentive here but even at a distance one could do much, especially if the children can visit a good social history museum. I have already discussed *The Second Shepherds' Play* as a basis for playmaking, the Corpus Christi procession still takes place in Newbury and other ancient towns, while the plays themselves are now performed as cycles annually in York and elsewhere. The Lorenzo di Medici medal referred to in the story is in the Victoria and Albert Museum.

The next best known of Cynthia Harnett's novels, *The Load of Unicorn*, is equally valuable as a project centre, for it has the same gripping quality of story and a similarly intelligent and sympathetic boy hero. There is geographical detail about journeying from London to Stratford on Avon, up towards Warwick and then back to London, and topographical detail about London and Westminster, in which two cities the story mainly takes place. This brings out their separateness and individuality and invests what are familiar names to Londoners, Millbank, for instance, and Horseferry Road, with their concrete origin. There are also descriptions of new industrial processes, this time of printing, and of the routine of a school day at St. Paul's, which the hero is on the point of leaving. The plot concerns the attempt by reactionary fifteenth-century scriveners to disrupt the emergent rival trade of the printer, Caxton, who had set up at the Sign of the Red Pale next to the Chapter House of Westminster Abbey. Unicorn was the name of a watermark of the best quality paper, which at that time had to be imported from Holland, and one important load of which the villains try to prevent reaching Caxton.

Project work on this might well start in a study of the London and Westminster of the day, made more actual by a visit where feasible to the Abbey or St. Paul's. Jonathan Cape's *Jackdaw* series can be of help here too, for its ninth issue, *Young Shakespeare*, has a reproduction of contemporary maps of the two cities given side by side. One would want to study modern printing processes, if possible at first hand in a local printer's, and also see that children knew something of revolutionary modern developments, which so far have only affected the national Press. Children growing up in a television age are probably more able to appreciate the sweeping nature of the revolution caused by printing than earlier generations, who comfortably accepted it as the only possible large scale means of communication. They can certainly be made to consider in what way it is still indispensable.

Elizabethan England

There is a wealth of material here of interest to children, particularly in social history. I have already mentioned players and the theatre as a centre of interest, and Rosemary Sutcliff's early book, *Brother Dusty Feet*, as a story that could lead to playmaking. Margaret Jowett's *A Cry of Players* has a similar appeal for rather older children. Margaret Jowett is not as good a writer as Cynthia Harnett or Rosemary Sutcliff, but nevertheless the story is quite interesting and she is genuinely concerned to give accurate information about the development of the theatre companies and life in London at the time. The story ends with the hero joining Shakespeare's company, which makes it go well with a project on Shakespeare's London. If one was lucky enough to see the quartercentenary exhibition at Stratford on Avon, one has an inspiring starting point. Children are fascinated by details about the Plague, enjoy making a model of the Globe Theatre, and collages of Elizabethan costume, and if one's school is near London it is possible to arrange guided tours round the London Museum in Kensington Gardens, where there is much relevant material. I have already suggested a possible dramatic content for such a project.

Later Periods

Children were not important in the seveneenth and eighteenth centuries and their climate of thought is much more remote for modern children in many ways than that of earlier times. Few modern historical writers for children have chosen to set stories in those periods, although the nineteenth-century classic, *Children of the New Forest* is still liked by children, especially in dramatised form on radio or television. A story like *Moonfleet* gives a realistic background to eighteenth-century smuggling, which is usually treated in a lurid and conventional way. On the whole, however, the feeling in both these books is much more suited to secondary children than juniors. The aspects of the history of these periods that teachers most concentrate on, the Civil War, the Great Plague and Fire of London in the seventeenth century, and the varied panorama of social life in the eighteenth, are best illustrated by their selecting from adult sources. They remain periods difficult for a child to enter into although they can explore the externals of life with much success. A figure like Alexander Selkirk makes a deep impression. Children are always interested in life at sea, and there is also much material in the accounts of voyages like those of Captain Cook and Fletcher Christian, or of the dramatic mutiny against Captain Bligh of the *Bounty*, that can be the centre of project work. The appeal of islands is very strong, and in the recent Pitcairn Islanders' enforced exile to this country and the subsequent choice of most of them to go back to their island a new chapter has been written that focuses awareness on many contrasts in values and conditions. Geography and history fuse in much of this work as they so often do in projects but the appeal of many stories is strong and not to be treated simply as useful background material. One can read excerpts from books like Sir Arthur Grimble's *A Pattern of Islands* or Conrad's *Typhoon*, and possibly from *The Kontiki Expedition* and *Robinson Crusoe*, without regard to the appeal and power of the whole, but *Coral Island* and *Treasure Island* are enjoyed in a different way. Unfortunately the story of their twentieth-century allegorical descendant, *The Lord of the Flies*, is quite unsuitable for juniors and would seriously disturb them if read, yet it is far too good a story simply to be quoted from. I know a teacher who embarked on reading excerpts as background to an exciting project on *The Bounty* mutiny and then had a very difficult job, when the children clamoured for her to go on, explaining and justifying her refusal.

The Victorian age sees the beginning of children's literature, which must be considered in its own right. Few stories have much direct connection with any work on the social history of the time, although in so far as the age is accessible to children it is almost entirely so through their strong humanitarian instincts. But they always need some point of entry in their imaginations if they are to conceive what it was like being a child in another age and there is much moving testimony in adult books about the childhood suffering of characters in them which can be relevant. Dickens, as I have suggested, is very significant here and while I would never choose to read him simply to help any exploration of social conditions in his time, his energy and power are such that children want to go on. *A Christmas Carol*, for instance, has this effect, as has *Oliver Twist* and to a lesser extent *Nicholas Nickleby*, both of which can be creatively adapted by teachers who know and love them. There is an account in *Using Books in the Primary School* of the work of a Nottingham school, which was much helped by its coinciding with a production of *Oliver Twist* at the Nottingham playhouse and a Dickens Exhibition. The actor who played Fagin visited the school. London and Kent teachers start with great advantages also in being able to concentrate on some vivid milieu in his work, the Pool of London, for instance, or the Dover Road, or Clerkenwell, but there were workhouses all over England and more than one school like Mr. Creakle's. In any case, place is not particularly important for children. Arnold Bennett is not a writer for them but there is a very moving account in *Clayhanger* of how Darius Clayhanger, a hard man, unsympathetic to his son's ambition to be an architect, and not a printer like himself, started work at seven years old in the potteries:

The next morning at half-past five, Darius began his career in earnest. He was 'mould-runner' to a 'muffin-maker', a muffin being not a comestible but a small plate fashioned by its maker on a mould. The business of Darius was to run as hard as he could with the mould, and newly created plate adhering thereto, into the drying-stove. This 'stove' was a room lined with shelves, and having a red-hot stove and stove-pipe in the middle. As no man of seven could reach the upper shelves, a pair of steps was provided for Darius, and up these he had to scamper. Each mould with its plate had to be leaned carefully against the wall, and if the soft clay of a new-born plate was damaged, Darius was knocked down. The atmosphere outside the stove was chill but owing to the heat of the stove Darius was obliged to work half naked. His sweat ran down his cheeks, and down his chest, and down his back, making white channels and lastly it soaked his hair.

His other job was clay-wedging. In this — he took a piece of raw clay weighing more than himself, cut it in two with a wire, raised one half above his head and crashed it down with all his force upon the other half, and he repeated the process until the clay was thoroughly soft and even in texture. At a later period it was discovered that hydraulic machinery could perform this operation more easily and efficiently than the brawny arms of a man of seven. At eight o'clock in the evening Darius was told that he had done enough for that day, and that he must arrive at five sharp the next morning to light the fire, before his master the muffin-maker began to work. When he inquired how he was to light the fire his master kicked him jovially on the thigh and suggested that he should ask another mould-runner . . .

Darius reached home at a quarter to nine having eaten nothing but bread all day. Somehow he had lapsed into the child again. His mother took him on her knee, and wrapped her sacking apron round his ragged clothes, and cried over him and cried into his supper of porridge, and undressed him and put him to bed. But he could not sleep easily because he was afraid of being late the next morning.

This is the kind of material which, like the account in *The Bonnie Pit Laddie*, arouses children's sympathies and at the same time implants particular details in strongly retentive minds. Against such a background of concern about the age and the life of children in it, one could read a story like *The Secret Garden* with added relevance. For the picture it gives of very different childhood lives, quite apart from their human value in themselves, deepens children's perceptiveness of life then as a whole.

History did not stop in 1939, although it tends to in text-books. Children have little conception of what the Second World War meant to people in Europe nor very much of what it was like living through it here. Teachers may well not wish to make this real for them at this stage, but if they do there are two very good stories for children worth exploring: Ian Ser-raillier's *Silver Sword*, about the survival and escape from Poland of a group of children, and Naomi Mitchison's *Rib of the Green Umbrella*, concerned with children caught up in the work of the partisans in Italy. With either of these in their minds, and some exploration on their own account into wartime life in this country, which can be based on recollections of parents and grandparents, the war will begin to be seen and felt rather differently from the conventional thrills of their comics. It would be in such an atmosphere that a picture like Paul Nash's *Dead Sea* reproduced in plate 5 would have its most powerful imaginative effect as a starting point for writing.

GEOGRAPHICAL PROJECTS

Most children's stories take readers exploring in some way, often far from home geographically. Many are set from the beginning in foreign countries, being translations from native originals. Whether this is so or not, good stories are realistic and truthful in physical and social detail and, particularly in the latter group, intimately of the country in atmosphere and presentation of human relationships. It is well worth teachers themselves exploring here, for if children are engaged on a project about another country, it adds greatly to their interest, degree of involvement and capacity to understand its way of life to have a really good story read to them during this time.

To interest eight or nine year olds in Australian Wool or New Zealand Butter, as I have seen attempted, solely through externals such as facts, figures, charts or photographs and educational films, is not easy unless they also have some means of realising emotionally what it is like growing up in those countries. And practically the only means open to children is the vicarious experience of a story. If one is concerned with Australasia, for instance, one can read a book like Joan Phipson's *Boundary Riders*, which begins by involving us in the life of children on a sheep farm, and ends with our sharing their awareness of the strangeness and hostility of the bush, or one of Nan Chauncey's stories about Tasmania. If a teacher has been to the country and talks vividly about his experiences there, this is in most children's eyes only another particularly fascinating form of story, concerning as it does that constant source of interest, their teacher's life outside the classroom. There is no guarantee that children will know more of geographical value because of this heightening of interest than they otherwise would, but it is an excellent fertiliser to mix round the roots of geographical knowledge.

As well as human interest, good stories about foreign countries also give children the kind of introduction to a country's social habits that foreign travel does, although of course much less vividly. Abroad for the first time, one is surrounded by much that is strange and new, which the inhabitants usually take for granted. The more perceptive inhabitants, though, realise what a visitor is struck by and can enlighten him, and be enlightened, in varying ways. The author in most children's stories tends to play the role of perceptive inhabitant and, by anticipation, to some extent sharpens perception in young readers or at least stirs curiosity. As for detailed physical description, one will not expect too much, for the writer who appears to be setting up as a tourist guide is usually a much less good story teller than the one who describes only what he needs for living background.

Some geography specialists do not encourage the use of story because it may be out of date in economic and social detail, and be romantically inexact in physical description. Where it is, they are of course right to be suspicious, but otherwise I would suggest not. Choice is clearly all important and teachers must be discriminating, particularly in their assessment of a writer's power to convey truthfully something of a country's way of life. As for plot, the main need is one likely to involve children not simply in the conventional events of an everyday adventure, for which the setting is more or less accidental, but in an action both probable and convincing, and that could not have happened anywhere else. The story chosen must also be one likely to be enjoyed for its own sake, with no feeling on a teacher's part that, were it not for his project, he would not 'waste time' on it. Finally, the story needs to be read aloud. Providing likely stories in the library or arranging for a special loan from a helpful local authority, though valuable, makes some children think of the reading as a kind of chore, and stories should never be seen in this light. Reading aloud, on the other hand, for a class that has come automatically to associate this with pleasure, focuses interest and makes it possible for the teacher to see that relevant detail is unobtrusively stressed. Story is never a substitute for the objective facts of a country's geography nor do I want to imply that one has to approach geography as a subject for juniors on a country by country basis. Story however can often be a valuable complement that engages them more wholeheartedly than a purely factual approach. In the same way a good teacher will use a country's folk music, art or ballad poetry where they are likely to interest and inspire children, for instance in work on Australia or America.

With America particularly, if a teacher is interested and prepared for the work involved, there is tremendous variety, excitement and interest for children, with stories and other writing that is part of the history. They immediately respond to the adventure of America's development, the recurrent note of pioneering, whether one concentrates on the earliest stage of Columbus's discovery, which C. Walter Hodges has written about for children and also strikingly illustrated in *Columbus Sails*, or the life of the Puritan settlers, or the opening up of the West, or various great modern technological achievements. Classic American children's stories like Mary Dodge's *Hans Brinker* and P. Travers's more modern *Mary Poppins*, appeal to young children without in any way making them aware of America. On the other hand a story like L. I. Wilder's *Little House in the Big Woods*, now available as a Puffin book, gives quite young readers a real sense of Laura's experience as she grows up away from cities, yet not in a fairy-tale forest. Girls still love Louisa Alcott usually without knowing what war it is that takes the March girls' father. One would not read *Little Women* to give children insight into the Civil War. On the other hand the favourite anthology ballad, Whittier's *Barbara Frietchie*, makes realistic and stirring reading if a class is at the same time concerned with the war, while excerpts from Stephen Crane's *Red Badge of Courage* can make the fighting more real. This story is not for children, but it can be drawn on by a teacher who knows it. Much more valuable and immediately accessible to children is Esther Forbes's *Johnny Tremain*, set in Boston at the time of the outbreak of the Revolution, for this is essentially a moving and exciting story that happens incidentally to be very illuminating as history.

However, probably more than her history, it is the size and variety and openness of America that stir children's imaginations, as they have done those of many of her writers. In this context, the holiday pioneering of children's favourite stories takes on what Conrad called 'the romantic feeling of reality'. The sweep and power of Walt Whitman brings this out when he writes of his country:

> this land
> My own Manhattan with spires, and the sparkling and hurrying
>   tides, and the ships,
> The varied and ample land, the South and the North in the light,
>   Ohio's shores and flashing Missouri,
> And ever the far-spreading prairies cover'd with grass and corn.

With the right class, the quiet watchful eye of Robert Frost provokes thought in a poem like *The Line-Gang*, about men who are taking telephone and telegraph wires across the continent:

> Here comes the line-gang pioneering by,
> They throw a forest down less cut than broken.
> They plant dead trees for living, and the dead
> They string together with a living thread.

In a poem like *Virginia*, T. S. Eliot is not difficult and full of allusions, but immediate:

> Red river, red river
> Slow flow heat is silence
> No will is still as a river
> Still.

Still more strongly American in Eliot is 'the sea howl and the sea yelp' of *The Dry Salvages*, and teachers who know and enjoy his poetry will find that passages from this poem have a mysterious and strong appeal if children are concerned with the New England Coast, with 'its true owner, the tough one, the sea-gull', and possibly with the excitement and danger of whaling such as Melville describes in *Moby Dick*.

One can bring America to life for children without her poets and writers and in any case most children already have much visual awareness of the country from the cinemas and from television Westerns and serials. But teachers who care to explore will find much to deepen and particularise these generally stereotyped images. Mark Twain running away from home to work on the great Mississippi steamboats, which he describes in his *Life on the Mississippi*, the Welshman, W. H. Davies, writing of his life as a hobo in his *Autobiography of a Super-tramp*, the small town atmosphere of Sherwood Anderson's *Winesburg Ohio*, this is the kind of deepening I have in mind. It is a great pity that the story of Jack Schaefer's *Shane* is too adult for juniors because the impact of the stranger on the boy narrator from the moment he rides into the valley from the open Wyoming plain beyond is immediate and fascinating to them, as much as to adolescents:

> He rode easily, relaxed in the saddle, leaning his weight lazily into the stirrups. Yet even in this easiness was a suggestion of tension. It was the easiness of a coiled spring of a trap set.

And this fascination fixes every detail of his clothes, horse and arms in the boy's and reader's mind, just as it does the detail of the boy's own homestead background:

> He drew rein not twenty feet from me. His glance hit me, dismissed me, flicked over our place. This was not much, if you were

thinking in terms of size and scope. But what there was was good. You could trust father for that. The corral, big enough for about thirty head if you crowded them in, was railed right to true sunk posts. The pasture behind, taking in nearly half of our claim, was fenced tight. The barn was small, but it was solid, and we were raising a loft at one end for the alfalfa growing green in the north forty. We had a fair-sized field in potatoes that year and father was trying a new corn he had sent all the way to Washington for and they were showing properly in weedless rows.

I have quoted this deliberately because the impressionable openness of the boy, with the fixing of detail that this entails, is very close to the intent receptiveness of a good class if their imagination is fired by some documentary aspect of a project. If one wants a story that one *can* read to ten year olds, with something of the background and appeal of *Shane*, I would recommend *My Friend Flicka*, where the young hero's feelings are deeply centred in his horse and in the ranchers' open way of life. However, *Tom Sawyer* probably remains the best starting point for juniors, whether for work about the Mississippi or something more extensive.

Where their own *local or environmental* studies are concerned, teachers will naturally take advantage of any outstanding original writing to reinforce the main active exploration of the project. There is a particularly interesting account in *Using Books in the Primary School* of the work of an Oxfordshire school based on the life of William Morris, which took the children into diverse realms of social history, art and craft. Kelmscott is in Oxfordshire, but Morris was born in Walthamstow and always had a strong feeling for Epping Forest, so that the possible scope of his appeal in a local sense may be wider than is realised. For the most part, though, this work will not depend much on story or playmaking but will be a valuable stimulus to children's writing. In the same way studies of the natural world will not need story, though good animal stories may sometimes be an exception. This is a sphere where some poetry comes in naturally. Not nature poetry in the Romantic sense, in which nature is often only the occasion for the expression of a variety of personal feelings by the poet, but the poetry of writers like Clare and Hardy, and sometimes Edward Thomas and D. H. Lawrence. R. S. Thomas and Ted Hughes among more modern poets are worth exploring, as is Crabbe among past ones, especially for teachers in East

Anglia, while John Masefield in a story poem like *Reynard the Fox* speaks far more powerfully to children than in his anthology pieces.

FRANCE AND JUNIOR SCHOOL FRENCH

More and more junior children are beginning to learn French and are therefore very interested in the country and its life. Most teachers probably devise some kind of project work to develop this interest and may want at the same time to read their class a good children's story by a French writer. For this, more than anything, helps children to understand through its child characters what life is like in France. Paul Berna's *Hundred Million Francs*, for instance, is ideal for eight and nine year olds, having a convincing gang of Paris children, an exciting plot and Great Train Robbery connections. I would also recommend for older juniors Van der Loeff's *They're Drowning Our Village*. The significant thing here is the validity of the situation. A whole village in the French alps is to be destroyed so that a large area may be supplied with hydro-electric power. There is exploration of what this means to people of different generations in terms of memories, prejudices, hopes for the future. There is a splendid, cantankerous, irrational, old grandfather, who leads a family deputation to Paris to try to halt everything, and one therefore sees Paris through the eyes of country people to whom all is strange and rather frightening. The central young character, Pierre, is old enough to realise something of the complexity of the situation. He himself wants to be an engineer, is of the new world, not the old. Yet 'What did he want? What did he really want? The new that attracted and frightened him? Or the old, to which he had been used all his life, and which he now, and at this distance, felt he loved more than he had ever realised.' This story raises issues that concern children, even at ten and eleven, as well as making them aware of the distinctive quality of French life.

SPACE PROJECTS

These stir the imagination of modern children, often producing a kind of creative excitement that needs an outlet. Particularly they will want to make models, and explore their reactions in painting. One may like to read them during this time a good science fiction story for young readers, one that shows some concern for the human values involved as well as bringing out the excitement of human achievement. Paul Berna's *Threshold of the Stars*, or its sequel, *Continent in the Sky*, Dennis Suddaby's *Lost Men in the Grass*, H. G. Wells's *First Men in the Moon*, these are all possibilities. Children may well like to write their own science fiction story, for they are often highly inventive at this age. They may like to write their own Moon poetry, if they have enjoyed Ted Hughes's *The Earth-Owl and other Moon-People*, or create their own Diary or Wall Newspaper for a thousand years hence. They may like to create plays which bring inhabitants of other planets here or take us to other planets, and will probably turn to *Dr. Who* for inspiration. The framework of this serial is ideal for the kind of exploration children love, although its contents are stereotyped.

MAGAZINES AND WALL NEWSPAPERS

Apart from various library and book projects designed to increase children's interest in reading, these are probably the only specifically 'English' projects in the junior school. Ironically, unless imaginatively handled by a teacher, they tend not to produce children's best writing. For there are so many second-rate models to fall back on, and imitative articles on pop stars and fashion reveal little that is personal or individual in their authors. However, the incentive is sufficiently real and potentially interesting to be worth development. It is best to aim at simple objective reporting and one can encourage children to explore the local and school possibilities. Accounts of an interesting school visit or journey, an ambitious project, a school concert or open day; reports of interviews, carefully thought out and prepared with the young reporters beforehand, of willing victims such as head teachers, school secretaries, transient students, these are possible assignments. Simple questionnaires on subjects like pocket money, favourite television programmes, preferences in reading, can be answered by the class and then a group of children can assess and write a report of the results. Letters to the editor, if taken seriously and answered where necessary, are usually popular, while there is much scope for work on hobbies, holidays, future careers. Layout and presentation are particularly important and offer scope to children who may not be very keen on writing. One hears quite often of class newspapers but some adventurous and imaginative head-masters have seen the value, once in a while, of producing a school newspaper, with different classes responsible for different features and with the school hall becoming for several days the news centre where various editors receive copy and 'sub' it

before it goes to press or Banda. Other children will be responsible for advance advertising and distribution.

DIARIES

These are often advocated as a good way to help children
with little to say to write more freely. Compilers of text-books
urge them like this:

> Practice makes perfect. The more sentences you write, the better
> you will write them. A good way of getting practice is to keep a
> diary. If you have no diary you can make one like *My Word Book*.
> All you then have to do is to write the date and say what you did on
> that day. Why not begin one now and write a few sentences every
> evening? You can draw too.

This compiler is at least honest about motive. You don't keep
a diary because you really want to but because it will give you
a chance to practise your sentences, like your scales if you
happen to learn the piano. Most of us can probably remember
diary keeping in our childhood. The Christmas present of a
diary, the high enthusiasm of the first entries during the
holidays, when one had some activities to report, then increasing
tedium, gaps, rededication, finally abandon and relief. Unearthed years later, its banality is comic: 'Went to Joan's.
Played Monopoly. Uncle Victor came.' Sometimes its unconscious perception has the ring of truth. For instance: 'Dad
tried to mend window.' Then the next day's entry: 'Man came
to fix window.' But the writer's powers of expression are not
much developed through this. As soon as a child has anything
to say in a diary, a girl anyway, it concerns people and relationships, and becomes her most secret property. A child of eight
or nine would probably write quite freshly for a few days, but
then the very breadth of the instructions – 'say what you did
on that day' – would dull the edge of husbandry. Routine
would set in.

On the other hand, given a more relevant reason for keeping
a diary in connection with some kind of project, children profit
from it and write well. A nature diary, for instance, kept by a
child really interested in what he is watching and describing,
is usually exact in observation and sensitive in expression. The
log of a voyage, the diary of a child in a past age, or centuries
ahead, these are more testing, in that they ask for imaginative
projection and need genuine assimilation of the experience of

history or space project. But the objective validity of the form encourages most children to make an extra effort.

DISCUSSION

One of the most valuable aspects of project work is the opportunity it gives for discussion, the demands it makes on spoken English. All kinds of issues arise naturally from the experience of the project which children want to follow up and talk about. For instance, how children live in another country compared with themselves, whether they would rather have lived in the time of the project than now, education for children in a past age compared with their own, their views on hunting, or looking after animals, the advantages of some scientific advance, like the hydro-electric power of *They're Drowning Our Village*, and its disadvantages: these are only a few possible subjects. There will usually be a slightly greater sense of occasion in some of these discussions than children are used to, which makes some of them suddenly shy and tongue-tied, but it helps to meet and overcome this early on. Children are always full of particular instances in their discussion but a good teacher can help them as they grow older to move on from this towards making more general points. There may also be occasions in a project when the leader of a group has to report in some way, or for all the members of it to say something individually about their activities. All this helps build up a child's confidence in his use of language and his powers of expression.

LANGUAGE WORK GENERALLY

Teachers are well aware how, throughout project work, valid occasions frequently arise for children to write, and how this strengthens their other language work and can be related to it. It is not so fully realised that preparation for this work, especially in training children to select relevant detail from factual books and to reproduce it in their own way, as distinct from unthinking copying, is valid objective training in comprehension. Children need practice in close reading if they are to make progress in their 'research' for project work. They must early learn the need to select what is important in a passage. Problems of ordering of an individual kind constantly arise, as do more practical external ones of setting out and labelling. There is invariably an end product of interest and value to the child. He feels he has written to some purpose.

English of all kinds contributes vitally to project work but the controlling factor remains the teacher's imagination. This must be not only active, as I suggested at the outset, in the conception, personal exploration and creative presentation, but as the work progresses be constantly aware of children's reactions. The value of any project remains what the children get out of it and some very ambitious ones that if summarised sound extremely impressive may in the classroom and in children's minds and memories amount to rather less. Imagination is needed to prevent any set method or external pattern being imposed on teachers and particularly not on students in training. Some maturity and breadth of mind is needed which eighteen and nineteen year olds rarely have, confidence must be built up over a period of time, experiment encouraged and basic principles considered in relation to what they are discovering about learning generally. Even more important, training courses generally should in some measure demonstrate at student level an awareness of the relatedness which is at the heart of the project approach. Then any subsequent work students do with children, on a small or large scale, is more likely to be based on individual insight rather than taken over externally from a sense of duty.

8

PROGRESS IN READING

CHILDREN come into the junior school proud to be no longer infants and eager to do well in an exciting new world. They are often already aware that this depends to an alarming extent on their reading ability. Some children read fluently already, many are near to doing so but equally many have a good way, and some still very far to go. The initial teaching alphabet may well transform the situation. Certainly its first experiments seem very encouraging but it is far too early to be very sure and widespread change will not occur rapidly. For many years to come, unless the Plowden recommendations are implemented quickly, teachers of first-year juniors will still have the immensely challenging and important job of consolidating and extending a child's reading ability so that he becomes really fluent as quickly as he can.

Many seven year olds, and of course older children too, seem to read well when one hears them, yet one knows that the substance has little meaning for them because they are concentrating so much on the actual process of reading. There is no inner response from them that turns the words on the page into experience in the mind and imagination. I know that this ignores the achievement and the creative attitude towards books in many infant schools, but I think that it remains valid comment on many children entering the junior school.

I am convinced that *meaning* in this context is largely independent of the actual method used to teach a child to read, although clearly one method may achieve it more quickly and naturally than another. It is the teacher's job to assess as far as possible what is best for each child, just as it is the researcher's to explore and test new means of easing difficulties. Yet meaning is usually assumed to be at the heart of the still unresolved controversy between the main methods, those who favour sentence and look-and-say rather than phonic arguing that words and sentences grasped whole have more meaning for the child than ones built up in stages, because this is how children learn to speak and to understand speech. It is true that whole words and sentences bear a more immediate relationship to a child's experience than parts of them, but the difficulty remains that the former methods give the child no means of recognising these wholes except his visual and aural memory, and his interpretation of his teacher's (frequently leading) questions. As most teachers know, a good deal of random guessing occurs. Most children need some other means of translating the symbols on the page into the sounds that they recognise in speech, which is why most teachers use a combination of methods adapted as far as is humanly possible to the needs of individual children. The creative act still remains for the child. The text must come alive for him in his mind. It must become meaningful in relation to his experience. What some teachers and compilers forget, in their genuine concern to bring the child to this point of recognition, is that this will happen more swiftly if the content absorbs the child, arouses his feelings in some way, is of interest to him and concern. Lilian Hollamby in her book, *Young Children Living and Learning*, speaks of a not very bright six year old who went to his new class having been on a particular reading card for several weeks. When his teacher asked him what words were at the top of his card he said, after long hesitation, 'I think it is something about an old tin can!' Lilian Hollamby goes on, 'In fact the words at the top of the card were "my" and "can" – two isolated words with no relationship to each other or to Freddie's own life or thought at that moment.' She concludes, 'This is the kind of reading which leads to mechanical sounding of words, with children sometimes reaching the junior school stage and not even then realising that the pages of their own reading book are telling them a story.' She reminds us that in their play, too, children sometimes produce a special sing-song voice for intoning from their 'reader'.

In the junior school such children will progress more rapidly if their teacher helps them associate reading with being absorbed in a good story, or with finding out exciting facts about something that they are already interested in through an imaginative introduction in other lessons. Whatever methods teachers adopt to give children the frequent oral practice that they need, more will be achieved if it is assumed by everyone that the real aim of reading is quiet individual enjoyment. Some ways of testing progress, such as reading aloud in turn in groups, do not foster this at all. Indeed, they actively combat it.

In the first year, of course, teachers are under special pressure to increase skill because so much else depends on this. In other skills practice and technique are all-important, so teachers are naturally tempted to concentrate on these aspects of reading. For some teachers method begins to take precedence over stimulus. What is objective and measurable, so many pages of a bright-looking graded reader neatly entered by the child on his individual card after the daily 'tool' reading lesson, unconsciously at least becomes more important than what is subjective and not measurable: the driving force of interest and involvement in what is read. I am not saying that system and vigilance are cramping and should be jettisoned. Far from it. The child needs order and a sense of purpose. But it is a question of emphasis and priorities. It is possible to be both practical and imaginative. Reading is certainly a basic skill but it is very much more. It is itself an activity, although not a physical one, and it involves with differing degrees of emphasis and intensity a child's mind and feelings.

Above all, *reading is not a kind of race,* although the approach of some classroom techniques must condition many children into thinking that it is. This includes well-intentioned questionnaires about their reading. Undoubtedly the slowness of many children is due to sluggishness but my contention is that if the average content were more absorbing, these children would be less sluggish, or lazy, or whatever word one prefers to describe their dawdling. The drill books that exist specifically to increase speed, with titles like *Reading Faster,* show in a more extreme form what is apparent in some reading series, and is to some extent symptomatic of the scientist's approach to programmed learning of all kinds: reliance upon external techniques and not enough regard for human needs.

Ironically, in my experience, it is usually in schools where the head is most proud of his system of recording progress that progress is most halting, that graded readers continue to be the children's staple diet right through the school, and that class libraries are least attractive and adequate. I met an extreme instance of this recently, when the headmaster of a new primary school, after explaining his system of cards and checking and colour grading for supplementary readers, took me to see the new library. The basic stock of fiction, for the moment at any rate, was entirely made up of additional sets of graded readers. Often, too, it is in schools like this that the atmosphere in reading lessons least encourages quiet enjoyment. The children may be divided into groups according to ability, and be reading aloud in turn, while the teacher hears one group. This system, particularly, encourages the mechanical sing-song voice Lilian

Hollamby deplored. In more individual systems children may not be allowed to go beyond a certain page or move on to a new book, before they have been tested by their teacher, which inevitably means time spent in queueing up and agreeable chat while one waits. In some schools in the first year only the good readers are allowed proper story books and may be seen in absorbed isolation, while the majority, the ones most needing valid personal proof that stories can be absorbing, cheerfully distract each other in between plodding through their particular graded reader. These are not always bright attractive publications either. I have seen quite as many dog-eared linen-covered nondescripts.

In the infant school primers are closely linked with basic teaching method and are based on recognisable principles of phonic complexity, word frequency and sentence structure. Method and reader naturally reinforce each other. Good teachers, though, see that their primers are supplemented by attractive picture story books and imaginatively conceived simple picture non-fiction. An hour in a good children's library immediately brings the possibilities alive.

This applies even more at junior school level and many education authorities give practical help and stimulus, having permanent well chosen up-to-date collections that are open for teachers to visit, or sending exhibitions of books round to schools who want them. Schools sometimes link such visits with parents' evenings, so that there is awareness at home as well as at school of what will give most interest and pleasure to children at infant and junior stage. There is much variation between local education authorities in insight and provision in this field and there is room for action from teachers, who if they discover that their own authority does little can jolt it into doing more.

It is all important to have an exciting class library. It may be helpful to have a class reader with simple controlled vocabulary, but words used creatively, in however simple a form, in an individual story in which the writer himself is imaginatively absorbed have a life and power to fascinate not found in readers. Children love long words, strange words, words a little beyond their comprehension; but these inevitably are what graded readers don't provide. In fact, as a book like *Words Your Children Use* has shown, they tend to condition children to the unadventurous and ordinary. In the same way simple rhythms that come naturally from the pressure of creativeness in the individual story teller will always be more pleasurable than ones composed to fit a pre-arranged conception of the need for repetition. Above all, there are stories to be found that involve a child's feelings in a valuable way and give him a foretaste of the central pleasure of fiction, discovering about life through immensely varied vicarious experience of it.

Despite all this, many junior schools continue to depend on graded readers for their children's main contact with stories well beyond the first year and have class libraries in some instances whose supplementary value is negligible. Most series are designed for all four years, which is hardly surprising given the plumpness of this particular sitting-target for publishers and compilers alike. There usually remains some statistical control of sentence complexity and word frequency, to confer a pseudo-scientific standing upon what may well be very trivial subject matter; but by the third and fourth years this tends to dis-appear, sometimes to be replaced by various kinds of questioning, again often vouched for by research, whose relation to the purpose of extended reading is often very dubious. The compilers may hint at their real aims in their introduction or accompany-ing teacher's book, but their titles usually emphasise the pleasure of what they offer. *Gay Way, Radiant Reading, Happy Trio, Happy Venture, Sunbeam, Gleaming Road*: such insistence suggests some insincerity, there often being little in the content likely to arouse feeling, excite interest and give pleasure. Other compilers are more realistic. *Reading for Information, Reading for Meaning, Read and Think*, such titles give a reasonably accurate indication of approach and attitude. I noticed yet another, recently, *Reason for Reading.* One might as well be completely honest and come out with *Read and Pass Your 11+, Read Your Way to the Top*, or – even more depressing – *Read And Be Kept Occupied.* For many of these readers test much that is extraneous to the interest of sustained content, on the assumption that something practical and utilitarian justifies the activity more adequately than a story. The best graded readers, however, present children with quite good simple stories, containing increasingly complex sentences and vocabulary and usually increasing in length, so that by book four of most series one has something approaching a short novel.

Apart from this last aspect of grading, which is useful in leading children on to gradually more sustained effort, I see little value in using readers extensively beyond the first year, except that teachers are saved the individual effort of building up a really good class library, and head teachers and local

authorities the expense of paying for it. The advantages of
various kinds of statistical control of languge right through
the junior school seem to me to exist in a vacuum in the minds
of some educationalists and teachers who have not genuinely
considered the alternatives. I have never met any cogent
definition of them. Adults who like and understand children
never find it difficult to talk to them, for their ability to enter
a child's world and understand his imagination provides the
necessary control. Good writers for children do this instinctively when they write, invariably with more imaginative
effect and consequently more power to involve and influence
a child than any statistically controlled composition will have.
Ironically, the tone and attitude of a number of readers does
not suggest this kind of imaginative interest in and capacity
to understand children. Teaching children to read, many of
them imply, is a job to be made easier by using the most
up-to-date scientific techniques. Teachers must decide for themselves how far they think that this is true. I only suggest that
they do so in the light of honest recollection about their own
most vivid experience in reading, whether early or late, and
by putting themselves with all the understanding and imagination they possess at the receiving end of the readers they most
depend on.

It is usually argued that without graded readers one cannot
measure a child's progress and so assess his reading age. Granted
that one considers it important and valuable to know this,
graded readers alone won't give it. With them one can only
measure a child's progress in relation to other children in his
class and school, which statisticians are quick to point out has
little worth as an objective assessment. For that one must resort
to one of the standard reading tests. Not all teachers seem
aware that these are only diagnostic, not remedial. They show
what is wrong, whether faulty visual or aural co-ordination, or
lack of phonic knowledge. But they are only valuable as a basis
for treatment in specialist hands. Sometimes more time and
energy are expended in a school on establishing a child's reading
age than in providing any kind of remedial treatment. Yet
when a mother finds that her child has a temperature of over
a hundred, she doesn't waste time writing this down, nor in
taking the temperatures of her other children. She sends for the
doctor. (If her children are well, she is not always concerned
about their temperatures either, which may not be an entirely
valid analogy but has, I suggest, some bearing on attitudes

towards reading.) The important thing surely is for all head teachers to try to provide backward and slow readers with sympathetic remedial help in small groups, where everything possible is done to create confidence and the desire to progress, and where psychological understanding takes precedence over specialised method.

With average children good junior teachers will strike a creative balance between stimulus and technique, probably using more than one reader in the first year, supplemented from the beginning, as in good infant schools, with an attractive and generous supply of story books, imaginatively conceived non-fiction of all kinds, in which the writers are genuinely excited by whatever facts they are concerned with presenting to children, and by the most exciting poetry books for children they can discover. All these can be made genuinely interchangeable, so that the child who progresses best with a graded reader feels no stigma attach to this but where the guiding factor is more often one's knowledge of the child's interests and needs than arbitrary adherence to any division according to difficulty; although this, if not overstressed, can happily exist as a guide. The more story books one knows personally, the more one can stimulate an individual child's interest and find the right book for him at a particular stage. There is no substitute for this personal know-ledge, which takes time to build up, yet is in itself often very rewarding. The more living experience of books one gives a class all the time in school, the more one has something pleasurable and real to relate their reading practice to, and the more likely children then will be to *want* to get on in their private reading. Whatever teaching 'method' one favours with first-year children, I am sure that, like all teaching habits, it should be looked at often, so that one asks oneself what inherent value it has *for the child*, what imaginative vision it gives him or her of the whole world of books. Sympathetic understanding on the teacher's part and personal vision will be far more inspiring than the most up-to-date method. In the light of such scrutiny, some practices such as having markedly different quality reading matter – I mean quality of format and general desirability here, quite as much as of content – for A and B children would disappear. But as I said earlier, it is often a question of emphasis. What is perfectly sensible as suggestion becomes depressing and retarding as arbitrary division. The important thing is to keep the general attitude positive and creative and individual. The important thing is for teachers to use their imaginations in this most practical sphere as actively as elsewhere. If they are temporarily asleep, let them be stirred by the realisation that young children themselves are often highly critical, sub-consciously at least, of the unreality of their so-called 'happy' readers. One six year old I read of recently, for instance, was found by his father having crossed out the heroine's name, Dora, throughout his book, and written 'Bora' instead – a spirit of rebelliousness the father hoped his teachers might respond to. It remains up to them.

9

BOOKS AND LIBRARIES

'I FOUND my first real Primary School Library in Manchester in 1944 a wonderful *tour de force* in a difficult year.' So wrote Mr. Blackie in *Good Enough for the Children*. It is now widely accepted that books and pleasant easy access to books are as vital in junior as secondary schools, especially in those where most children get no encouragement to read at home.

Yet the Newsom Report found that twenty per cent of secondary modern schools had no library, and although I have no figure for primary schools it may well be comparable, if by library one means a stock of books housed together in a separate room or part of the school. But all junior schools have some books, even if only locked in a cupboard. There is a great gap, though, between good and average here, which is not only a question of physical conditions. Some schools have little beyond additional sets of graded readers, others have a range and quality that is better than many small public library children's departments. Some schools have regular library periods and in all kinds of ways make their libraries attractive and enticing places. Others do not allow children to take books home and have their libraries shut save during odd periods. Some are obviously very keen for children to develop the habit of reading but find strangely unimaginative ways of doing this: making it compulsory, for instance, for children to borrow one book per fortnight or not allowing children to change their book until they have written a report on it.

It is a great deal of work to build up and run a library not only efficiently, but creatively, and I think that head teachers should be as generous as is in their power over recognising this financially. I have heard, for instance, of schools with a grant for helping with boys' games but nothing for the librarian.

Local authorities, too, differ considerably in their generosity, practical encouragement and general insight where libraries are concerned. The best are very good indeed; the average provide quite helpful facilities without the extra dynamic that will stir teachers' imaginations in making use of them. Of the two kinds of grant given to schools, those authorities which give a separate library allotment seem to me the more stimulating, for it is still open to head teachers to supplement this as they think fit from their all-purpose or text-book allotment. But with a separate grant, the library cannot be completely overlooked. Some authorities, including London, have made special grants, spread over a number of years, specifically to raise the standard of infant and junior libraries and most now make some initial library grant to new junior and infant schools. But difference in provision between junior and secondary remains wider than I think is justified. In initial grants, for instance, one county allows £300 to a junior school but £2,000 to a secondary. One does not want the secondary grants cut down but every recognition of the great importance of a good library lower down as well.

Everything of course depends on how the money is spent; and this is in the hands of teachers, particularly of head teachers. Some authorities, London, for example, provide a helpful practical advisory service, concerned with siting, shelving, display, layout, etc. Most give some kind of advice over choice of books but here variation in quality is great. Some authorities make the library service one of the concerns of a particular inspector. Others run an independent library advisory service with gifted and enthusiastic specialists in charge, who realise that annotated lists are of limited value unless teachers get ample chance to see the books themselves, and to choose only after personal consideration. A number of authorities have very good permanent collections at their headquarters. More adventurous ones supplement these by taking collections into schools. Leicestershire, for example, sends out collections of over 500 books, which are on display in a school hall from early afternoon until just before lunch next day. This kind of stimulus is tremendously valuable in provincial centres where bookshops only carry limited stocks, and where these are usually some way off from country schools. This kind of display is supplemented by special advice and provision for a particular project, this last service with good county or local authorities being rapid and comprehensive. It would be invidious to mention names here. Sufficient to suggest that if one works in an area where such a service is poor or non-existent, one should press for improvement. Most authorities also provide some kind of mobile service from which schools can borrow for a term or part of a term, to add to their permanent stock. This service tends to be widely used for fiction and some schools obviously prefer to spend all their grant on topic books or books of reference or information.

I have spoken so far of a school's library, without saying anything of the all important class collections and their relation to the central one. There are differences of emphasis here, often the result of the authority's policy. Leicestershire, for instance, believes that class libraries should come first and that the central collection is a sort of depot from which class teachers can draw. There is the danger where this is reversed that the central library may be more of a show piece than an integral part of the life of the school. There is certainly something wrong when a school suggests, after adding to its central library, that the books no longer needed or worth having there can now be passed on to the class libraries. Yet I have heard of schools where this has been suggested. However, the possession of a really good central store of books from which teachers can draw is necessary and valuable.

Class libraries are essentially the creation of individual teachers and their quality can therefore vary enormously within a school. Whatever the general standard, and however little encouragement a teacher may get, he can see that there are books in his classroom, attractively set out, kept clear of dusters, chalk and empty inkwells. (Looking through one dog-eared collection recently, I even came upon a carton of lavatory paper, to be doled out on demand, since it got stolen if left in the lavatories.) Puffin books are not expensive. One can always pester headmasters and headmistresses with small book lists. Some have been known to say that money is allotted but their staff do not come forward with requests. Where staff feel that the head lacks imagination in this sphere, they can usually exert some pressure. There can even be some two-way action here. One county adviser told me how, having enlisted the head-teacher's support, more in theory than from conviction, for some major additions to the school's library, he was amused when the head so succeeded in stirring up his staff that they proceeded to disturb his composure and, as my informant put it, 'heave him back into action'.

One's aim in all this, surely, is to encourage children to use books widely and freely and to find pleasure in so doing. One should always remember that for many children this is their only contact with books. Where it is satisfying, they will become readers. Colour and sometimes fine quality in production are important unconscious influences. Books to hand, in the class-room, in the corridor, in some convenient alcove of the hall where children know that they can sit and read, it is to this kind of environment that nine and ten year olds best respond. Much depends on the school building. In some, given a suitable room where children know that they are welcome to come and go freely, a library may flourish and contribute more to the life of the school than if it has to be fitted in to cramped corridors. More important than siting is having the books attractively arranged at children's eye level and a simple borrowing system that children can help operate. Cork notice-boards for displays of new dust-covers and racks so that new and interesting books may be laid out flat and not seen only from their spines are very valuable, while clear marking of the different sections attracts children and helps them find their way about.

There are a number of books and Schools Library Association pamphlets to give more detailed guidance to teachers wanting to build up a good junior school library, while *Using Books in the Primary School* to which I have frequently referred is most helpful in basic ways as well as in its main consideration of project work. The only issue I am concerned with here as of special concern in connection with English is the attitude to fiction. As with children's television programmes, the non-fiction in most school and class libraries is of a higher quality and is obviously considered more important by a majority of teachers. Students have commented on how dated the fiction often is in class libraries, while new topic books of various kinds abound. Many schools have no permanent fiction, only what they borrow from their authority's loan service. This last is useful certainly for additional reading, and for supplying popular authors much enjoyed by children, although very stereotyped in plot and conventional in language. But I am convinced that a good library needs, as do good class libraries, the best supply of good fiction and poetry books for children that one can give it. This can only be the result of personal exploration and choice, although there are books about children's reading to help one and most authorities circulate some lists of recommended books. The latter vary, though, from completely uncritical brochures, which include course books, typically conventional uninspiring school anthologies and graded readers, to the perceptive lists circulated in Hertfordshire, for instance, where there is a real attempt to make teachers aware of the areas of experience brought to life in story, and where the books chosen, both prose and poetry, have obviously been genuinely assessed by the Children's Librarian. This county also arranges, as do some others, special 'Library Weeks', with competitions for children, exhibitions of good children's books in bookshops, talks by authors, visits to printing works. The Children's Librarian plays an active part in these activities and talks to many schools and to students in training colleges. But not all counties show this kind of awareness and concern. Too much of the comment in so-called annotated lists, including much in books about children's reading, goes little beyond the pointless effusions of publishers' blurbs. Janice Dohm, for instance, in *Young Writers, Young Readers*, itself an interesting compilation of children's writing, together with articles about their reading, and about particular poets and story writers suited to them, gives a full book-list with comment. But the comment is about as discriminating as, say, *The Observer* 'Briefing.' Mary Norton's *The Borrowers*, for instance, is 'a tremendously convincing and original creation, toughly realistic', while *National Velvet* she calls 'an *adult* book much favoured by children' (my italics). But it is unhelpful to carp. Teachers who can do no more in a busy life than find time to choose books on the basis of this kind of comment will still give pleasure to many children. If they have time for book reviews, these are usually more discerning. As well as twice-yearly reviews of children's books in *The Times Literary Supplement*, there are always extensive ones at Christmas and occasionally at other times in *The Observer* and *Guardian*, and there are also two special reviews, *The Junior Bookshelf* and *Growing Point*, obtainable to order. Janice Dohm gives details of where to write. Some of the suggestions made in this book may also be helpful.

Any real interest in children's fiction and poetry books for children must be personal, based partially at least on one's own reading. Where a teacher has enjoyed a book, this is always infectious and children want to read it for themselves. If one has this interest and also the chance to shape a school's library or simply one's own class library, it can express itself there in a particularly valuable and creative way.

10

CONCLUSION

It would be rash to underestimate the opposition to the conception of English and imagination I have been concerned with. A student commented recently on a fourth-year class, in which thirty-five out of forty children had just passed the eleven plus: 'The language work is geared to passing an exam – it is very successful but starves the children of any of the aesthetic qualities of English.' The headmaster remarked in the same connection: 'The proof of the pudding is in the eating.' One cannot be scornful of this kind of strategy nor of the complacency of the headmaster, while our society's values remain so governed by success. Children would happily endure aesthetic starvation even if they knew they were undergoing it, which of course they don't, in order to get the only kind of education that has so far counted. According to Dr. Clifford Allen in his book, *Passing School Examinations*, parents will reasonably regard examination success 'as more important than any other acquisition . . . (a child) will get at school'. It will be of little satisfaction that the child learns to enjoy literature if he fails 'the examination that will open the doors of the grammar school to him, and ultimately the university'. Above all it is overidealistic 'to risk his failure trying to *inculcate responses* at the expense of the knowledge essential for examination success'. (My italics.)

The end of our present secondary system offers parents and teachers the chance to repudiate this monstrous choice. There is no need for us to set fact against fiction, knowledge against literature, success against natural and full development as a human being. They can and should nourish each other, and this nourishing will be essential if we are to create truly comprehensive schools. When one helps children to enjoy English, whether in the junior or the secondary school, one is not concerned with some clinical process of emotional indoctrination such as Dr. Allen envisages in his jargon phrase, *inculcate responses*, but with their individual development as human beings. Junior school teachers here have no less opportunity than secondary ones, in many ways more. In giving English a full content, all help children to think and feel for themselves, and so be less likely to grow up into the kind of people who accept Dr. Allen's values without disquiet.

Ironically, awareness is growing that a 'successful' society needs imaginative minds as well as trained analytical ones. So people like Dr. Allen are now devising 'open-end' tests to replace I.Q. tests and measure imagination. It is too early to say what value these may have but one is sceptical. This smacks of 'composing legalism', of imposing a pattern or yardstick from without. If we truly want more imaginative minds, we must trust the imagination and allow every scope for genuine creative activity in our schools. Imagination cannot be taught any more than can intelligence but there is strong evidence that both can be strengthened through a sympathetic environment and education, and that the imagination, especially in children, can be fostered through the imagination of teachers and the power of other, more exciting imaginations in literature, music and art. It was no genetic freak, for instance, that one student teaching in a town offering no richness of environment should be struck by the 'good imaginations' of her class, while others in neighbouring schools noticed nothing of the kind. Wordsworth had a strong regard for fact as well as a powerful imagination. He knew that teachers were not only concerned with books but with things. The good ones, he wrote, had the skill

> To manage *books and things* and make them act
> On infant minds as surely as the sun.

Bad teachers he called 'the keepers of our time', 'the wardens of our faculties', concerned only with our intellects. They confined children

> like engines
> To the very road that they have fashioned.

There is no sense of confinement in our junior schools but there are still some dreary crocodiles along the road in English, conducted by teachers who have not discovered what the woods and fields have to offer. Some people will argue that if one has to get from A to B it is best to go by the most direct route. More relevant, I think, is that teachers should consider in what sense children ever have to reach a given destination as a group in English. It is rather a question of what kind of approach will most strengthen their individual capacity as walkers. 'The true educators,' said Henry Miller, 'are the adventurers and wanderers.' An Outward Bound approach or a crocodile, in the Junior School the choice is as simple and direct as that. And for the children being educated it is the individual teacher who decides.

Most junior school teachers, I am convinced, are educators and would like to go in this if in nothing else with Henry Miller, but some still blame their head teacher, their local authority, selection tests, the 'unpromising' material of the children in their area, for their being so unadventurous. Teachers may not be able to plot the whole course for a class, but the essential nature of the exploration for the children, what they look for, what they see, and what they make of what they see, this largely depends on their teacher. More specifically, it depends on their teacher's imagination, both in its power to see and its power to shape. No subject in the junior school is more important than English in such exploring, for it largely creates the climate for it and the spirit in which it is done. It is needed for all straightforward communication and for more intimate exchange and growth in understanding. It also plays a vital part in recreation, that creative life without which no one benefits very deeply from the voyage. Its varied activities, though, must be seen whole by the teacher. He or she must see the connections, and trust the imagination as a compass with power to guide.

R

Appendices

I

Suggestions for teachers' reading

NOVELS AND STORIES

Childhood and boyhood

Keith Waterhouse, *There is a Happy Land*

Dannie Abse, *Ash on a Young Man's Sleeve*

Dylan Thomas, *Portrait of the Artist as a Young Dog* and *Early One Morning*

Joyce Cary, *Spring Song* and some of the other stories in the Penguin volume with this title

—— *Charley is my Darling*

Katherine Mansfield, *The Doll's House* (a long short story)

James Kirkup, *Only Child*

David Daiches, *Two Worlds — An Edinburgh Childhood* (David Daiches is the son of a rabbi)

Laurie Lee, *Cider with Rosie*

Flora Thompson, *Lark Rise* and *Lark Rise to Candleford*

Like *Cider with Rosie* also about a country childhood but much bleaker and less nostalgic.

Maxim Gorki, *My Childhood* (Oxford World's Classics and Penguin Books)

Richard Wright, *Black Boy*

Mary Macarthy, *Memories of a Catholic Girlhood*

Adolescence

There is no definite division between this group and many of the books suggested in the former one. But these concentrate more intensely on this time of life, recalling its extremes of confidence and uncertainty, sadness and excitement, and underlying idealism:

Carson McCullers, *Member of the Wedding*

J. D. Salinger, *Catcher in the Rye*

Anne Frank, *The Diary of Anne Frank*

Nadine Gordimer, *The Lying Days*

Jeremy Brooks, *Jampot Smith*

Parents and Children

This relationship has naturally been a major concern of many of the books mentioned so far, but some explore it for its own sake, revealing selfishness and hypocrisy in some parents' attitudes, as well as love without understanding, often on both sides. It is not accidental, I think, that some of the most significant books here are by Victorian writers:

Edmund Gosse, *Father and Son*

Samuel Butler, *The Way of all Flesh*

Henry James, *Washington Square*

Arnold Bennett, *Clayhanger* (this is wider and fuller as a story than a single theme suggests)

D. H. Lawrence, 'Mother and Daughter' (a short story, contained in the third volume of his *Complete Short Stories*)

Simone de Beauvoir, *Memoirs of a Dutiful Daughter*

Raymond Williams, *Border Country*

A fine novel about a railway worker's life in Wales during the twenties, but also concerned with the modern, often sad situation of separation caused by education. The son has been cut off intellectually and socially from his emotional roots in his family and whole early way of life. The action leads to his rediscovering them at least in part.

I would mention here two major novels concerned with all these themes, in both of which there is obviously much very personal material, but which it would be narrow to categorise:

George Eliot, *Mill on the Floss*

D. H. Lawrence, *Sons and Lovers*

Marriage

'Reader, I married him,' says Jane Eyre at the beginning of the last chapter, and it is frequently assumed that Victorian novels never went any further than this. True, their general attitudes to sex usually prevented their writing honestly of adult relationships between men and women, either within or outside marriage. Yet many of the greatest novels of this time were concerned with marriage in a mature sense: for instance,

Tolstoy, *Anna Karenina*

George Eliot, *Middlemarch*

Henry James, *Portrait of a Lady*

Thomas Hardy, *Jude the Obscure*

Marriage is the philosophical centre of much of Lawrence's work, but before recommending his two major novels, *The Rainbow* and *Women in Love*, I would suggest two or three short stories that reveal his attitude in a simpler, unobsessive way: for instance, 'Odour of Chrysanthemums', 'The Daughters of the Vicar', 'The Captain's Doll'. Less books about marriage than stories of specific marriages are Scott Fitzgerald's *Tender is the Night* and Penelope Mortimer's *The Pumpkin Eater*.

Some people through circumstance or temperament stand aside

APPENDICES 263

from marriage: Rickie, for instance, E. M. Forster's hero in *The Longest Journey*, Jake Barnes in Hemingway's *The Sun Also Rises* (alternatively known as *Fiesta*, the title of the first English edition), Miss Vorontosov in Sylvia Ashton-Warner's *Spinster*. The latter teaches in a Maori infant school; Rickie for a time in an English public school, with whose ethos Forster is deeply out of sympathy.

Success and Happiness

Growing up usually involves some search for identity and growth in self-knowledge, together with some measuring of oneself against one's immediate surroundings and often against society as a whole. Young writers are often full of confidence, their books extrovert and comic, success stories probably satirical at the expense of contemporary trends, but with no fundamental questioning of success as a value to live by: H. G. Wells in *Kipps*, for instance, Kingsley Amis in *Lucky Jim*, Malcolm Bradbury in *Eating People is Wrong*. The interesting Irish-Canadian writer, Brian Moore, appears to use the same approach in *The Luck of Ginger Coffey*, but for rather deeper exploration.

Profounder books, usually by older writers, are less content to celebrate the surface of life, but concerned to reveal its quality and question its values. Wells in *Mr. Polly* and *Tono Bungay*, E. M. Forster in *Howards End*, Lawrence in *Women in Love*, diverse though these are in their authors' underlying philosophies and power as writers, come together in this. Similarly concerned with American society between the wars, though in very strongly contrasted ways, are Scott Fitzgerald's *The Great Gatsby*, John Steinbeck's *The Grapes of Wrath* and Sinclair Lewis's *Babbitt*.

Rejection or Acceptance and Compromise

Questioning implies eventually one or other of these attitudes, quality here usually being closely related to how far the issue is of genuine personal significance to the writer, and not simply a fashionable theme to be exploited. The emphasis, though, in the following suggestions is always very strongly on the personal story of the hero.

REJECTION

Graham Greene, *Brighton Rock*

Alan Sillitoe, *The Loneliness of the Long Distance Runner*

Albert Camus, *The Outsider*

ACCEPTANCE OR COMPROMISE

John Braine, *Room at the Top*

Alan Sillitoe, *Saturday Night and Sunday Morning*

Stan Barstow, *A Kind of Loving*

David Storey, *This Sporting Life*

Colour and Race Prejudice

Conrad, *Heart of Darkness*

E. M. Forster, *Passage to India*

George Orwell, *Burmese Days*

Joyce Cary, *Mr. Johnson*

These four are all set against a background of the exploitation and injustice of white imperialism. The next are by South African writers, in some ways more tragically trapped in their own situation:

Alan Paton, *Cry The Beloved Country*

Dan Jacobson, *The Evidence of Love*

Nadine Gordimer, *Six Feet of the Country* (a book of short stories)

—— *A World of Strangers*

I have mentioned Richard Wright's *Black Boy*, but the most powerful American Negro writer today is James Baldwin. *Go, Tell it on the Mountain*, in many ways primarily a religious novel, concerned as much with the hero's soul as with his colour, springs from the varied, complex, mainly ugly experiences of growing up a Negro in America, when for many coloured people their only hope seemed to lie not in this world but in the next. *The Fire Next Time* starts with an autobiographical account of James Baldwin's own experience of growing up in Harlem, and ends with a polemical essay that repudiates Christianity and proclaims the need for strong action now. The greatest modern American writer, however, for whom colour is an inevitable part of his world was the white Southerner, William Faulkner. Often difficult because of his rhetorical style, he rewards perseverance. I would suggest first his book of short stories, *Go Down Moses*, particularly the title story. Of his many novels I would suggest *As I Lay Dying* and *The Wild Palms*.

Other kinds of prejudice and exclusion continue to be active and hurtful, especially where class and education are concerned. One does not expect good novels to be about these themes objectively, but if they are about ways of life very different from our own they should enlarge our understanding and disturb any inbuilt feelings of superiority or complacency that may be narrowing our lives.

Where prejudice against the Jews is concerned, Christopher Isherwood's *Goodbye to Berlin*, written just as Hitler was coming into power, remains a very disturbing and revealing book.

War

THE FIRST WORLD WAR

Robert Graves, *Goodbye to All That*

Hemingway, 'A Natural History of the Dead' (a short story in the Penguin volume called after the later story, *The Short Happy Life of Francis Macomber*)

THE SPANISH CIVIL WAR—a war that inflamed passionate ideals as the futility of the Great War never did:

Hemingway, *For Whom the Bell Tolls*

George Orwell, *Homage to Catalonia*

Not a novel, but an account of Orwell's own experience.

The only novel of distinction that I know about the Second World War is Norman Mailer's *The Naked and the Dead*.

Middle-age

Graham Greene, *The Heart of the Matter*

—— *The End of the Affair*

Angus Wilson, *The Middle-age of Mrs. Eliot*

Virginia Woolf, *Mrs. Dalloway*

James Joyce, 'The Dead'

A long short story in *Dubliners*, which makes us share the middle-aged hero's sudden desolating feeling of separateness from his wife, after an occasion of warmth and festivity, of self-satisfaction and apparent happiness.

The Search for Meaning

Ultimately one is often aware of such a search behind a novel, or inherent in its pattern of action. The answer may be bleak and despairing, the nada or nothingness of Hemingway's 'A Clean Well-Lighted Place', a short story in the same volume as 'A Natural History of the Dead' about two waiters in a café late at night, one anxious to get home, one more anxious to stay, who have just turned an old man out into the street who had tried to commit suicide the week before because he had nothing to live for. Or one could turn to Virginia Woolf, who in *To The Lighthouse* in a quite different way also searches for meaning behind highly individual experience, suggesting some stay in the power of an individual person, here her central character, Mrs. Ramsay, to irradiate the lives of others even after she has died; and through the experience of Lily Briscoe, the amateur painter, in the artist's power to create something permanent out of transience, however imperfect her achievement contrasted with the vision in the mind. Or one can read *The Tree of Man*, by the Australian novelist, Patrick White, I think the greatest of living novelists writing in English. Here there is an underlying faith in the endurance and courage and power of achievement of ordinary, very simple people. Most of them suffer a good deal, their lives are limited in many ways, but the book leaves one feeling that something of value in itself has happened by their living.

Visions of the Future

The unease of modern times has led many writers to explicit allegory, not only asking what life adds up to, but warning where it seems to be heading. My three very obvious suggestions in this final section are chosen because I think they indicate, beyond their great intrinsic interest, some of the same divisions in attitude I have been noticing at a more individual level. There is cynicism behind Aldous Huxley's *Brave New World*, written with remarkable foresight as early as 1932, which sees man conditioned by his scientific inventiveness to a life of manipulated sensation rather than face the pain of full thought and feeling. There is nightmarish rejection in Orwell's *1984*, which sees even the most indomitable individuality succumbing in the end to the rule of power used entirely for its own sake. William Golding in the *Lord of the Flies* to some extent retells the Christian story of the fall of man, suggesting that even if we could start all over again we should end up much as we are now; he does, though, make us feel the lasting power of certain positive human qualities. However, as Wordsworth reminds us, it is 'Not in Utopia . . .

> Or some secreted island heaven knows where,
> But in the very world, which is the world
> Of all of us, the place in which in the end
> We find our happiness or not at all.'

I therefore find more complete and satisfying truth in a novel like *The Tree of Man*, rooted as it is throughout in what the author makes us feel to be actual experience; and for me it is in its capacity to explore and reveal experience in this way that the novel's central value lies.

DRAMA

Immediately one thinks practically of grouping plays according to their themes, the absurdity of it is apparent: *Taste of Honey*, for instance, is about adolescence, and so is *Romeo and Juliet*; Ibsen's *Doll's House* is about marriage, but then so, in large part, is *Look Back in Anger*, not to mention *As You Like It* and Edward Albee's *Who's Afraid of Virginia Woolf*; Chekhov's *The Three Sisters* is concerned with the disillusions of middle-age as John Osborne is in *The Entertainer* or *Inadmissible Evidence*. But seeing any one of these plays in the theatre would rarely make us call to mind the others. If I offer such groupings, then, it is to be deliberately and I hope creatively provocative, to make one open to the variety of drama and the importance of its total effects, for which no play reading, however good, is adequate substitute. For drama is concerned not with written words, but speech and action, with silence and inaction, with movement, gesture, set and lighting, all controlled by the interpretative, shaping power of the producer and enacted for us, not as individuals, but as members of an audience, by living actors. This experience is concrete in a way that that of the novel or poetry cannot be, the stimulus, emotional, intellectual and physical, more concentrated and powerful, our corresponding response more immediate and usually stronger. It is concrete, also, in a way television drama cannot be, moving though the latter's best productions are, and tremendously valuable though television has been in extending the audience for drama and awakening an appetite for it. For there have always been elements of ritual, of ceremony and participation in drama which, when they work on us as part of an audience, release and exhilarate in a way that cannot happen at home in the sitting-room. I am not arguing that there is no place for good drama on television, but that one should not take it as true theatre.

Stress on drama's primitive origins and the power of its emotional effect is misleading unless it brings out how much this has always been concerned with ideas, how much in drama has always sprung from powerful intellectual passion. Aeschylus, Marlowe, Ibsen, Shaw, Brecht have all affected audiences not simply by feeling, but by ideas charged with feeling. Drama has always been more philosophical, and also more immediately political than the novel. In all significant periods of dramatic activity there has been intimate contact between the concerns and themes of playwrights and the issues that genuinely matter in their society and time. The theatre has always shown, as Hamlet put it, 'the very age and body of the time its form and pressure'. Government actions against the players in Shakespeare's own time, the significance of Verdi for the Italians during the Risorgimento, the impact of the first years of the Abbey Theatre in Dublin, all are instances of strong interaction. When the theatre matters, people are affronted as well as excited, they walk out or boo, as well as acclaim, they take sides.

It is this kind of involvement which makes the theatre of the last ten years in England significant, quite as much as the varied interest and quality of individual writers. Admass labels like 'Kitchen Sink' or 'Angry Young Men', and more pretentious intellectual categories like 'The Theatre of Cruelty', or 'The Theatre of the Absurd', simply remind one that the theatre has always been a partly commercial art, and that a certain posturing is an inherent element of the theatrical. Nevertheless, new plays in the last ten years have reflected a much wider area of life in social and individual terms, and at a deeper level, and have been more honest generally about how people actually think and talk and behave than most plays between the wars or immediately after 1945. Reactions have been strong because to confront us now with some of our deepest concerns means in part attempting to dramatise the very antithesis of drama, usually thought of as essentially *shaped* action. Rawness, drift, apathy, aimless violence, inarticulateness, a questioning in some writers of the point of any action: where lies the *shape* in all this? Certainly not in the conventional, well-constructed, three-act play, that by its very form and associations belies the nature of this material. New kinds of patterning had to be found and are still being explored. Which does not mean that there is no future for the more conventional form, itself of no great age, but that there is nothing sacrosanct about it either; only a strong commercial interest in preserving two long intervals for spending money in the bars, and for saving it with small casts and few changes of set.

To enjoy drama, then, one needs to be open to the variety of dramatic experience, which in practice means, surely, taking advantage of the best that comes one's way, and of going out of one's way sometimes to pursue the best. Mystery and chronicle plays, presented often now at summer festivals; good productions of Shakespeare and other Elizabethan and Jacobean playwrights; productions in the round; a good production of Chekhov, whose patterning through mood and atmosphere is far closer to some modern writers than Shaw or Ibsen, these are instances of the variety I mean. Many teachers find their greatest pleasure in taking part in a production themselves. Certainly some experience, in no matter what capacity, of what happens when the different elements fuse and one senses that something new is being created: this particular production of whatever play it is, is vital for a full understanding of the theatre (which is not the same, exactly, as drama) and of great value practically in one's work with children.

It is with all this much in mind that I offer the following suggestions of themes and plays:

War

Shakespeare, *Troilus and Cressida*
Sean O'Casey, *The Plough and the Stars*
Bertolt Brecht, *Mother Courage*
John Arden, *Sergeant Musgrave's Dance*
Willis Hall, *The Long and the Short and the Tall*

Social Responsibility and Social Morality

Ibsen, *The Pillars of the Community*
Shaw, *Widowers' Houses*
Arthur Miller, *All My Sons*

Capitalism, Work and the Individual

John Galsworthy, *Strife*
Elmer Rice, *The Adding Machine*
Walter Greenwood, *Love on the Dole*
Arnold Wesker, *The Kitchen*

The Acceptance of Reality

The strong conviction in Arthur Miller and Arnold Wesker that society should be changed is profoundly disturbed by doubt when individual lives and circumstance are fully explored: how far can people be changed? how far can they face the truth about themselves or even begin to see it? to what extent do they need a faith, an ideology, a dream, to live by? Miller's *Death of a Salesman* and Wesker's trilogy of plays, *Chicken Soup with Barley*, *Roots*, and *I'm talking about Jerusalem*, move us considerably through this awareness. Other plays have been concerned with human dependence upon illusion, with no implicit social message. For instance.

Ibsen, *The Wild Duck*

Eugene O'Neill, *The Iceman Cometh*

Tennessee Williams, *The Glass Menagerie*

Robert Bolt, *The Flowering Cherry*

There is a profound and continuing source of individual conflict here: the point where the knowledge that, in Donne's words, 'No man is an island' meets the personal experience that in many ways essentially he is. It has generated great drama in the past, with resolutions differing according to the underlying philosophies of their creators:

the medieval *Everyman*

Marlowe, *Faustus*

Shakespeare, *Hamlet*

Ibsen, *Master Builder*

Three of the most remarkable modern plays, I would suggest, spring from a related concern:

Samuel Beckett, *Waiting for Godot*

John Osborne, *Luther*

Harold Pinter, *The Caretaker*

Harmony and Delight

Not a theme, simply a suggestion of effect, the exhilaration, release and final sense of balance which the best productions of good comedy can bring. This has little at the time to do with subject matter. *As You Like It, What You Will, Much Ado about Nothing*: Shakespeare's casualness over his titles here shows that he realised this. It has much to do with the pattern of the situations and the moods they cause in the audience, with the power of the language in poetry and wit, and also the particular rightness of rhythm and tone in the playing. The plays may be as diverse as *Love for Love, The Importance of Being Earnest* or *Twelfth Night*, but one recognises the connection in the sort of satisfaction one feels.

POETRY

There is a poem called *Days* by the modern poet, Philip Larkin, which runs:

> What are days for?
> Days are where we live.
> They come, they wake us
> Time and time over.
> They are to be happy in:
> Where can we live but days?

> Ah, solving that question
> Brings the priest and the doctor
> In their long coats
> Running over the fields.

Here is an individual voice speaking to each of us at a level of our being
that we usually ignore in our actual everyday living. The concentration
of the poet's thought and feeling opens out in each of our minds and
imaginations in a personal and individual way: the days each of us live,
or don't live, now; days we have lived, or failed to live, in the past; paths
across fields to lych gates, along city roads to crematoria, a wreath of
bronze chrysanthemums in a warm October. Individual images spring
up, for me against an oddly surrealist background in which landscapes
from pre-war French films merge into hospital corridors. But for each of
us, experience of the past, awareness of the present, apprehension of the
future are stirred.

There is a poem by another modern writer, Norman Nicholson, called
Five Minutes:

> 'I'm having five minutes,' he said
> Fitting the shelter of the cobble walk
> Over his shoulders like a cape. His head
> Was wrapped in a cap as green
> As the lichened stone he sat on. The winter wind
> Whirred in the ashes like a saw.
> And thorn and briar shook their red
> Badges of hip and haw;
> The fields were white with smoke of blowing lime,
> Rusty iron brackets of sorrel stood
> In grass grey as the whiskers round an old dog's nose.
> 'Just five minutes,' he said.
> And the next day I heard that he was dead,
> Having five minutes to the end of time.

Here the concentration is seemingly entirely outward, on a particular
old man, whom the poet lets us live with for a few minutes in a sharply felt
and visualised situation. The full reverberation for each of us comes with
the last two lines; again there is a stirring of our individual awareness. 'A
poem begins in delight and ends in wisdom,' was how the American poet,
Robert Frost, chose to express it in prose. Or as the Irish poet, Yeats,
wrote in middle-age, from the depth of personal experience, in a poem he
called *The Coming of Wisdom with Time*:

> 'Though leaves are many, the root is one;
> Through all the lying days of my youth
> I swayed my leaves and flowers in the sun;
> Now I may wither into truth.'

Wherever the stress falls, on the greenness or the withering, the delight or the wisdom, a good poem usually increases our apprehension of both. One seems to hold for a moment in the mind a kind of truth. If one calls it *poetic*, this has nothing to do with its being about any special kind of 'poetic' subject, or with the poet's using any special kind of 'poetic' language. It has everything to do with the intensity of the poet's own apprehension and his power to find particular words and images and rhythmic control of his expression to convey this exactly to us. When he succeeds, the pressure of what he has to say will so fuse with the way he finds to say it, that his poem exercises what Ted Hughes has well called 'its final sway over the mind'. Never to read poetry means missing this particular kind of experience.

Many teachers will have had it already. Others who want to make poetry alive for children and who begin to explore some of the anthologies I have suggested will discover something of what I mean. It is up to them to go on from there; not to stay content with experience limited by the emotional range of children. For them, I offer the following further suggestions, many of which are available in paperback editions. I think one wants to own one's poetry books. They are not to be read with a return date in mind, but need to be to hand, to stir one in different ways, often with long gaps in between. For the reasons I gave in speaking of the novel, I concentrate mainly on modern writers.

Anthologies

New Lines, edited by Robert Conquest (Macmillan)

Poets of Our Time, edited by F. E. S. Finn (John Murray)

Dawn and Dusk, poems of our time, chosen by Charles Causley (Brockhampton)

An anthology made for boys and girls of secondary school age, which nevertheless gives adults wide range of choice for further exploration.

The Faber Book of Modern Verse, recently reissued with a quite full contemporary section

It offers a good representative selection of twentieth-century poetry up to the war, though surprisingly omits Robert Frost, who often makes a strong appeal to people hitherto impatient of poetry.

Poets

Paperback editions of individual authors include:

Thom Gunn and Ted Hughes, *Selected Poems* (Faber)

Penguin Poets, a series including a number of important poets, among whom are W. H. Auden and D. H. Lawrence

The impact of the latter, especially, is direct and immediate, particularly if one has always associated poetry with a set form and rhyme. Robert Frost is also published in this series.

Vista Books Pocket Poets, John Betjeman, Laurie Lee, Edward Thomas

The latter particularly, I think, would appeal to many teachers for his quiet strength and truthfulness in recording what at first seem very simple personal experiences. Killed in 1917, he was never directly a war poet, writing most of the country, and his own thoughts and feelings, stirred by observation and memory.

A Miscellany of Dylan Thomas (Aldine Press), both poetry and prose is a good introduction to this poet. *Under Milk Wood* (Dent)

W. B. Yeats, *Selected Poetry* (Macmillan). Especially the poems from the books called *Responsibilities, Wild Swans at Coole* and *The Tower*

T. S. Eliot, *Selected Poems* (Faber). Often highly complex and difficult, but not to be approached with awe. If one starts with *Preludes,* say, or *Landscapes,* or *The Journey of the Magi,* or *Animula,* about the simple soul of the child, and the growing pain and complexity of experience, one will realise how direct and moving he can be.

Among poets at the moment still only published in hardback editions, particularly recommended are:

Philip Larkin, *The Less Deceived* and *The Whitsun Weddings* (Faber)
Keith Douglas, *Selected Poems* with an introduction by Ted Hughes (Faber)

Douglas was killed in Normandy in 1944; some of his finest poems, though, are about his experiences in Egypt and the desert.

Adrian Mitchell (Jonathan Cape). His themes are often public, his treatment satirical, the effect often exciting and moving.

In addition to these, I would also like to recommend particularly the Penguin Series, *Penguin Modern Poets,* eight of which have so far come out, each containing a selection from three modern writers not yet as established as those of their *Penguin Poets* series, but nevertheless of great interest, and considerable achievement; most seem peculiarly close to present moods. A glance through the subjects: 'Death of a Son', 'Bed and Breakfast', 'Absence', 'Winter Sunday', 'On a Tube Train,' suggests the variety. There is both continuity in what is permanently a source of deep feeling, the loss of death, or absence; and also a kind of poetic awareness felt in the most everyday situations, obviously imbued with the particular flavour of our time, which many people sometimes feel, although they never write about it. The first poem in the first of the series, 'A Prospect of Children', by Lawrence Durrell, should evoke immediate response in teachers. It springs from his feelings as he sits writing letters at his window, 'smoking up there alone', while children play in the park below. Part of him envies them, 'gruesome little artists of the impulse', yet part does not. Christopher Middleton, in the fourth

volume, has a poem called 'For a Junior School Poetry Book', in which
the freshness of childhood and the routine of experience are dancingly
confronted. Which does school really encourage, he seems to hint, for
by the end the children are waiting outside school for the mothers to
come out, and odd things have happened to the tenses of the verbs:

> The mothers had eyes that see
> boiled eggs, wool, dung and bed.
> The children have eyes that saw
> owl and mountain and little mole.

What does school do to the seeing eye of childhood? What has life made
fill the vision of adults? Edwin Brock has a poem in the eighth volume
called 'Symbols of the Sixties' which starts,

> On a quiet Sunday
> when the sun is out
> you can drive to
> a village in Kent
> which boasts a
> coffee bar with plastic
> tables.

There 'Boys in plastic jackets' fidget with 'beehive girls', the chickens
taste as factory-made as the table-tops, while at the heart of the poem,

> a bird in a
> painted cage says
> Ban the bomb ban
> the bomb ban the
> bomb ban the bomb.

Once one realises how close poetry can come to one's own life, one
will want to read it sometimes for the special kind of illumination it can
bring. One may well want to discover, or rediscover earlier poets. A
good anthology, such as Denys Thompson and Raymond O'Malley's
Rhyme and Reason (Chatto & Windus), Janet Adam Smith's *The Faber
Book of Children's Verse*, a fine collection but going well beyond the
level of children in much of its content, or James Reeves's *The Poet's
World* (Heinemann), could be a starting point from which personal
inclination can lead one on. I make few suggestions of what teachers
would be likely to enjoy. I am only sure that, if one has read no poetry
since having to at school, and did not much enjoy it then, one will be
surprised and moved by certain writers rarely encountered there, or
encountered before one was mature enough for understanding. My few
suggestions are:

Donne, love poetry. A selection is available in *Penguin Poets*

S

Blake, his *Songs of Innocence* read side by side with the *Songs of Experience*

Batsford paperback selection has an excellent introduction by Professor de Sola Pinto.

Wordsworth, his description of a joyously free boyhood in the Lake District, in the first two books of *The Prelude*

Coleridge, two poems far less well known than *The Ancient Mariner* or *Kubla Khan*, but more intimately personal: *Frost at Midnight* and *Dejection: an Ode*

Keats, *The Odes*, read as a group, and seen as vitally concerned with important aspects of experience,

Clare, quietly and exactly perceptive of life in nature, very fresh and personal like Edward Thomas, but without his tendency to flavour an experience for its own sake. There is a good selection by James Reeves (Heinemann) and a useful pamphlet by J. H. Walsh (Chatto & Windus)

Hardy, particularly 'Moments of Vision' and 'Late Lyrics and Earlier', in his *Collected Poems*

But whoever one turns to, the important thing is to be free of preconceptions and open to what the poet is saying, to the experience at the heart of the poem.

II

Books on the Teaching of English in the Junior School

First of all books central to my thesis: that English should be the creative centre of a child's experience in school, and that for this to happen some vision is essential in the teacher. Many of these books are particularly concerned with children's own creative expression through writing, but the overall stress is on interrelatedness. The other sections give details of books usually equally aware of this but more specialised in their application.

ENGLISH AND IMAGINATION

Blackie, John, *Good Enough for the Children* (Faber)
Clegg, A. B. (editor), *The Excitement of Writing* (Chatto & Windus)
Ford, Boris (editor), *Young Writers, Young Readers* (Hutchinson)
Hourd, Marjorie, *The Education of the Poetic Spirit* (Heinemann)
—— *Some Emotional Aspects of Learning* (Heinemann)

APPENDICES   275

—— with Gertrude Cooper, *Coming into their Own* (Heinemann)

A study of a verse-writing project carried out with ten-year-old children.

Jackson, Brian (editor), *English versus Examinations — A Handbook for English Teachers* (Chatto & Windus)

The first part is concerned with the Primary School.

Langdon, Margaret, *Let the Children Write* (Longmans)

Marshall, Sybil, *An Experiment in Education* (C.U.P.)

Pym, Dora, *Free Writing* (U.L.P.)

An account of pioneer work in the 1950's in Wiltshire.

· Sampson, George, *English for the English* (C.U.P.)

Thompson, Denys (editor), *The Use of English* (quarterly, Chatto & Windus)

Practical and imaginative in the most helpful way, and becoming increasingly concerned with junior school work, i.e. junior teachers are beginning to write for it.

I would also draw attention to two official publications:

English in the Primary School, the evidence of the National Association for the Teaching of English presented to the Plowden Committee, July 1964, obtainable from NATE.

English, Working Paper No. 3 of The Schools Council, 1965 (H.M.S.O.)

POETRY

I include here several studies of children's poetry which might equally have come in Appendix III, on books for use in the classroom, but which have a wider value in helping teachers realise the involvement that occurs when an experience matters to the writer, and the kind of experience that concerns children. This kind of book, even though about adolescents' writing, deepens one's insight into the nature of poetry.

Baldwin, Michael (editor), *Poems by Children 1950–1961* (Routledge and Kegan Paul)

—— *Poetry without Tears* (Routledge and Kegan Paul)

Concerned with the secondary school, but of interest and practical value if one has to take over top juniors with little or no genuine experience of poetry.

Beckett, Jack, *The Keen Edge*. An Analysis of Poems by Adolescents (Blackie)

Of very great interest, especially for the poetry.

Druce, Robert, *The Eye of Innocence*, Children and their Poetry (Brockhampton)

More comment from the author than in the preceding book, and a particularly interesting chapter on *What is Poetry?*

Hughes, Ted, the introduction to *Here Today* (Hutchinson)

Hourd, Marjorie and Gertrude Cooper, *Coming into their Own* (Heinemann) (already cited in the previous section)

Poems from Bristol Schools, an Anthology compiled by the Bristol Association for the Teaching of English, beginning with age-groups six to ten

Reeves, James, *Teaching Poetry* (Heinemann)

—— 'Writing poetry for children', Chapter 12 in Part II of *Young Writers, Young Readers* (cited in previous section)

Woodley, C. C., 'Primary School Poetry' in *Use of English*, Vol. XVII No. 2

Interesting and helpful in a practical and imaginative way.

A number of anthologies meant for older children, and individual poets usually thought of as not for juniors, are nevertheless likely to be of value and a source of pleasure to many teachers, who as they explore will discover many poems that they recognise would work with their class, be exactly right in the context of what they are doing, offer something beyond what any class anthology contains. These might include:

Anthologies

Adam Smith, Janet, *The Faber Book of Children's Verse*

Causley, Charles, *Dawn and Dusk* (Brockhampton)

—— *Modern Folk Ballads* (Studio Vista)

Holbrook, David, *Iron, Honey and Gold I–IV* (C.U.P.)

Here Today, compiled jointly by Hutchinson and Jupiter Recordings Ltd, and available also on record

Oxford Book of Ballads, for instance, 'Binnorie', 'The Daemon Lover', 'The Wife of Usher's Well', 'The Twa Corbies', 'Sir Patrick Spens', 'Get Up and Bar the Door', 'Thomas the Rhymer' (to give one a sense of the power of the ballad)

Read, Herbert, *This Way Delight* (Faber)

Reeves, James, *The Poet's World* and *The Modern Poet's World* (Heinemann)

Thompson, Denys and O'Malley, Raymond, *Rhyme and Reason* (Chatto & Windus)

Poets (for some of their poems):

Auden, W. H., 'Night Mail', a few ballads; Blake, *Songs of Innocence and Experience*; W. H. Davies, Emily Dickinson, Robert Frost, Robert Graves, some ballads; D. H. Lawrence, *Birds, Beasts and*

Flowers; Dylan Thomas, 'Fernhill', 'The Hunchback in the Park'. Other more modern poets, referred to in the Poetry chapter, I have given details of in Appendix I.

STORY BOOKS AND WHAT THEY MEAN TO CHILDREN

Britton, James, the teacher's books issued with his *Oxford Book of Stories for Juniors*, particularly No. 3, and *What Happened Next?*

Fisher, Marjorie, *Intent Upon Reading* (Brockhampton)

Jay, Richard, 'The Average Child', an article in *Young Writers – Young Readers*, which also has critical articles on Enid Blyton, Biggles Books, comics, school stories.

Some of their writers worry overmuch, I think, about the lack of discrimination at this age, which is a time of appetite not taste.

McElroy, W. M., 'Books for the Under Twelves' in *Use of English*, Vol. XIII, No. 3

A very interesting article, followed by a most comprehensive and helpful book list.

Shavreen, David, 'Reading and Imagination in the Junior School' in *Use of English*, Vol. XVI, No. 3

Written from close contact with children, encouraging in its insistence that children, in their own way, want their story books to have some truth to life.

Trease, Geoffrey, *Tales out of School* (Heinemann)

DRAMA

Alington, A. F., *Drama and Education* (Basil Blackwell)

Barr, Enid, *From Story into Drama* (Heinemann)

Most warmly recommended for the variety and quality of the stories chosen, the vivid power with which they are told, and the writer's active sense throughout of the manysidedness involved in dramatisation.

Bruford, Rose, *Teaching Mime* (Methuen)

Haggerty, Joan, *Please, Miss, can I play God?* (Methuen)

Hodges, C. Walter, *Shakespeare's Theatre* (O.U.P.)

Most attractively produced, illustrated in colour by the author, giving a vivid account of conditions of playing in medieval as well as Shakespeare's time: the mystery cycles, mummers' plays, as well as Elizabethan ones, are set in a living context that brings out the mingled elements of ceremony and festival in drama.

Holbrook, David, *Thieves and Angels*, Dramatic Pieces for Use in Schools (C.U.P.)

Also concerned with ceremony and festival. Probably most valuable to junior teachers as a source of ideas. 'The Programme about Childhood', for instance, with which it ends, may suggest exploration with different material but along similar lines.

Hourd, Marjorie, *The Education of the Poetic Spirit* (Heinemann)

Raised again here because of its great concern with the value of dramatisation as a maturing influence.

Slade, Peter, *Child Drama* (U.L.P.)

Ward, Winifred, *Playmaking with Children* (Appleton-Century)

—— *Stories to Dramatize* (Children's Theatre Press)

Two very good books by an American writer, concerned with aims and values as much as methods.

CHILDREN'S WRITING AND GROWTH IN LANGUAGE

Because of their central significance, I have already suggested the important books on children's writing, in the first section. Here I would add:

A. B. Rowe, 'Writing Prose and Verse' in Brian Jackson's collection, *English versus Examinations* (Chatto & Windus)

and two BBC *Radio for Schools* programmes, running at the time of writing:

Living Language, edited by Joan Griffiths, for children of nine to eleven

Listening and Writing, edited by Moira Doolan, for eleven to thirteen year olds

The broadcasts may be over, and in any case the second series was not meant for junior children, though many of the poems and stories were of immediate interest to them. The booklets, however, and particularly the teachers' pamphlets for the second series, if still obtainable, remain of much practical and imaginative value to junior teachers. The stress throughout is on the need for a sensitive response to what is heard, for talk, for related and helpful work of a more detailed kind, and then the individual child's search to create for himself from his own experience as called forth by the broadcast. The illustrations, often reproductions of paintings, are most exciting to children. Other programmes of similar quality may exist at the time of publication, and even if they cannot be fitted into one's own school timetable, one can get ideas from them for one's own use.

Recommended as a background to children's growth in language are:

Edwards and Gibbon, *Words Your Children Use* (Burke)

Hollamby, Lilian, *Young Children Living and Learning* (Longmans), particularly the section, 'Development of Language'

Marshall, Sybil, 'English and Idiom in the Primary School', an article in *English in Education*, edited by Brian Jackson and Denys Thompson (Chatto & Windus)

Opie, Iona and Peter, *Lore and Language of School Children* (O.U.P.)

Sullivan, Anne Mansfield, her account of her experience in teaching Helen Keller, given in the appendix of the latter's *Story of My Life* (Hodder)

LIBRARIES AND BOOKS FOR PROJECTS

The School Library Association provide ample practical help to teachers. I would mention only their Primary Schools Sub-Committee publication, *Using Books in The Primary School*. In addition to its accounts of and ideas for projects of varied kinds, it gives useful lists of non-fiction books related to these.

Two other books giving much helpful practical advice, though both tend to think of books primarily as sources of factual information, are:

Cutforth and Battersby, *Children and Books* (Blackwell)

Purton, Rowland W., *Surrounded by Books*, The Library in the Primary School (Educational Supply Association)

III

Books for the classroom or the library

POETRY

I include anthologies (marked with an asterisk) for a class to possess, and poetry books to have in the class library for children to explore and enjoy individually.

BBC Radio For Schools Series : two current ones, *Stories and Rhymes*, meant for younger juniors, arranged by William Mayne, and *Adventures in English*, arranged by Michael Baldwin. Both offer teachers poems and ideas for poetry programmes of their own, even if they cannot arrange for their class to follow a series, and no doubt subsequent programmes will do the same. For instance, three of the themes for *Stories and Rhymes* for Spring, 1966, which was called *Meetings*, were 'Animals I have met', 'Things I have met', 'Things I have done', and the accompanying booklet was most attractive to young children, not only in layout and typography of the poems, but because of some delightful black and white illustrations by Sheila Robinson.

Berg, Leila (editor), *Four Feet and Two* (Puffin)

Blishen, Edward, *Oxford Book of Poetry for Children*

Expensive, but a lovely book, with original illustrations in colour by Brian Wildsmith, suitable in its choice of poems for juniors of all ages.

*Britton, James (editor), *The Oxford Books of Verse for Juniors I–IV*

Clark, Leonard, *Drums and Trumpets* (Bodley Head)

De La Mare, Walter, *Come Hither* (Constable)

—— *Peacock Pie* (with drawings by Edward Ardizzone) (Faber)

—— *Tom Tiddler's Ground* (Bodley Head)

Eliot, T. S., *Old Possum's Book of Practical Cats* (Faber)

Farjeon, Eleanor, *The Children's Bells* (Oxford)

—— *Silver, Sand and Snow* (Michael Joseph)

—— *Then there were three* (Michael Joseph)

Graham, Eleanor, *Puffin Quartet of Poets* – Eleanor Farjeon, James Reeves, E. V. Rieu, Ian Serraillier

Graves, Robert, *The Penny Fiddle* (Cassell)

*Grisenthwaite, Nora (editor), *Poetry and Life I–IV* (Schofield)

Uneven in quality. Intended for class use, but as with most anthologies one needs to think hard before committing oneself to bulk purchase.

Hughes, Ted, *Earth-Owl and Other Moon-People* (Faber)

—— *Meet my Folks* (Faber)

MacBeth, George, *Noah's Journey* (Macmillan)

Most attractively produced, though the striking colour illustrations by Margaret Gordon seem aimed at much younger readers than the text.

Opie, Iona and Peter (editors), *Oxford Dictionary of Nursery Rhymes*

—— (editors), *The Puffin Book of Nursery Rhymes*

Reeves, James, *The Wandering Moon* (Heinemann)

—— (editor), *Merry-go-round* (Heinemann)

—— (editor), *Orpheus, A Junior Anthology* (Heinemann)

Serraillier, Ian, *Beowulf the Warrior* (O.U.P.)

—— *Everest Climbed* (O.U.P.)

Walsh, John, *Roundabout by the Sea* (O.U.P.)

—— *The Truants* (Heinemann)

*Wollman, Maurice and Grugeon, David (editors), *Happenings* (Harrap) now available on Record).

*Wollman, Maurice and Hurst, D. M. (editors), *Junior Book of Modern Verse* (Harrap).

Young, Andrew, *Quiet as Moss* (Hart-Davis)

Poems about nature and the countryside, with wood engravings by Joan Hassall.

Poetry on Record

An increasing number of good recordings exist, and can do much to bring poetry to life in the classroom. Above all they serve to remind us that most poetry is intended to be heard, not read silently. James Gibson has written an interesting article, as well as giving a helpful list of recommended records, in *The Use of English*, Vol. XVII, No. 4 (Summer, 1966). For primary schools he suggests:

Poems and Songs for Younger Children, Part 2 — Jupiter JEP OC30, intended for children of seven to nine, and containing an outstanding rendering of *The Daniel Jazz* by a primary school

Hutchinson's *Jupiter Book of Verse* — two 10-inch records, JUR OOB1, 3 and 5 (called on record *A Junior Anthology of English Verse*)

The poems in *Here Today*, the joint compilation already referred to, are available in full on Jupiter JUR OOA6 and OOA7, many read by their authors, which children find particularly fascinating. Argo issue four records of poetry and song, called *Rhyme and Rhythm* to accompany Macmillan's four volumes of the anthology of that name. The numbers are: ARGO RG 414–417 (12-inch).

Head teachers who realise the value of investing in some of these and teachers who explore recordings beyond those meant primarily for junior children, will make children actively look forward to poetry in school in a way few do now; and also give them an incentive and high standards to aim at in making up their own programmes of poetry and music.

STORY IN THE JUNIOR SCHOOL

Fable and Fairy Story

Aesop — retold in *Fables from Aesop* by James Reeves (Blackie)

Andersen, Hans, editions by Bodley Head and Faber

Also a very attractive recent one by Cape, illustrated by Grabianski.

Amabel Williams-Ellis, *The Arabian Nights* (Blackie, Andrew Lang, Longmans)

Farjeon, Eleanor, *The Little Bookroom* (O.U.P.)

Grimm, J. and W., *Tales*, Routledge Complete Edition, various other selections

Lang, Andrew, various collections (Longmans)

Folk-Tales

English Fables and Fairy Stories by James Reeves

Irish Sagas and Folk-Tales by Eileen O'Faolain

Scottish Folk-Tales and Legends by Barbara Ker-Wilson

Welsh Legends and Folk-Tales by Gwyn Jones

French Legends, Tales and Fairy Stories and *German Hero-Sagas and Folk-Tales*, both by Barbara Leonie Picard

Scandinavian Legends and Folk-Tales by Gwyn Jones

T

Red Indian Folk and Fairy Tales by Ruth Manning-Saunders (all O.U.P.)

Four others of interest are *Old Peter's Russian Tales* by Arthur Ransome (Nelson), *The Magic Drum: Tales of Central Africa,* retold by W. R. P. Burton (Methuen), 'The Tales of Till Eulenspiegel' in *The Owl and the Mirror,* trans. by G. Freeman (Blackwell), and 'The Tales of Hans Sachs', retold in *Through the Cobbler's Window* by E. U. Ouless (Pitman)

The Greek World

LEGENDS

Graves, Robert, *Myths of Ancient Greece* (Cassell)

Green, Roger Lancelyn, *Tales of Greek Heroes* (Puffin)

Hawthorne, Nathaniel, *A Wonder-Book for Boys and Girls* (Dent)

—— *Tanglewood Tales* (Collins, and Dent)

Hyde, Lilian Stoughton, *Favourite Greek Myths* (Harrap)

Kingsley, Charles, *The Heroes* (Blackie, and Macmillan)

Penn Warren, Robert, *The Gods of Mount Olympus* (Muller's Legacy Library)

Warner, Rex, *Men and Gods* (Heinemann)

HOMER—THE ILIAD

Green, Roger Lancelyn, *The Tale of Troy* (Puffin)

Picard, B. L., *The Iliad of Homer* (O.U.P.)

Warner, Rex, *Greeks and Trojans* (Heinemann)

Wormald, R. D., *The Trojan War* (Longmans)

THE ODYSSEY

Fadiman, Clifton, *The Voyages of Ulysses* (Muller's Legacy Library)

Lang, Andrew, *Adventures of Odysseus*

Picard, B. L., *The Odyssey of Homer* (O.U.P.)

Selincourt, Aubrey de, *Odysseus the Wanderer* (Bell)

For teachers who want a fuller background, I would suggest reading part at least of a full adult translation: E. V. Rieu's, for instance, in the Penguin Classics. Also worth exploring are:

Limebeer, *The Greeks* (C.U.P.)

M. I. Finley, *The World of Odysseus* (Pelican)

Leonard Cottrell, *The Bull of Minos* (Evans)

Marjorie and C. H. B. Quennell, *Everyday Things in Ancient Greece* (Batsford)

Roman Britain

Duggan Alfred, *The Romans* (Brockhampton)

Sutcliff, Rosemary, *The Eagle of the Ninth* (O.U.P.)

—— *The Mark of the Horse Lord* (O.U.P.)

Treece, Henry, *Legions of the Eagle* (Bodley Head)

—— *The Eagles Have Flown* (Bodley Head)

The Norse World

BEOWULF – Prose translation for children by Rosemary Sutcliff, with drawings by Charles Keeping (Bodley Head)

In a modern verse retelling, *Beowulf the Warrior*, by Ian Serraillier (O.U.P.)

PROSE SAGAS

Eric the Red and other Icelandic Sagas by G. Jones (O.U.P.)

Grettir the Strong, retold by Allen French, with drawings (gruesome) by Bernard Blatch (Bodley Head)

MYTHS AND LEGENDS

Green, Roger Lancelyn, *The Saga of Asgard* (Puffin), also in a hard-back edition under the title *Myths of the Norsemen* (Bodley Head)

Keary, A. and E., *Heroes of Asgard* (Macmillan)

Picard, B. L., *Tales of the Norse Gods and Heroes*

Wilmot-Buxton, E., *Tales from the Eddas,* (Harrap) also the O.U.P. volume already referred to, by Gwyn Jones, *Scandinavian Legends and Folk-Tales*

NOVELS AND STORIES for young people about this period include:

Boucher, A., *The Path of the Raven* (Constable)

Kipling, R., the chapter called 'Joyous Venture' from *Puck of Pook's Hill* (Macmillan)

Mitchison, Naomi, *The Land the Ravens Found* (Collins)

Tolkien, J. R. R., *The Hobbit* (Allen and Unwin, also Puffin)

Original and independent, but rooted in Norse mythology.

Treece, Henry, *Viking's Dawn, The Horned Helmet, The Last of the Vikings* (Bodley Head)

THE ACTUAL NORSE WORLD

For teachers I recommend *The Vikings* by Johannes Brønsted (Pelican)

For teachers and children, Naomi Mitchison's *Travel Light* (Faber), which follows their journeying from Denmark to Byzantium

Recent revelations about Lief Ericson and the crossing to America are likely to lead to writing for children before very long.

ELSEWHERE IN ENGLAND AND EUROPE AT THIS TIME

Oman, Carola, *Alfred, the King of the English* (Dent)

Serraillier, Ian, *The Ivory Horn*, a prose retelling of the *Song of Roland* (O.U.P.)

Sutcliff, Rosemary, *The Shield Ring* (Bodley Head)

The Medieval World

ARTHURIAN LEGEND

Cooke, B. K., *King Arthur of Britain* (Ward)

Green, Roger Lancelyn, *King Arthur and his Knights of the Round Table* (Puffin)

Picard, B. L., *Stories of King Arthur and his Knights* (Oxford Children's Library)

Ridley, M. R., a modern English prose version of *Sir Gawain and the Green Knight*, illustrated by John Galsworthy (Ward)

THE CRUSADES

Hampden, J. (editor), *Crusader King* (Ward)

Treece, Henry, *The Children's Crusade* (Puffin)

Welch, Ronald, *Knight Crusader* (O.U.P.)

CATHEDRALS AND MINSTRELSY (ceremony and festival)

Gilbert, Joan, *Imps and Angels* (Warne)

A good historical story for young juniors.

Jewett, Eleanor Myers, *Told on The King's Highway* (Harrap)

Power, Rhoda, *Redcap Runs Away* (Penguin)

ROBIN HOOD

Green, Roger Lancelyn, *Robin Hood* (Puffin)

Oman, Carola, *Robin Hood, Prince of Outlaws* (Dent)

Sutcliff, Rosemary, *Chronicles of Robin Hood* (O.U.P.)

For teachers to have some taste of the originals, the Robin Hood Ballads, Part II, Book V of *The Oxford Book of Ballads*.

CHAUCER

The Prologue to *The Canterbury Tales* and selected tales

Some reading, however brief, of the original, if one can. There is a good recording, Argo RG 401, in what scholars think approximates to the original pronunciation, worth trying to hear to catch the movement and the life.

Modern translations include a prose version by David Wright (Barrie and Rockliff), and Neville Coghill's lively verse one (Penguin Classics).

For reading to children and the class library:

Brewer, Derek, *Chaucer in His Time* (Nelson)

Farjeon, Eleanor, *Tales from Chaucer* (O.U.P. and Oxford Illustrated Classics)

Hieatt, A. Kent and Constance, *The Canterbury Tales of Geoffrey Chaucer* (selected and adapted), illustrated by Gustaf Tenggren (Golden Press, New York, distributed by Books for Pleasure Ltd.)

Malcolmson, Anne, *A Taste of Chaucer* (Constable)

A selection re-presented in the original metre, with modernised words, and with attractive woodcuts. This writer has also published *Seven Medieval Plays for Modern Players*, with eleven year olds in mind, which junior teachers would find helpful for their own dramatisations.

Fifteenth Century

Harnett, Cynthia, *The Woolpack* (Methuen, and Puffin)

—— *The Load of Unicorn* (Methuen, and Puffin)

Sixteenth Century

Hodges, C. Walter, *Columbus Sails* (Bell)

—— *Shakespeare's Theatre* (O.U.P.) (discussed in Part I, Drama Section)

Jackdaw No. 9, *Young Shakespeare* (Cape)

Jowett, Margaret, *A Cry of Players* (O.U.P.)

Sutcliff, Rosemary, *Brother Dusty Feet* (O.U.P.)

Seventeenth and Eighteenth Centuries

A few stories for older juniors already interested in and finding out about life in these times. There is plenty of social realism to help teachers in writers like Defoe, in *The Journal of the Plague Year*, in Smollett, in Fielding, or in artists like Hogarth and Rowlandson, but they must make this real for their class in their own ways.

SEVENTEENTH CENTURY

Avery, Gillian, *The Warden's Niece* (Collins)

This, much more suitable for girls than boys, starts in Victorian Oxford, but the plot is concerned with the earlier period.

Marryat, F., *Children of the New Forest* (Dent)

Sutcliff, Rosemary, *Simon* (O.U.P.)

EIGHTEENTH CENTURY

Beatty, John and Patricia, *At The Seven Stars* (Chatto & Windus)

An exciting story by two American historians of a late Jacobite plot, which shows more awareness than most stories set in this period of what life was like for ordinary people living in London (though it also manages to bring in a number of famous ones). The hero is a fifteen-year-old American boy anxious to get back to Philadelphia. The authors have another book coming out in the autumn of 1967 about the Civil War, called *Campion Towers*.

Defoe, Daniel, *Robinson Crusoe* (O.U.P.)

Meade, J. Falkner, *Moonfleet* (Arnold)

Stevenson, R. L., *Treasure Island*

The last three have little connection for children with any history they may be concerned with, but belong in their minds and ours with books like the following:

Ballantyne, R. M., *Coral Island* (Schofield, Blackie)

Duvoisin, Roger, *They Put Out to Sea: The Story of the Map* (U.L.P.)

Gibbings, Robert, *Coconut Island* (Dent)

Heyerdahl, Thor, *The Kontiki Expedition* (children's edition published by Longmans Bridge Series)

Hodges, C. Walter, *Columbus Sails* (Bell)

Komroff, Manuel, *Marco Polo* (Methuen)

Wyss, Johann, *The Swiss Family Robinson* (Collins, and Fontana)

These, whether brought together for some project on *the Sea* or *Exploration*, or simply put in the path of older juniors, appeal strongly to their spirit of adventure, have for them what Conrad called 'the romance of reality'.

Nineteenth-Century Literature for Children

These are given alphabetically, since the elements of fantasy, allegory and realism are too strongly intertwined to make divisions profitable, and in any case have already been discussed in the chapter on *Story*. I include the books which I think still live for children, in different ways.

Andersen, Hans, see Fairy Story on page 281

Dickens, Charles, *A Child's History of England* (O.U.P. and New Oxford Illustrated Dickens)

Well worth teachers knowing for the way it helps us realise how children look at history.

—— *A Christmas Carol* (Michael Joseph, illustrated by Ronald Searle)

—— *David Copperfield as a Boy* (Dent) (unabridged)

—— *David Copperfield's Boyhood* (Nelson) (unabridged)

Burnett, Frances Hodgson, *The Secret Garden* (Heinemann, and Puffin)

Carroll, Lewis, *Alice's Adventure in Wonderland* (Allen and Unwin)

—— *Through the Looking Glass* (Macmillan)

—— *The Hunting of the Snark* (Chatto & Windus)

It is worth, if possible, having one edition in the library with Tenniel's original illustrations.

Collodi, Carlo, *Pinocchio, the Tale of a Puppet* (Collins Classics and others)

Dodge, Mary Mapes, *Hans Brinker* (Collins) also abridged as *The Silver Skates* (Dent: Children's Illustrated Classics)

A wonderful story for children that ought to have the classic status here that it has in America, the central story having the kind of human involvement and appeal of, say, *The Secret Garden*, or *Black Beauty*. Its author obviously believed, also, that where the feelings are involved one learns, for she sets out to give children some incidental geography lessons about Holland.

Grahame, Kenneth, *The Wind in the Willows* (Methuen)

Grimm, J. and W., see Fairy Story on page 281.

Hardy, Thomas, *Our Exploits at West Poley* (O.U.P) (Hardy's only story for children, discovered quite recently)

Kingsley, Charles, *Water Babies*

Kipling, Rudyard, *The Jungle Book* (Macmillan)

—— *The Second Jungle Book* (Macmillan)

—— *Puck of Pook's Hill* (Macmillan)

—— *Animal Stories* and *All the Mowgli Stories* (Macmillan)

Nesbit, E., *The Railway Children* (Benn, and Puffin)

—— *The Phoenix and the Carpet* (Benn, and Puffin)

Ruskin, John, *The King of the Golden River* (Macmillan, New York)

An attractive picture-book size edition, illustrated by Sandro Nardini.

Sewell, Anna, *Black Beauty* (Harrap, and others)

Spyri, Johanna, *Heidi* (Collins, and others)

Modern Stories for Children

I begin with modern fantasy and allegory, along the lines of the divisions discussed in the chapter on *Story*, and then give alphabetically writers who seem to me worth most for children in various ways, probably in their private reading. All these, I would suggest, have some genuine imaginative life at the level for which they are written. Finally, I group some particularly realistic adventure stories in a way I have suggested may add to the impact and interest of some topic and project work. They can easily be enjoyed, with no such connection, by the readers in the class but enjoyment through this association may be an incentive to some children not very fond of reading to be more adventurous on their own.

MODERN FANTASY

Lewis, C. S., *The Chronicles of Narnia*, particulary *The Lion, the Witch and the Wardrobe* and *The Silver Chair* (G. Bles)

Tolkien, J. R. R., *The Hobbit* (Allen and Unwin) (traditional and extrovert)

Norton, Mary, *The Borrowers* and *The Borrowers Afloat* (Dent) (individual and extrovert)

Boston, Linda, *The Children of Green Knowe* and its sequels (Faber)

The best, because something real for children emerges from it, is, I think, *The Stranger at Green Knowe*.

Pearce, A. Philippa, *Tom's Midnight Garden* (O.U.P.)

(Realistic in setting but introspective in their heroes.)

Many other good modern stories still contain strong elements of fantasy, the marvellous and the magical quite frequently occur, but in the main arise naturally from a realistic and credible setting. Those particularly suitable for younger juniors are asterisked.

Barrett, A., *Songbird's Grove* (Collins)

*Bemelmans, Ludwig, *The High World* (Hamilton)

A good story of the author's childhood in a mountain village in Austria.

*Berg, Leila, *A Box for Benny* (Brockhampton)

*Capek, Karel, *Dashenka: the Life of a Puppy* (Allen and Unwin)

Church, Richard, *The Cave* (Heinemann)

*DeJong, Meindert, *Dirk's Dog, Bello* (Lutterworth)

*—— *Hurry Home, Candy* (Lutterworth)

—— *The Wheel on the School* (Lutterworth, and Puffin)

Dillon, Eilis, *The Island of Horses* (Faber)

A good book, with genuine insight into the relationships involved, as well as power to recreate the fine natural setting off the west coast of Ireland.

Enright, Elizabeth, *The Saturdays* (Heinemann)

*Gallico, Paul, *The Small Miracle* (Michael Joseph)

Grey Owl, *The Adventures of Sajo and her Beaver People* (P. Davies)

*Kästner, Eric, *Emil and the Detectives* (Cape)

—— *When I was a little Boy* (Cape)

The latter deserves to be more widely known. The author spent his childhood in Dresden.

*King, Clive, *Stig of the Dump* (A Puffin Original, illustrated by Ardizzone)

Lynch, Patricia, *The Turf-Cutter's Donkey* (Dent)

Probably better known than the other Irish writer for children, Eilis Dillon, but not I think so genuinely perceptive.

Pearce, A. Philippa, *A Dog So Small* (O.U.P., and Puffin)

—— *The Minnow on the Say* (O.U.P., and Puffin)

Pullein-Thompson, Diana, *The Boy and the Donkey* (Collins)

Ransome, Arthur, *Swallows and Amazons* (Cape)

Spring, Howard, *Tumbledown Dick* (Faber)

A book realistically set in Manchester before the First World War.

*Travers, P., *Mary Poppins* (Collins)

Williamson, Henry, *Tarka the Otter* (Putnam, and Puffin)

Much enjoyed by some junior children who love animals.

Story Books for Projects

These, being specially good stories, belong just as much in my earlier list.

MINING

Grice, Frederick, *The Bonnie Pit Laddie* (O.U.P.)

JUNIOR SCHOOL FRENCH

Berna, Paul, *A Hundred Million Francs* (Bodley Head, and Puffin)

Bosco, Henri, *The Boy and the River* (O.U.P.)

The hero, Pascalet, is a small boy who lives on a farm in France, near a great river.

Loeff, Rutgers van der, *They're Drowning Our Village* (U.L.P.)

FLOODS AND DISASTERS

Hartog, Jan de, *The Little Ark* (Hamilton)

A moving account of the terrible floods in Holland in 1953. I would also recommend *The Lost Sea*, about the author's boyhood in a village on the Zuider Zee.

Loeff, Rutgers van der, *Avalanche* (U.L.P. and Puffin)

THE LAST WAR

Benary, Margot, *The Ark* (Macmillan)

The story of a family reunited in Germany just after the war.

Dejong, Meindert, *The House of the Sixty Fathers* (Lutterworth)

The story of a Chinese waif's escape from behind the Japanese lines.

Mitchison, Naomi, *The Rib of the Green Umbrella* (Collins)

About the partisans in Italy.

Serraillier, Ian, *The Silver Sword* (Cape)

AMERICA

I include here some books that belong as well in my list of good nineteenth-century stories. Most of the others associated with projects, even if they are set in the past, are by modern writers.

Denison, Muriel, *Susannah of the Mounties* (Dent, and Puffin)

—— *Susannah of the Yukon* (Dent)

Enright, Elizabeth, *The Saturdays* (Heinemann)

Good if one wants to give some idea of life in New York for middle-class children now.

Forbes, E., *Johnny Tremain* (Constable)

The story of a boy who grows up in Boston during the Revolution.

Loeff, Rutgers van der, *Children on the Oregon Trail* (U.L.P.)

Morrow, H. W., *The Splendid Journey* (Heinemann)

O'Hara, Mary, *My Friend Flicka* (Atlantic Books, Dragon Book Series)

O'Steele, William, *The Far Frontier* (Macmillan)

Steinbeck, John, *The Red Pony* (Heinemann)

Twain, Mark, *Tom Sawyer* (Dent, and Puffin)

Wilder, Laura Ingalls, *Little House in the Big Woods* (Methuen, and Lutterworth) and others in the series

AUSTRALIA

Phipson, Joan, *The Boundary Riders* (Puffin)

—— *It happened one summer* (Angus and Robertson)

Spence, Eleanor, *Lillipilly Hill* (O.U.P.)

—— *The Summer in-between* (O.U.P.)

Nan Chauncy has written a number of stories set in Tasmania. The natural and topographical details are quite well described but the characters and plots tend to be rather stereotyped. I would recommend *World's End Was Home*, which has a good account of a Christmas spent in midsummer.

SPACE PROJECTS

Berna, Paul, *Threshold of the Stars* (Bodley Head)

—— *Continent in the Sky* (Bodley Head)

Heinlein, Robert, *Farmer in the Sky* (Gollancz)

Severn, David, *The future took us* (Bodley Head)

Suddaby, Donald, *The Death of Metal* (O.U.P.)

—— *The Lost Men in the Grass* (O.U.P.)

—— *The Star Raiders* (O.U.P.)

Walters, Hugh, *Blast off at Woomera* (Faber)

Wells, H. G., *The First Men in the Moon* (Dent)

BOOKS OF STORY

Britton, James (editor), *The Oxford Books of Stories for Juniors I–IV.*
Book III particularly recommended.

By the end of making a compilation like this, one begins to think that the categories are more important than the contents. Yet this only proves the truth of one of my main arguments, that everything depends upon the insight of those who 'use' the list, on their imagination in setting children adventuring more excitingly than many would alone.

LANGUAGE BOOKS

'How we all hated those endless pages of English Exercises especially. The book was called *First Aid in English* for some obscure reason which we never managed to work out, and was thick and blue. The first thing we did after finishing the examination (11 +) was to ceremoniously throw these books into the waste-paper basket. I cannot remember their fate.' (Training college student, writing in 1966.)

Many course books don't deserve this much contempt, but I suggest only four that have a consistently positive value:

Deadman, Ronald, *Enjoying English* (Rupert Hart-Davis)

Only one volume has appeared at the moment of writing, which shows unusual awareness and understanding of how children's minds and imaginations work. I like particularly the use made of photographs, and of good black and white illustrations conceived with the text genuinely in mind.

Eyre, Wallace, *Imagine and Write* (Basil Blackwell)

In some ways a more original book, and also more uneven. Children, and teachers, are led to imagine, to see things in new ways, and much interesting material has been drawn on. Reproductions from such artists as Hogarth, Rowlandson, Hieronymus Bosch, give some idea of the quality of stimulus. Surprisingly, though, together with some good modern drawings, are sprightly strip-cartoon type ones.

Jackson, Brian, *Good English Prose, Books I and II* (Chatto & Windus)

These are intended to set teachers free of text-books which is why there are only two in the series, instead of the usual four.

Rowe, A. W. and Emmens, Peter, *English Through Experience, Book I* (Anthony Blond)

The first of a course designed for secondary schools, so not suggested as a class book for juniors. But it offers teachers of older juniors many suggestions and a framework not of abstract categories, but of the senses and the child's developing experience.

INDEX